ROMANTIC IDEALISM AND ROMAN CATHOLICISM

Romantic Idealism and Roman Catholicism:

Schelling and the Theologians

THOMAS FRANKLIN O'MEARA, O.P.

UNIVERSITY OF NOTRE DAME PRESS

NOTRE DAME   LONDON

Library of Congress Cataloging in Publication Data

O'Meara, Thomas F., 1935-
Romantic idealism and Roman Catholicism.

Includes bibliographical references and index.
1. Theology, Catholic—History—19th century.
2. Tübingen School (Catholic theory) 3. Schelling, Friedrich
Wilhelm Joseph von, 1775-1854. I. Title.
BX1747.06   230'.2   81-40449
ISBN 0-268-01610-0   AACR2

Manufactured in the United States of America

Contents

Preface

THE FOLLOWING STUDY is a history of the interplay between faith and culture in the first half of the nineteenth century. Although these pages describe the past, their time has an enduring quality, for it was a time when the Catholic spirit understood how to live in a historical world and how to be faithful to tradition while fashioning a theology that spoke to a particular age. With the past as forecast, this history becomes a justification for the present.

The author's thanks are due to the Association of Theological Schools and to the Dominican Province of St. Albert the Great (USA) for grants sustaining research. Special thanks go also to Dr. Francis Fiorenza and Mr. James Langford for substantive and nuanced literary counsel.

Introduction

Roman Catholic Theology in the Nineteenth Century

THE NINETEENTH CENTURY is the most recent epoch in Western history; we know its entirety, its origins and its conclusion. The nineteenth century began, roughly speaking, with the French Revolution and ended with the First World War. As a cultural age, it was parent to our own unfinished century. For those interested in the search for the numinous and the absolute, which philosophy and religion assume to be their concerns, or for those interested in the grounding patterns of our culture, the nineteenth century remains an intriguing age.

At the end of the eighteenth century, contrary to the expectations of those who were living contentedly in an enlightened Europe, a counter-movement emerged. It drew upon the freedom and subjectivity of the age of light, only to replace it. The very events of politics and philosophy that the Enlightenment helped to bring to life—for example, the thought of Lessing and Kant, the revolutions in America and France—impelled Europe into a new age. This period, beginning with the 1790s, proved to be not a brilliant coda to the Enlightenment but a transition to a different world, Romanticism. Romanticism offered not reason but intuition, not mathematics but electricity and chemistry, not only republican society but the freedom of the solitary hero, not reasoned plan but turbulent nature.

In Germany the early nineteenth century presented a panorama of great movements, individuals and groups. For music, literature and poetry it was an era almost incomparable. The philosophers saw their mission to be heralds of a new era of freedom, to ground and synthesize science, art, history and religion. Their intuitive systems would explain, arrange and expand all that the human spirit could create. Right or wrong, poets and philosophers were swept up in the conviction that they were not only changing the world but changing consciousness, changing how men and women would perceive cosmos and godhead. Philosophers and theolo-

1

gians rushed into print with a dialectical network of systems, original and grandiose blueprints for human history, even for the life of God.

> The immediate effect of the philosophy of Kant was to send modern metaphysics into its second great period of richness. In the short space of two, three decades a pleroma of metaphysical constructions of outstanding style and considerable depth were put together, coming so close upon each other that this period is unique in history. It is the final . . . great epoch of metaphysics to this day.[1]

In philosophy, Kant, Jacobi, Fichte, Schelling, Hegel and dozens of lesser figures such as Windischmann, Eschenmayer, Niethammer worked on the final great period of metaphysics. Goethe, Schiller, Novalis, Tieck, the Schlegels altered the style of literature; Schleiermacher, Sailer, Görres, Baader applied literary criticism and scientific philosophy to religion. The systems that followed each other in abundance during the decades surrounding 1800 aspired to set free a modern world, to do justice to both reason and mystery, to unite Graeco-Roman and Gothic cultures.

Not too many years before this remarkable time burst upon the European scene, one of its precursors, J. G. Herder, wrote: "The Church of Rome resembles an old ruin where one cannot expect new life."[2] Frightened, aloof, angry, misunderstood and misunderstanding, Rome had watched cultures come and go. These individualistic children of Luther, these final stages of the Enlightenment—would they not also pass away? Should not these figures more radical than Descartes or Kant be ignored if not condemned?

The fear, almost panic, that spread in the years following the Reformation caused in the Counter-Reformation a conserving reaction. This altered the intellectual life of what had been the Western church; the openness of discussion in the medieval church (where Thomas Aquinas and Albertus Magnus could disagree with papal views on Aristotle) ceased. From the point of view of Roman Catholic intellectual life, Immanuel Kant was Martin Luther applied to philosophy; both furthered the triumph of subjectivism. The scenario begun at the Reformation had two acts, and Luther and Kant were their protagonists. What Luther began, Kant completed. The haughty secularity, the mechanism, the natural rationalism of the Enlightenment seemed to Rome a strong argument that, whereas modernity might find congenial some form of contentless, subjective faith, it had nothing in common with a historical revelation, a powerful

faith, a permanent church. The worlds of Protestantism and Enlightenment had brought down the curtain upon the richness and aesthetic sacramentality of the Catholic baroque. Rome, despairing of the directions of
rationalism, retreated from culture to the patristic and especially to the
medieval.

Soon Rome convinced the world that it neither wanted nor had any
modern history. Both Origen and Thomas Aquinas had said that the water
of Greek philosophy could be transformed through revelation into the
wine of theology. The water of Leibniz and Spinoza, of Descartes and
Voltaire, seemed to lack the sparkle and limpidity for such a metamorphosis. Rome rejected not only the institutions of the modern world—
democracy, science, development—but rejected new forms of cultural
life such as subjectivity, evolution, freedom. Rome dreamt and cultivated
happier, theonomous, sacramental times of the past.

In Germany, however, Roman Catholicism stood on the edge of a new
era, one of creativity and potentiality. The flow of Enlightenment into
Romanticism attracted Catholics, and after 1790, as Catholicism underwent a rare renaissance, a period of theological vitality burst forth. The
successors to Kant in idealism and to Herder in Romanticism offered life
to the "old ruin." The last great restructuring of Catholic theology before
our own times happened in the first half of the nineteenth century.

> The nineteenth century in Germany is an epoch of great theologians
> and of great theology. The achievement of Catholic theologians
> seems all the more impressive if we consider the beginnings of that
> age, the catastrophe of the church of the Holy Roman Empire.
> Catholic theology was in a crisis: the philosophy and theology of the
> high Middle Ages were forgotten, the scholasticism of the baroque
> was gone, the Enlightenment had come with serious effects. . . .
> The history of theology in the eighteenth and more in the nineteenth
> century mirrors the attempt to build new, solid foundations, to pre-
> sent the old faith in a new time in a believable way, to reconcile the
> hostile siblings, belief and knowledge. This great task was recog-
> nized and accepted by the more significant theologians of the past
> century.[3]

The history of Roman Catholic theology and philosophy of religion in
the period between the French Revolution and the year of widespread
revolution, 1848, has until recently been unresearched, ignored. It was
presumed that no significant Catholic theology existed from that time, no

meeting with the makers of the modern world. We need to take seriously this real and seminal encounter of Catholic intellectual life with Romantic idealism precisely because, between Trent and Vatican II, it was a rare event. In its goals and style it begins and molds Catholic theology in the modern world.

Friedrich Schelling and Roman Catholic Theology

This book is a study of Roman Catholic intellectual history in the early decades of the nineteenth century. Our focal point will be the German philosopher Schelling, for in the history of his thought the reader can find a schema for the history of German Catholic life at that time. Schelling was the mentor of German Catholic intellectuals. In its perduring influence upon German Catholicism, his long career gives us a framework, the outline of a chart for early nineteenth-century Roman Catholic thought. Artists and scientists, theologians and bishops, government ministers and kings saw in Schelling an embodiment of the new (what came to be called the modern) world, an embodiment that seemed congenial to the Catholic spirit. In Schelling Catholic philosophers and theologians first accepted Romanticism and idealism, and the philosopher's influence lasted for over three decades. By treating the inspiration of much of Roman Catholic theology at this time we reach not only the chronological history of the period but a genetic exposition of the sources, shifts and movements of this age.

In the Roman Catholic dialogue with Schelling, we find an important message: during the four centuries from 1562 to 1962, from Trent to Vatican II, Roman Catholicism was not a well-planned garden with a neoscholastic statue at its entrance and closure. For at least one segment of that history, Catholicism creatively engaged with the culture of the time. Catholic thought and life assumed it could find a new synthesis through post-Kantian idealism as it had previously with Plotinus and Aristotle.

Schelling's philosophy not only belongs to a historical period, it created that time. His thought was an answer to the questions and aspirations of the nineteenth century. It was an incarnation of the years when Romanticism and transcendental philosophy were new and powerful.

We will be looking at Friedrich Wilhelm Joseph Schelling as he influenced Christian theology, and at Roman Catholic intellectual history as it drew inspiration from Schelling. For a while some Protestant theologians were attracted to him—for instance, Karl Daub and Philip Marheineke —but Hegel drew them away. After all, Hegel gave a central position in the history of thought to Luther and the Reformation, and he was openly contemptuous of Roman Catholicism. In his critical logic he was more sympathetic to Lutheran spirit and form than were the Romantics, who sailed along the coastline of sacramentality and mysticism. Schelling, however, was an alternative to Hegel, and his Catholic disciples found through him a way of conceiving their theology and philosophy in the style of the nineteenth century. Schelling is, in this book, a symbol for the culture of his time, just as for Catholics in the past century he was the mentor of the modern understanding of self and history.

Schelling was a philosopher of the self. He accepted the Kantian revolution from object to subject and sketched further the cartography of the personality's active forms as they influence our perception of the world; he affirmed that the highest knowledge was contact with, insight into, the highest knower, the absolute. Schelling, however, was also an affirmer of the world of nature and history. Our self and its world, he often wrote, were stages where the *Iliad* and the *Odyssey* of the spirit were being enacted. Nature and spirit were two sides of a process; history, natural science, religion and art were fields where this dialectic of process became concrete.

Schelling was a Romantic. He was recognized as such in 1798 by the founding circle of Jena. Schelling's interest in natural science, neoplatonism, mysticism and myth—even in Christianity—betrays the usual stance of an idealist philosopher, but shows also that Schelling's mind was profoundly Romantic. His work presupposed Kant in theory and the French Revolution in practice; still, the new sciences of chemistry, electricity and magnetism, the Romantic tone in literature and art, as well as the expansion of Europe's religious horizon eastward through Asian languages and mythologies were enduring forms in Schelling's philosophy.

Until recently the name of Schelling held almost no meaning except as a philosopher whom Paul Tillich revered and described as a precursor of existentialism. By and large, histories of philosophy repeated the puzzling entry that Schelling, Fichte and Hegel were the giants leading from Kant to Nietzsche and Freud, but then those textbooks gave only the skimpiest summary of Schelling's thought, drawn entirely from his early systems. Schelling's entry into religious issues after 1804 was omitted; his view of God and will in the *Essay on Freedom* (1809) was overlooked; the later philosophy, the system of world-mythology culminating in

Christianity, was not mentioned at all. This Schelling of the philosophy textbooks, a dreamer of a Fichtean cosmos where only the mental counted, could hardly have been a catalyst for Roman Catholics. It is the complete Schelling, the thinker of will and unfolding mind, of myth and godhead, who interests us; it is the Schelling of religion who is a catalyst for theology. For him, religion was not church concerns or dogmatic allegiances but a mystical wrestling with the nature of a highly immanent God whose deity is revelation and whose being is history.

A Schelling renaissance began in 1954 and continues to deepen and expand. Nevertheless a book on Schelling in English is still rare.[4] So we must struggle to hold our spotlight on Schelling *and* upon the Roman Catholic thinkers he helped to fashion. By approaching this complex thinker, rather forgotten and often misrepresented, we hope to illumine our task: an outline of Roman Catholic intellectual history in the first three decades of the past century, a history that can be arranged around his career.

Schelling's philosophical persona was not ashamed of change, and his thinking passed through several mutations. We find both continuity and change in a man who for almost sixty years served as a prophetic metaphysician for German culture, who lived beyond Fichte for forty years and who survived Hegel by a quarter of a century. Schelling, through the variety of his thought, was a major factor in the span of the century after the French Revolution. As the new century began, he attended with Goethe in Weimar a premiere of Haydn's *Creation*, and fifty years later he left his lecture hall through groups of students that included Kierkegaard and Karl Marx. After Schelling's death in 1854, Kierkegaard lived only for one year and Schopenhauer six.

There is a certain unanimity among experts concerning the four major periods in Schelling's thought. In the first, reaching from 1794 to 1798, he was already expanding, with the help of Spinoza, the transcendental philosophy of Kant and Fichte. Next, with his discovery of the new natural science at Leipzig and through his contacts with the Romantics in Dresden and Jena after 1798, he became not only a leading idealist philosopher but a famous philosopher of nature and, in the synthesis of the two, the philosopher of Romanticism. In a third period, from 1806 to 1821, Schelling pursued Romantic idealism into the world of religion; there was more emphasis upon objectivity and process, studious learning from theosophy and mysticism. The subject of his philosophy was not the knowing self but the mysterious, dialectical will of the godhead. The fourth period is that of the system he expounded at Munich after 1827 and at Berlin after 1841: a philosophy of existence but also a Christian philosophy where the life of God realizes itself in mythology and Christian revelation. At the end of his life, lecturing to the students in Berlin, this final system seemed hopelessly antique. For Kierkegaard, it was too abstract; for Engels, it was too Christian.

A focus upon self, freedom, system, the absolute, insight in mind and process in universe and history, art and myth—these held Schelling's interest in one arrangement or another from his first publication at the age of nineteen until his death at seventy-nine. What are the breakthroughs in philosophy, developed or introduced by Schelling, that might be important for the history of theology?

First, in the early *System* of 1800, he introduced into German idealism process and history. History was raised to the equal of nature, as consciousness was presented as becoming. A modern view of God was sketched: the being and activity of God were moved from the objective to the subjective realm. Schelling wanted to counter Kantian criticism as much as Christian dogmatics. God cannot exist, he wrote, as a being in the objective world, for then he would either be less than God or preclude our existence. God's existence is viewed as a kind of revelation, and how many modern theologians begin with this theological approach.

Secondly, with the *Essay on Freedom*, Schelling introduced into idealism indeterminacy and will. The absolute is not simply reason, finite or infinite, but will: indeterminate, necessary and free. This shift from the rational to the volitional had long-lasting effects. The structure of reason before and after Kant cracked under the weight of the problem of freedom and necessity. All of the elements of psychological life that Kant and Fichte had spotlighted were now studied in the primal, surging, unfolding will of the godhead.

Thirdly, with the Munich lectures of 1827, Schelling offered a last system of universal scope. Fundamentally idealist in retaining much of his earlier philosophy, it explored the developing subjectivity of God, drawing into a vast system idealism, myth and particularly religion.

Teacher and guide, prophet and sun—all these titles were given to Schelling at one time or another by Catholic intellectuals. In our study Schelling stands for modern philosophy itself, for idealism, for subjectivity, for the revolution that decided to begin its worldview with thinking rather than being.

Romantic Idealism and Roman Catholicism

Schelling was the point of passage from the Romantic approach to art and life to the Catholic tradition of mysticism and symbol. Parallels and compartmentalizations must be developed carefully when we deal with Romanticism and idealism. We want only to show how some philosophers and theologians moved through these currents.

"The Romantic"—it is not possible to arrive at a precise definition of the term: a metaphor for that movement would not be a stream but an arrangement of volcanos. Romanticism did not stay the same but changed each decade. The Romantics were writers, artist and philosophers grouped in their circles. A shift in meaning, a new pathos, emotion and insight as well as reason, attention to the individual in the cosmos, a preference for the Gothic over the Hellene—these revolutions in style were applied by the Romantics to literature, science, art, music and religion.

> Romanticism stands over against a world which the Enlightenment robbed of its magic: the marvelous, the healing powers of the depths, feeling, awe, the unconscious . . . the opposite of what is reasonable, lucid and orderly, rational. . . . What was decisive in the entire voyage of Romanticism was that it found its way to the theistic and the Christian, and so fashioned a great Christian renaissance.[5]

The Roman Catholic renaissance was the product of men and women who were working within a fairly circumscribed epochal change around 1800. The Romantic movement that played so central a role in Catholic life then was German. Horst Fuhrmans has written:

> The time at the turn of the eighteenth century was indeed the great hour for the Germans, the hour for them to shine: for poetry through Klopstock, Lessing, Goethe, Schiller, Kleist, Hölderlin; for German music and for German philosophy. After Kant, through Fichte, Schelling and Hegel, system quickly followed system. . . . In all of this Schelling had his unavoidably important place—he is in fact the person who drew out and founded German idealism.[6]

German Romantic life touched England, France, America (through Coleridge, Schelling influenced various English divines[7]), but the following study is limited to Germany, where, simultaneous with the birth of idealism and Romanticism, there was a Roman Catholic renaissance.

The Romanticism which influenced Roman Catholic theology profoundly at the turn of the nineteenth century was Romanticism at its birth. Imagination and insight, polarity and process, limitless nature and limitless self, freedom from the power of the self—these were its characteristics. They would undergo metamorphoses in other countries and later years. The idealism which is our topic stands between Fichte and Hegel. An objective idealism, it explored the self and the absolute as the unfolding of all reality in a dialectical process. Schelling esteemed himself to be much more than a theoretician of Romanticism and he viewed his thought as a philosophy of existence, a synthesis transcending that of his contemporaries; nevertheless, in him these two currents came together, and in him they spoke to the theologians. The cultural world we are examining, even in its influence after 1835, is that of the first decades of the nineteenth century.

Perhaps the lasting and diverse influence of Schelling upon Roman Catholic theology was due to the intersection in his own life of the loftiest systems of intellect with a mystical exploration of the divine abyss. Hans Urs von Balthasar writes: "He is really an apocalyptic figure for whom all is arranged around revelation, around the disclosure of mystery, around breakthrough into the mysteries of God. From this magical and visionary style, so different from the ascetical Fichte and the cool Hegel, emerges the fact that he is a prophet and a poet."[8]

Catholics saw Schelling as anti-Enlightenment and pro-Romantic. They were supported in this by his growing interest in mysticism lived out in nature and religion. Once he had allowed the arational and the mystical to complement idealism's research of the mind, he could guide others through the world of self to "that temple of the godhead, nature," as the Romantics put it. Feeling and insight as well as logic opened up the iconic world of nature and history. The Romantic thought-form is tied to the ascendancy of the Catholic spirit. Romanticism was the right moment, the *kairos*, for a searching Catholic culture and led not to cathedral dogmatics but to a clearing where the believer awaited a new encounter with a revelatory presence as real as it was divine.

As we mentioned, Romanticism burst upon the European scene as something of a surprise; it emerged in circles of artists, philosophers, scientists. At Jena in 1797, the Schlegels drew Schelling to their circle; Heidelberg, where German folk literature came again to light, had its own circle, as did Berlin, whose members drew in Schleiermacher. Schelling himself wrote "of the school of Baader, of Görres with which I have a high sympathy."[9] Romantic circles of Catholic men and women ranged from Westphalia to Austria, from the Rhine to the Alps. In Münster, the center was Princess Gallitzin and Count von Stolberg. The Vienna circle in the 1830s included figures as disparate as St. Clemens Maria Hofbauer and Anton Günther. The early Landshut movement, the later Coblenz-Rhine axis, even the Catholic Tübingen faculty were schools of men and women rethinking faith and society.

Munich was a special center because there the long-term union of Romanticism and Catholic life had been prepared by an active Enlightenment Catholicism. Schelling came to Munich at the age of thirty-one in 1806. There he experienced the times of Enlightenment, of high Romanticism, of dark and uncertain Romanticism. It was with the crowning of Ludwig I in Munich, in 1827, that contemporary Catholic renewal became a state enterprise. Munich would be an Alpine Florence, which could boast that its architecture was as numinous as its restored monasteries, that its metaphysics of the godhead could be understood by a young, enlightened monarch.

We understand Roman Catholic intellectual life in the past century only by entering into the fullness of the different Catholic-Romantic circles of the half-century that began toward the end of the eighteenth century and ended at the fateful year 1848.

Charting Catholic Theology in the Nineteenth Century

Nineteenth-century religious thought has commonly been considered in English-speaking countries as predominantly a Protestant domain. The rare efforts of Catholics in modern religious philosophy seem to have ended up in "modernism" condemned by one or more of the popes; or, one might presume that Catholic intellectuals of the past century fell under the general designation of insignificance: "*Catholici non leguntur*"—a slogan heard as late as 1960.

We hope to challenge a number of these widely held presuppositions: (1) nineteenth-century theology and philosophy of religion is, above all in Germany, a Protestant enterprise; (2) Schleiermacher is the most typical example of a Christian theologian using the philosophy of early idealism and Romanticism; (3) examples of nineteenth-century Catholic thinkers are most easily found outside Germany—Newman or de Lamennais; (4) Roman Catholicism after Luther and Trent was neoscholastic up to the theological agitation leading to Vatican II; (5) the very few Roman

Catholics who struggled with the thought-forms of the modern world—for instance, Günther and Hermes—had inevitably failed and had earned well the label "modernist" for their deployment of philosophy after Kant.

Until fifteen years ago the histories of philosophy and of Christian theology in the nineteenth century were almost exclusively the work of German Protestants and they seldom if ever acknowledged the existence of a parallel Roman Catholic endeavor. The presumption was that the serious movements and figures were as Protestant as they were German. The century itself, because of its elevation of freedom and subjectivity to high places, was an application, a radicalization, of the Reformation. Before the magisterium of Rome the writings of so many thinkers from Lessing to Ritschl must be, if not Lutheran in their evangel, Protestant in their logic. More or less this is what Goethe and Hegel believed and what the anniversaries of the Reformation in 1819 and 1869 celebrated.

The origins of a subjectivity that is critical and creative may well lie within the cultural ambiance of German Protestantism. Clearly the dominant and numerous figures from Herder to Harnack were in their background, if not their practice, Protestant. But the five presumptions briefly sketched above are too carelessly assumed in studies of the nineteenth century. They misrepresent Roman Catholic thought at that time. The correction for this view is a broader and deeper picture of Catholic intellectual life in the early nineteenth century. Schelling is the bridge between idealism/Romanticism and Catholicism.

Roman Catholics too contributed to this incomplete picture. Studies of the Tübingen theologians often neglect their cultural context and sources. We learn little of where the Catholic Tübingen school came from and why it faded into a time of neoscholasticism. The Tübingen theologians appear to have lived in a vacuum, without contact with the Enlightenment or Romanticism; or, their activity is deemed worth studying only to the extent that it recalls Hegel.

Kant, Hegel and Schelling were Protestants, but transcendental criticism, Romanticism and developmental, objective idealism were not exclusively so. Perhaps Schelling is particularly symptomatic of Christianity in an idealist-Romantic format because his career pursued this goal for almost fifty years. Thinkers such as Franz von Baader, Friedrich Schlegel and F.A. Staudenmaier offer lucid, developed examples of the Romantic-Christian synthesis because they saw the new philosophy not as a substitute for, but as an expression of, revelation.

Theological periods depend upon cultural epochs. It is not easy to arrange Roman Catholic figures and movements to parallel the history of Protestant theology in the nineteenth century.[10] In Germany, both Catholic and Protestant philosophy of religion and theology flowed out of the same cultural forms, but contacts between the two church traditions were infrequent (the double faculty of Tübingen was an exception). Roman Catholic life had its own rhythm even if it drew upon modern philosophy for insights and frameworks.

There are, in the cultural history of the nineteenth century, two great segments; the middle of the century, particularly the years leading to 1848, separates them. The following pages chart the first segment; in many ways the rest of the century—modernism, late Romanticism, neo-scholasticism, socialism—are a reaction to the creativity of the first decades.

a) *Three Generations* Between 1798 and 1848 there were three genera-tions of Roman Catholic thinkers open to the culture of that age. They were not only theologians, exegetes and philosophers but scientists, histo-rians and artists. Most of them confronted Schelling as their mentor, or later as a venerable personification of an era passing.

The *first* generation of Catholic disciples of Schelling reaches back into the last years of the eighteenth century. J. M. Sailer and members of the faculties of science at various Bavarian schools accepted Schelling's first writings with enthusiasm. Independent thinkers of the stature of F. Schlegel and J. Görres represent another kind of influence accepted. The *second* generation includes giants such as Franz von Baader and J. S. Drey, the founder of the Catholic Tübingen school. Drey's disciples: Staudenmaier, Kuhn and Möhler—a third generation—related to Schel-ling in different ways. Staudenmaier was intent upon a faithful Catholic system that would build upon Hegel and Schelling. By the 1830s, how-ever, the younger *Tübinger* such as Möhler and Kuhn had moved away from Schelling; critical of both Hegel and neoscholasticism, they pre-ferred history to system. Martin Deutinger and Ignaz von Döllinger rep-resent in different ways the late Roman Catholic interest in Romantic idealism. These two Munich professors are the resolution of the third generation; they form not a school but a testimony to influences that were once powerful and promising, but now in decline.

We will treat the influence of Romantic idealism in the history of Roman Catholic theology chronologically. Each of the three periods—the years after 1798, 1806 and 1827—marks changes in the prominence of subjectivity and process in culture. Schelling's intellectual life reflects them all and each corresponds to a period in the history of German theology.

b) *Two Focal Points: Subjectivity and Revelation* To write a history of German Roman Catholic theology from Kant to Nietzsche, from idealism to existentialism, would be the work of several decades. We do not offer the following chapters as a substitute for that history, nor are they only a segment of that history. The philosophers and theologians around Schelling up to 1848 enact the first period in nineteenth-century thought, perhaps the most important one. They assert and describe an active Roman Catholic theology after 1750. The value of this history comes not from its complete record of personages and books but from its exemplification of a culturally engaged theology. The subject of this book is then not only the theologians or philosophers but their thinking and writing as a mirror of the times.

One is always in danger of getting lost in the mountains of Teutonic systems. Like an inexperienced traveler in the Himalayas, the researcher as well as the reader experiences vertigo before the quantity of pages by Schelling or Görres, before the massiveness of a single system by Schlegel or Staudenmaier. To avoid wandering in the encyclopedias of this age, two focuses have been selected to help guide our way. They are *subjectivity* and *revelation*: one is the principle of modern, transcendental philosophy; the other is the foundation of Christianity. Both lie at the center of idealism and Romanticism.

German idealism means many things but particularly it means a shift to subjectivity. Whether this began with Martin Luther or with the Italian Renaissance and how it continues on to the psychiatrist Sigmund Freud and the composer Alban Berg need not concern us here. Idealism began by affirming the primacy of subject and it chose thinking as its field of study. Being was to be related to thinking and objectivity would be explained out of the subject. Under Fichte, the self was all, and then for Schelling all reality had the nature of a self.

Roman Catholicism had long been the defender of objectivity. Subjectivity implied excessive freedom, relativism, the absence of obedience to God's word and the church's voice. The influence of Aristotle and the shock of Luther reinforced in Catholicism a supreme allegiance to the object. The German Catholic intellectual community, on the other hand, without eschewing church and doctrine but reacting against the Enlightenment's secularity, accepted the shift to subjectivity. In the following pages, "idealism" does not mean a metaphysics that denies a world of objects but a transcendental (in the sense of Kant) analysis of subjectivity as the point of departure. The idealism that attracted Catholics was one that included the significant variations of *Romanticism* and *objective idealism*. In that combination young Schelling had replaced Fichte and various Kantians.[11]

Our second focus is revelation. What is revelation? For the nineteenth century this question was not just a topic of private piety but the point to which all the roads of philosophy led. Is revelation the necessary and evolving life of God present in our consciousness and world, or is it an entrance by a perfect and sovereign God into a distinct, relatively independent and needy human pageant? The goal of religious thought in the decades around 1800 was to steer a course between these alternatives:

> Catholic theology, as it opens itself to idealist philosophy, faces a dilemma: on the one hand, it sees the new teaching about knowledge as largely justified and as capable of being employed in theology; on the other hand, it rejects the threat of agnosticism and of pantheism coming from Hegel and Schelling. Theology directs itself to the problems of fundamental theology and to the question of God. . . . Little by little, however, under the influence of Romanticism, drawing upon the motif of organic growth, there emerges a new focus upon history, upon the field of real events, and so a return to the fact of Christ and to revelation takes place.[12]

In treating the different thinkers and theologies active in a thirty-year dialogue with Romantic idealism, we will let subjectivity and revelation serve as magnetic poles bringing some arrangement to the discussion. At the same time, we will come to see that these two focal points were indeed not only at the heart of Roman Catholic theology in this period but expressed the deepest questions of the entire culture.

In the past two decades the Roman Catholic Church throughout the world has undergone changes unequaled in their extent and rapidity since the Reformation. Yet little is known about the century and a half of theology that led up to and culminated in Vatican II. Only recently have scholars—first in Germany and now in France and the United States—turned their attention to German Catholic religious thought during the eras of Enlightenment and Romanticism. Under the pressure of the contemporary world, Catholic theology has assumed an approach out of subjectivity and within process. In this Karl Rahner recalls F. A. Staudenmaier; Teilhard de Chardin or R. Panikkar continue the spirit of

Joseph Görres. There is a continuity between today and this first period of modern Catholic thought. In between lie other periods, but clearly the contemporary theological scene began not before or after the Second World War but a decade after the French Revolution. The upheavals in church and theology before and after Vatican II have their sources in this earlier renewal, a stream which rose in 1790 and ebbed after 1840 . . . only to rise again in our century.

PART ONE

Odyssey of the Spirit
1798 to 1806

1

The Jena Romantics

DISPLAYING ITS PARADOXICAL union of the medieval and the modern, the Lutheran church in Swabia in the eighteenth century still retained two beautiful old Cistercian abbeys, along with some of their monastic offices and customs. They served as minor seminaries that fed into the theological faculty at Tübingen. In alternating years, the young men who would be the future pastors and scholars of evangelical Württemberg would come from Bebenhausen and Maulbronn to the university on the Neckar for their education in divinity.

One of these abbey-schools Hermann Hesse describes in his novel *Under the Wheel*:

> This magnificent monastery, hidden beyond hills and woods, has long been reserved for the exclusive use of the students of the Protestant Theological Academy in order that their receptive young spirits will be surrounded by an atmosphere of beauty and peace. . . .
>
> Perhaps there was among their number one of those clever and stubborn Swabians who would push his way into the mainstream of life and make his ideas, inevitably rather dry and narrowly individualistic, the focal point of a new and mighty system.[1]

Born in a suburb of Stuttgart in 1775 and educated at Bebenhausen, Friedrich Wilhelm Joseph Schelling was one of those "clever and stubborn Swabians." Indeed, no one's systems were more grand or ideas more individualistic.

Schelling's father was professor of Semitic languages at the Bebenhausen abbey-school, an author of enlightened commentaries on Old Testament books. Both he and his colleagues recognized the talents of his precocious son. The faculty concurred that the young Schelling had no more to learn with them. After waiting a year at the request of the university, Friedrich, in 1790, at the age of fifteen, entered Tübingen.

Schelling's youth was spent in an atmosphere of vital Lutheranism. His father was a pastor and a scholar. Among his father's friends were men devoted to the eschatological pietism of the area; among his books were the writings of Protestant mystics and millenarians such as Bengel and Oetinger, perhaps even a copy of Jacob Boehme or Valentin Weigel.

The young Schelling entered the theological faculty but it was not certain that he would become a minister; an alternative was academia and scholarship.

The professors' courses repeated the dry Lutheran orthodoxy little altered for a century. Only one or two showed an awareness of the new trends, of Herder's philosophy of a unified history of the human race or of Kant's sensational writings, which had appeared frequently over the past ten years. Nevertheless, the spirit of the times roamed through the Tübingen seminary, the venerable *Stift*. Schelling's comrades and friends included two genuises: Hegel and Hölderlin. There was a group of students who studied on their own the revolutionary philosophy of Kant. The students asserted themselves in rituals of support for the ideas of the French Revolution. Eventually, because of this youthful stew of *Sturm und Drang* metaphysics and democratic politics at the *Stift*, the duke himself had to journey from Stuttgart, to give a paternal warning.

Schelling read Fichte's latest writings in Tübingen and there he had the opportunity to meet the philosopher himself. Both agreed that Kant, in his observation of the significant mental structures that modify our experience and knowledge, had gone only halfway on his journey to truth and freedom. Fichte intended to radicalize Kant. Schelling's seminary advisers counseled him not to write a dissertation on Fichte, and so instead he compiled a summary of Enlightenment biblical criticism upon the issue of myth in the first chapters of Genesis.

Schelling and his friends were conscious that they were standing on the edge of a new world, preparing for the next epoch. Their Tübingen years came to an end in the spring of 1795. Hegel wrote to Schelling: "The Kingdom of God is coming, and our hands are busy at its delivery."[2] Hardly twenty, Schelling was already publishing monographs in philosophy and more than one editor was interested in his writings. *On the Possibility of a Form for Philosophy* and *On the Self* were inspired by Fichte. He, Schelling argued, was the new direction: a genius who had seen that the effect of Kant's philosophy was not knowledge but total freedom; an arrow that passed right through the orthodoxy of church establishments and the sterility of the Enlightenment. If the self produced the world, the self was free in a radical way—and philosophy had joined revolution in a new era.

Schelling was also drawn to another philosopher, Spinoza. He wrote to Hegel that he was much taken with this man his contemporaries had described as someone "drunk with God." In Spinoza the Fichtean mental structures found a theory of world and absolute, found some material for their transcendental patterns. Schelling drew out all of being and thinking from the experience of consciousness and the unity of self. Everything that meets us, meets us in consciousness. Consciousness, too, is always greater than any object, greater than the entire world of facets and things that we encounter. The self is not only the world, it is the horizon and the atmosphere of the world. In the self, Schelling wrote, philosophy had finally found the one and the all, the *hen kai pan*, for which the philosophers had searched.[3] It remained to be seen how Schelling could combine the active all-creative self of our knowing with the all-encompassing absolute.

Just as Schelling completed his studies and was beginning to publish his first philosophical articles, a position opened up for him. As tutor for the two orphaned Barons von Riedesel, he would be assured of a trip out of Swabia. The youths were to attend the University of Leipzig, and the journey there would offer leisure to see other parts of Germany. Schelling visited Hölderlin in Frankfurt and saw something of the court of the elector of Mainz whose style was that of the French Enlightenment. Feeling himself akin to Martin Luther, the reformer, as he passed by the Wartburg, Schelling arrived in Leipzig in April 1796.

In Leipzig, something new intellectually and culturally attracted his attention: science. Not Fichte's *Wissenschaft* nor the mathematical physics of Newton but the new sciences of electricity, chemistry and magnetism. Quite recently Lavoisier had developed modern chemistry with his research into the role of oxygen, and Galvani had fathered electrophysiology. Mineralogy, magnetics, electricity had emerged, changing the very meaning of science. Schelling became a part of stimulating social and intellectual circles in Leipzig. We know little about his time there but we do know that he ignored the lectures in philosophy at the university and occupied his time with studies in physics, chemistry and medicine. They led him away from pure philosophies of the mind out into a changing and mysterious world. His reading fleshed out the abstract framework of transcendental philosophy and challenged its Fichtean presumption that the subjectivity of the knower explained the universe.

Within a matter of months Schelling believed he saw how the new science was the completion, the body of transcendental philosophy. All of these new phenomena seemed to point to a unity within the varied powers of nature and to the question of its relationship to the creative consciousness of the human knower. During the year 1797 he sketched out systems of natural philosophy and at Easter of that year *Ideas for a Philosophy of Nature* appeared. That and the publications that followed quickly made him famous as a philosopher of nature, of nature's science and its mystery. Most essays on the German Romantics treat their interest in the new directions in literature, but Romanticism entered Schelling's life with natural science. It was not the history of art or even the theory of the creative imagination but the new natural sciences that led him to become the philosopher of nature and Romanticism after 1797.

The Jena Romantics

In the last months of 1797, a position in Jena was offered Schelling. It was not a professorship, for he refused to pursue the requirements for a doctorate. His publications showed he was beyond that. He would come to Jena, lecture publicly without pay and count on his popularity to gain him a chair either in philosophy or in science.

En route to Jena, he accepted an invitation to join some of the circle of the Jena Romantics for a tour of the famous Dresden galleries. With the Schlegel brothers and the writer Tieck, accompanied by their talented wives, Schelling toured the famous collection of sculpture and paintings amassed under the two Electors Augustus in the Florence of Saxony.

Upon his arrival in Jena, he was quickly included in the circle of the Romantics. Goethe's journal at the end of May indicates that he had spent an evening with Schelling and Schiller in Jena.[4] Schelling's writings had gained the attention of Goethe, who was at work in Weimar on his own interpretation of nature. Goethe found Schelling's philosophy of nature attractive and he supported his presence at the Weimar Court University in Jena.

Scholars of German Romanticism describe the following few years—from 1798 to 1801—as a highpoint of German Romanticism, the Jena *Romantik*. Fichte, August Schlegel and his wife Caroline, Friedrich Schlegel and Novalis were members. Not far away, in Weimar, were Goethe and Schiller, friendly to the young thinkers and artists at Jena. In Berlin, Schleiermacher was kept informed of the latest opinions of the circle and their works in progress.

Schelling made an immediate, strong impression upon the Jena circle and upon all who met him. Powerfully built, of medium height, with blond hair and confronting blue eyes, he seemed a personality in which creativity was joined to substance. Schelling's gift for abstraction was joined to a rich imagination. His literary style was bright and compelling. Although he expressed his professional commitment to minister to reason's forms, he himself owned a fearfully strong will.

Like so many living at the turn of the year 1800, he was enthusiastic for all that was grandiose, for the system that included everything. Richly gifted, famous from early in life, he was proud and ambitious for his own position in the world. Yet his gift of imagination played havoc with the drive to fashion the ultimate system, and his weakness was lack of care and logic. He was quick to take offense, slow to forgive, often moody, the victim fairly early in his life of illnesses that too often were hypochondria. No one met Schelling casually; his personality shone through his Germanic features.

Schelling continued to work on his philosophy of nature, and the *World-Soul* was greeted in 1798 with widespread enthusiasm. Henrik Steffens, the Danish mineralogist, and G. H. Schubert, early devotee of natural science as mysticism, were among the first of his students. Johann Ritter, the founder of scientific electrochemistry, was an influential colleague (within less than a decade he would discover electroplating and invent the first batteries). Jena had just been the scene of an important conference on galvanism. In the *World-Soul*, the young philosopher abandoned the static mechanism of the Enlightenment's view of nature. Nature was organic, alive, growing. A tension from opposing powers moves the totality of nature through free, constant growth. Nature is not simply static or mathematical but a polar process toward the infinite with its own forms, its own language. To think about nature—Schelling wrote in articles flowing easily from his pen—means becoming aware of the unconscious productivity of consciousness and unconsciousness. Nature, objectively real, struggles through individual organism to become in consciousness the ideal. "True, chemistry teaches us to read the elements, physics to read the syllables and mathematics to read nature itself . . . but philosophy interprets what is read."[5] The transcendental self, he argued, must be realized in nature as more than laws expressed in numbers. The universe is a unity with a dynamic organization; its law is organic development. Schelling's goal was to admit the objectivity of nature (and then of history) without giving up the privileged framework of transcendental analysis. Nature differs from its counterpart, spirit, and as the objectively real it struggles through individual organisms to become in consciousness the ideal.[6]

The First System

If Schelling's writings at Jena first pursued the philosophy of nature, his lectures focused upon the "elements" and "general system" of transcendental philosophy. The time at Dresden, however, and the acquaintance in Jena with literary theoreticians such as August and Friedrich Schlegel led Schelling to incorporate art as well as nature into a transcendental framework. Fichte traveled to and from Jena. Teaching there along with his younger colleague Schelling, Fichte soon found the university closed to him because of his controversial views upon the absolute (which many interpreted as God) as the form or product of the knowing self. Perhaps during a visit in December 1799, Fichte observed sadly that his disciple was moving in a different direction. "Schelling's clear break with Fichte meant that the development of nature as an objective enterprise is the presupposition for transcendental idealism. . . . The philosophy of nature and transcendental philosophy exist not as opposed sciences but as parts of the system of philosophy."[7] To this, Fichte could never agree.

In 1800 at the Easter book fair, Schelling's first system appeared, *The System of Transcendental Idealism*. Its author was twenty-five years old. This system included material from the natural sciences and from painting and sculpture, sections that set it aside from the works of Kant or Fichte. Schelling's system announced parallel worlds: one of self, the other of nature. Idealism was an objective idealism; the world of nature was not a mental projection; the ideal needs the real just as spirit needs nature for the ultimate synthesis to occur. In this early work the two parallel histories of spirit and nature seem to be joined by a predetermined harmony and to lack the identity, ground or godhead that Schelling would later give them.

Equally important, Schelling's philosophy announces that consciousness has a history: it is genetic, developmental, syntheses following upon actions. "History as a whole is a progressive, gradually self-disclosing revelation of the absolute."[8] The self is not a mental scaffold but a process of unfolding and regrouping, and nature mirrors this process. Not even the absolute escapes process. "History is a theater in which the Spirit is the playwright, but we are the co-poets."[9]

The influence upon Schelling from the Romantics is obvious, for the system's climax is art. Art was the place where spirit became concrete. In the artistic imagination, realized in paint or marble, the idea assumed matter. The spirit of the knowing self was free and productive and empowered with intuition into absolute spirit; nature was hieroglyphics in which we could also read "the odyssey of the spirit."[10] In art, however, the tangible creation of the artistic mind, the synthesis of matter and form, mirrored the universe where the real and the ideal came together in history and play.

Romantic Nature: A Path to Religion

Romanticism, whether that of the philosophers or that of the novelists, flowed not only from the new sciences but from a new view of art and a new intuition into the powers of the human personality. While Schelling was viewing nature as the concretization of the epochs and powers of consciousness, the Romantics began to regard it as magical and mystical. In the new art and science of the years around 1800, nature is not a collection of things or a machine but a world that fashions experience prior to reflection and consciousness. Spirit needs nature to illumine its own structures; nature needs spirit as its higher, ideal realization. A dialectic of the life of the spirit is the primal form of everything in Romantic culture: human and divine, solitary and democratic, free and necessary, lost in the abyss and ecstatic with power.

For the Romantics, nature was religious, that numinous place where the cosmos was becoming spirit and where the ideal shone in the concrete. Panvitalism encouraged the pinnacle of conscious life, insight, to perceive the deeper structures and engaging presence of spirit within nature. Idealist panentheism (Schelling accepted the word) meant that the ideal, the absolute in spirit, dwelt not in heaven or in mathematics but in the history of self and in the dynamism of nature. Nature was the religion of the Romantics and mysticism was its eschatology.

The Romantics loved the image of the journey. Schelling's intellectual voyage, like that of Schlegel, Görres, Baader, Marheineke and many others, began with an embrace of freedom and subjectivity; it moved on to the new natural sciences with their organic, almost magic wonder at nature; art joined nature to serve as a mirror of spirit, and—equally important—to be a portal to the mysteriously infinite. The Homeric epic, Schelling wrote, was the poetic paradigm of the real world. In the journey of the individual and collective self we see Odysseus leaving home to become objectified and in his journey back to Ithaca he unfolds in history and life the ideal:

> History is an epoch whose poet is God. Its two main parts are found in the process of humanity; the first is humanity's emergence up to the highest point away from God; the second is the return. The first part is the *Iliad*; the second is the *Odyssey*.[11]

Oddly, science did not exclude mysticism but led to it. Natural philosophy was happy to examine not only the new results of experimentation but also the esoteric traditions of magic, alchemy and occultism. Mesmer's magnetism might be the discipline to unify the scientific and the suprarational. Against a Kantian abhorrence of nature's wildness and mystery, in the "atmosphere of a secret society,"[12] the parascientific was excitedly explored. Clairvoyance was given equal status with electricity; the seven sacraments might well be the highest form of magnetism.[13] Scientists were interested in alchemy. "In the course of the eighteenth century, the discovery of electricity as well as the discoveries of magnetic and galvanic phenomena brought a very significant transformation of the conception of God, of the understanding of the presence of God in the world. In the train of these ideas, there grew up a completely new understanding of the relationship of soul and corporality, of life and matter, of spirit and nature."[14]

When historians of the Romantic movement speak of its "mystical element," they do not mean a particular Christian spirituality or piety. The mystical is conscious insight. Schelling replaced the Kantian categories of reason with the intuitive power of the knowing self, which could reach to absolute spirit. The mystical too is a path to the divine disclosed in numinous creation. More than a symbol or an allegory, the materiality of life is the place or atmosphere where the human and the divine meet. Schelling and his Jena friends agreed that the numinous has three *loci*: nature, art and the depth of the free self. It only took a year or two for them to conclude that history also was numinous—and that implied revelation. Thus the Romantics came to look anew at religion long obscured by Protestant orthodoxy and the Enlightenment. "For the Enlightenment, Christianity was a surpassed form; for Romanticism it was the primal form. . . . The inner renewal of Christian consciousness is at this moment the decisive change for German intellectual history."[15]

Through a new philosophy of nature and through the many-colored world of the Romantics, religion approached Schelling. It is here that the history of the Roman Catholic dialogue with the cultural world around 1800—with Romantic idealism—begins.

Next we will look at Friedrich Schlegel, a Jena Romantic who in a few years moved from philosophy and literature to religion, mythology and Roman Catholicism. His personal way leads from Romanticism through Schelling's philosophy of nature to Christianity. Second, we will see how through scientists rather than Catholic theologians Schelling entered Catholic intellectual circles. The scientists set in motion a course of events that will establish Schelling as the philosophical mentor for Roman Catholic thinkers over the following thirty years.

Friedrich Schlegel

The younger Schlegel, Friedrich, born in 1772, belongs in Catholic intellectual history. Yet he is neither theologian nor churchman but universal thinker and layman convert. When Schelling joined him and acquaintances for a tour of Dresden, Schlegel had already published a theory of the new literature and had established a schema for the periodization of the arts. Early in the century he and Schelling were at the center of the circle gathered around Jena and Weimar; decades later both would labor over a definitive, Christian philosophical system. Schlegel's conversation with Schelling in religious thought was limited but always significant. In personal contact during the heady years of the *Frühromantik*, both strove for the same broad vision of self and nature and both concluded their careers with history and religion.

Schlegel first came to Jena in 1796, precociously drinking in the companionship of Goethe and Fichte, explaining his theories for the new literature. By moving to Berlin he entered the circle of the Mendelssohns, the Veits, the Tiecks, and he shared lodgings with Schleiermacher, who was at work on his translation of Plato. There he married Dorothea Veit, daughter of the philosopher Moses Mendelssohn. Dorothea was already married and the mother of two sons. In 1799, with the publication of *Lucinde*, rumor became sensation and the attention of Europe was gained. This novel (written as Schleiermacher was composing his *Addresses on Religion*) applied the philosophy of the Romantics to love and marriage; the heroine was clearly Dorothea fictionalized. August Schlegel's wife Caroline wrote from Jena in 1797 to her brother-in-law Friedrich about the life of the group . . . and about Schelling, who was quickly becoming the philosopher of Romanticism:

Schelling says he is going to wall himself in—to work. He is, however, more a man to break down walls. Believe me, my friend, he is, as a man, more interesting than you concede: a real, primal nature; in terms drawn from the world of minerals—granite.[16]

The junior Schlegel wrote back a question that was more a prophecy than he could surmise: "But where will he find female granite?" Friedrich arrived in Jena in the autumn of 1799 for a second stay. Only in his middle twenties, his writings were read in Europe and he was a close friend to Novalis whose *Hymns to the Night* presaged the course of Romanticism.

The circle of the Jena Romantics was complete. August Schlegel was translating Shakespeare; the theater intrigued them as much as science and philosophy. In Weimar, Schiller's *Wallenstein* was performed, as was also Friedrich's *Alarcos*. The circle read Spinoza, Plato, Jakob Boehme; they listened to Fichte, were visited by Goethe. Their motto was *hen kai pan*, their issue was subjectivity and freedom, their worlds the finite and the infinite.[17]

Young Philosophers

Schlegel already knew Schelling's writings, for in 1796 he had reviewed the first books *On the Self* and *Philosophical Letters*. Perceptivity is evident as he sums up the young philosopher: "The philosophy of Schelling—which one can call a critical mysticism—ends like Aeschylus' *Prometheus* in an earthquake."[18] Schlegel esteemed the young Schelling as Fichte's equal and Spinoza's successor, one worthy of a place in "the Parnassus of philosophy."[19] Schlegel worked to interest others in Schelling.

Schelling's next work, however, *On the World-Soul*, struck Friedrich as too theological, too superficial and hastily conceived. He wrote to Schleiermacher: "I have read the *Weltseele* of Schelling. He more and more resembles Leibniz in his presentation. There is a divine neglect in it. What he calls energy is only the feverish pallor of a sick person."[20]

Schlegel was caught up in his own plans and powers. His literary fragments do not conceal a skepticism toward grandiose systems. He also felt the introspective coolness that emanated from "the granite" and, as time in Jena passed, he came to dislike Schelling. Nevertheless, *Athenaeum*, the brothers' literary supplement for the Romantic movement, was happy to publish Schelling's writings, and Friedrich enjoyed the philosopher's tripping, sardonic poem of agnosticism "Heinz Widerporst's Confession of Faith.'' Despite Schlegel's indifference to Christianity and Schelling's mocking atheism, both were moving toward an appreciation of religion as revelation strong enough to hold their interest over future years.

Schlegel was accredited in the summer of 1800 at Jena University and he began to lecture there in October on transcendental philosophy. The previous spring, of course, Schelling had published his lectures under the same topic. Unfortunately, as he turned from literature to metaphysics, Schlegel's brilliance dimmed. Schelling's competition in philosophy was too strong and Schlegel, unsuccessful in the lecture hall, left for Berlin.

> Schlegel's philosophical connection with Schelling consisted in the themes of art, genius and productive imagination. . . . There was also the demand for a new mythology and the vision of a poetry which was both penetrating and at the same time unconsciously creating the cosmos. This led to his acceptance of that realism without boundaries which came with the natural philosophy born of idealism.
>
> While Schlegel developed his own viewpoint out of intellectual encounters with Kant and Jacobi, his relationship with Schelling seemed to be the opposite. He was of the opinion that he preceded Schelling in many of the ideas which they held in common during their lives. Schlegel influenced Schelling, and yes, at times he believed Schelling had looted his thought.[21]

From 1796 to 1806, Schlegel filled notebooks with excerpts from the worlds of the natural sciences and the humanities. Some of these fragments he published, some he intended to mold into the system the times called for. They offer a rich if scattered picture of his intellectual development during these exciting years at Jena. In a university lecture in 1804 he said, ''A person's philosophy is a history, a becoming, the progress of his spirit.''[22]

The journals have calculations similar to the charts in Schelling's philosophy of the natural sciences, but they refer to the structure of literature. Drawn from physics, they are a search for an *a priori* theorem, a last principle, for poetry. Before his early death in 1801, Novalis wrote to Schlegel about a philosophy of nature that would show just how symbolic and aesthetic were human perception and light. Both agreed that the problem was how to launch a probe into the ''infinite potentializations'' of the absolute in poetry.[23] And like Schelling, they glimpsed within the hieroglyphics of nature the odyssey of the spirit.

Schlegel wrote, "Idealism treats nature like a work of art, like a poem."[24] At first, a deduction of all reality from the Fichtean self seemed possible but, even more quickly than Schelling, Schlegel tired of the lonely mansions of the self; not only nature but literature, every history and religious movement, could serve as the realization of the ideal. Whereas Schelling emphasized the identity of all in God, Schlegel asserted that "the center of transcendental philosophy is not only the absolute identity of the real and ideal, but absolute diversity."[25]

Philosophy for Schlegel was not only the panorganizational form but the aesthetic product of an inner drive. Philosophy's essence was the search for the totality and beauty of the world as it was accessible to intellectual perception. Schlegel placed more emphasis upon the personal, upon the psychological. He had early concluded that of all philosophical groups the mystics have the genius for true science, for a science capable of total unification:

> Mysticism is nothing less than an uncritical *Wissenschaftslehre*. The identity of subject and object is an idea which comes naturally to the mystics . . . Christ was simply a mystic . . . , and it is from the mystics we must learn philosophy.[26]

In Schlegel's as well as Schelling's lectures on transcendental philosophy, religion and revelation were introduced. The chiaroscuro of the mystic Jakob Boehme (whose writings Tieck was circulating) presented to the Romantics another perspective on the identity of subject and object. The epochal hieroglyphics of nature and the complex lines of sculpture would find a synthesis in the horizon of the religious. How quickly Kant and even Fichte were becoming démodé. For the "lovable enthusiast," as Novalis called Schlegel, religion began to be more and more the vital center of life. Journal fragments show that Schlegel agreed with Schelling's conclusion to the *System* of 1800. "The work of destiny or nature was already providence imperfectly revealing itself. . . . When the final period exists, then God will exist."[27]

Schlegel repeatedly observed that he was living in a time of crisis and transition, that both scholasticism and the Enlightenment were inadequate for the tasks of the new age. There were three epochs in the Christian West, he wrote: Catholicism, Lutheranism and now idealism.

This is a new age but one hardly begun. We find ourselves between the times. . . . Idealism is the great phenomenon of the time. True idealism does not say simply that we make the object but that we construct the universe. It shows how we make the world, how we construct many objects and worlds.[28]

Unlike Schelling, Schlegel was hesitant to say that idealism solved all the problems of thought and religion. More and more his journals of apprenticeship in thought record the variety of human experience that speaks to the searching soul, selecting out of the variety of life the material for later systems. He was anticipating not only the next twenty years but the entire century. Schlegel was not content with the austere system and absolute of Schelling's writings published after 1798. He would take God and life more seriously. God should be depicted as a person; thought should include love; medieval mystics and Asian mythologies could be accepted as guides. And above all, there seemed to be more to the Christian tradition than philosophy had suspected.

In 1805—a boundary year between Jena and conversion to Roman Catholicism—Schlegel wrote:

True idealism has gone on since Christ—in the fathers of the church, the scholastics and members of sects. Creation *ex nihilo*, the Christian Trinity, the temporal beginning of the world can be explained only through the concept of a becoming godhead explained by a complete idealism.[29]

Schlegel and Dorothea left Jena for Paris to find a new career. Schlegel evaluated Schelling's publications after 1802 coldly. The dialogue *Bruno*, he wrote, lacked not only philosophical but literary distinction. Schlegel wrote to Schleiermacher that Schelling erred in letting systematization overpower his thinking; he was only repeating the cold terrain of Spinoza and Kant. "For Schelling, the *personal* is the last thing to enter. From this groundless nothing, from its perfect frigidity, there is no way out."[30]

In Paris, Schlegel studied oriental languages and searched out knowledgeable if obscure pioneers in Persian and Sanskrit. Through some mastery of those languages he gained access to the mythology and mystical writings of India—that is, to a new metaphysics, a new ontology of nature and religion. A book was soon begun on Asian religion.

The Romantic age was an age of conversion. In the time of *Sturm und Drang* one pursued the *numen* in the gifts of Graeco-Roman culture. When Romanticism replaced classicism, medieval gothic appeared as home and grace, and Roman Catholicism struck some as providing a desirable wholeness and luminosity. Among the more famous Romantic converts to Catholicism were Friedrich Schlegel and his wife Dorothea Mendelssohn Veit Schlegel. The road that led to Rome began in Paris with its paintings by Raphael and its Gothic architecture; it passed the rubble of Cologne art treasures damaged in the secularization of 1803, and wandered on through the Rhenish landscape that inspired Romantics from Tieck to Robert Schumann.

What is significant at this early point in our history of Roman Catholic culture in the early nineteenth century is not Schlegel's conversion to the church. (Later we will meet him again as a Catholic philosopher of world history.) Rather, the Romantics in a few years became dissatisfied with the enterprise of pure transcendental philosophy and its abstract ontology of the absolute. Romantic art and mysterious nature pointed to that deeper dimension; whether faith or church or scripture awaited the pilgrim there, remained to be seen. Nevertheless, the horizon and goal of the analysis of the times was neither the knowing self nor organic nature; it was to be religion.

Bamberg and the Physicians

Jena was prelude. Now we turn to the events of political and intellectual history which brought Schelling together with German Catholic intellectual life.

Already in 1799, in Jena, Fichte had become the subject of rumors and then of charges that questioned his very belief in God. If, after all, in the new philosophy the productive self was the absolute, where did that leave the question of the existence of God? In July 1799, Fichte felt compelled to leave Jena. The time with Schelling and the Schlegels had been so pleasant that he half-expected they would willingly come with him into exile and form a "colony" in Berlin.

How such a move would have altered Schelling's career! Although he was not anxious for a break, Schelling had realized that after his publications in natural philosophy he and Fichte were no longer on the same track. Their joint lecturing in philosophy at Jena did not give a completely accurate picture. Schelling, however, was not interested in moving to Berlin for another reason: he planned to further his scientific studies—in *medicine*! "If natural scientists are all . . . priests of the powers of nature, still the physician guards the sacred fire at the center."[31]

Fichte may have mentioned that Schelling might study medicine in Berlin at the Charité Hospital where Schleiermacher preached with growing success. But Schelling had decided on Bamberg in northern Bavaria where a prince-bishop ruled. "My plan is developed this far. I have decided to go for the summer to Bamberg. Röschlaub insists that I study there *privatissima*, and, as you can imagine, this is just what I want. The following year I'll spend in Vienna. What happens after that, time will show. So, I hope in one and a half years to be completely finished."[32]

What would be finished? A degree in medicine? Perhaps, more likely, studies in experimental sciences helpful to constructing their *a priori* system. Schelling solidified the plan to study at Bamberg intensely if privately, and to hold lectures there on the philosophy of nature. Marcus greeted the visit: "Bamberg was one of the first places where the public hospitals employed the Brown system. Now Bamberg will have the praise of applying in medical treatment that which your philosophy of nature is developing."[33]

The man Schelling chose to be his medical instructor, his first contact in Bavaria, was Andreas Röschlaub. In 1799 Schelling had published an article in Röschlaub's journal *Magazin zur Vollkommnung der Heilkunde*.[34] After studies in Würzburg, his dissertation *De febri fragmentum* won Röschlaub a doctorate from Bamberg. By 1798 he was ordinary professor and second in rank on the staff at the general hospital. In the history of German medicine, Röschlaub was the founder of a school with a method of treatment based upon the teachings of the Scotsman John Brown.

Adalbert Friedrich Marcus, director of the Bamberg hospital, was Röschlaub's co-worker and an admirer of Schelling. A Jewish convert to Catholicism and a favorite of members of the Bavarian government, he would be influential later in securing a position for the young philosopher at Würzburg where Schelling would work with him in publishing a medical journal.

The Catholic doctors Marcus and Röschlaub displayed no great interest in religious metaphysics, but the desire to find a unified system for the sciences as well as a set of transcendental principles to explain human life and disease led them to Schelling. They understood science as the source of new, almost magical powers behind which stood a power which also pervaded human consciousness; all of this was not far from the mystical, the religious.

For Brown, health consisted in the presence of the proper amount of stimulus.[35] There are only two kinds of diseases—those caused by a debility or by a superfluity of stimulation. Medical treatment consists in reestablishing the balance. Brown himself believed that most diseases were asthenic (lack of stimulus), and that stimulants (including opium) were apt for treatment. These principles were attractive to Schelling: the point of departure of his recently completed *System of Transcendental Idealism* was a history of consciousness displayed in the two mutually influential and developing realms of the real and the ideal.

Schelling plunged into medicine. His own forceful lectures strengthened his position among the Catholic doctors and students.[36] Rather than completing his studies in Vienna, however, personal and political changes led him to return to Jena in October where a time of mature productivity awaited him. The *System*, in print since Easter of 1800, so novel in its introduction of history, art and a developmental theology into transcendental philosophy, still bore, nonetheless, in its structure a Fichtean view of the productive, absolute self. Now Schelling would write *his* system: in 1801 he announced that the *Presentation of My System of Philosophy* would soon appear.

Schelling was at the height of his speculative powers in these first years of the century. Filled with ideas and formats, he published thousands of pages, close to half of what he would publish in his lifetime. The tasks he set for himself were huge but he was young and filled with energy, not afraid, as he put it, "to set out upon the open ocean of the absolute."[37] Schelling had united the transcendental philosophy of Kant and Fichte with a Romantic philosophy of nature and art; he had passed into the next period in his thinking, the time of objective idealism (1801 to 1803). He concluded that the absolute was not reason alone but a synthetic identity where the real and the ideal met and were one; the absolute—the source and identity of all—was the real-become-the-ideal.

During his years in Jena, Schelling reached his furthest point away from organized religion. The Lutheran orthodoxy and pietism of home and seminary were forgotten or repressed. He planned to write a parody of his education in the Tübingen seminary. His mockery of clerical and academic religion in the satirical poem "Heinz Widerporst" was a symptom of religious crisis, a sign of youthful revolt. Horst Fuhrmans describes Schelling's writings on the philosophy of nature and mind between 1795 and 1802 as "intentionally antireligious," and Xavier Tilliette calls the Widerporst poem "an impulsive and truculent profession of paganism in reaction to Schleiermacher's *Reden*."[38] And yet, for only a few years was religion fully absent from his books, and the absolute was always present. In the first system, God enters, albeit hesistantly and sparsely: a God who reveals himself and becomes existent in history and idealism.

When the mystery of nature flows into the epic of history there is not only religion but revelation. The *Lectures on University Studies*, written at Jena in 1802, invited Christianity to find a new interpretation within Schelling's own expanding idealism. And, in an article on the philosophy of nature, we find a striking passage:

> All the symbols of Christianity show a determination to present the identity of God with the world in images; the particular position of Christ is that of intuiting God in the finite. . . . We can call that mysticism.[39]

The new philosophy was the next stage in religion as well as in the culture of the world.

External events and decisions in his career were drawing Schelling in unexpected directions. A professorship in Jena was not available. Dissonance and departure broke up the harmony of life among the Romantics in Jena. In the south of Germany, however, other men and other circles had turned to Schelling.

Schelling in Bavaria

Bavaria was particularly ready for the philosophy of insight into the absolute, for the new philosophy of nature. The electoral duchy had taken little part in the classicism of Weimar. The Bavarian spirit was not captivated by the art of Greece or by the mathematics of England. The powers of Bavarian piety were latent, ready to emerge, in the Catholic south. The secular rationalism of the Enlightenment had never attracted fully the spirit that delighted in the interplay of nature and grace flowing through the cascade of baroque sculpture. The baroque spirit of southern Roman Catholicism, however, did find the characteristics of Romanticism congenial.[40] In the 1780s theosophic groups such as the Illuminati and the Rosicrucians sprang up; mystical and sacramental forces were alive again. Bavaria had been socially and culturally touched by the Enlightenment and this, paradoxically, was a preparation for the Romanticism to follow. There was by the 1790s an awareness that something new was approaching.

Schelling entered the south through his philosophy of nature, which symbiotically nourished and was nourished by Romantic currents. Although some saw in idealism and the philosophy of nature the mystical and the magical, Schelling expounded them as the concretization of the epochs and laws of self-consciousness. It was, then, not through theology or philosophy but through science that Shelling's thought began its conversation with Roman Catholic intellectual life.

Röschlaub and Marcus continued to evangelize the medical world for Schelling. The faculties at Jena, Würzburg and Vienna were enthusiastic. In 1801, questions for examinations in medicine at Bamberg included startling metaphysical theses drawn from Schelling's writings. The next year Röschlaub became professor at the Bavarian university in Landshut. He assured Schelling that more and more intellectuals were joining his school. "The best thing will be that smart people in ever greater numbers are understanding you better."[41] Only a few months after his arrival, Röschlaub was able to secure for Schelling a doctorate in medicine *honoris causa* from Landshut. "Your system is greatly studied here—of that you can be assured. I have found many friends of your work. The medical faculty, which is excellent, has the highest respect for your achievement. It would like to give you the diploma of a doctor of medicine. Their wish is unanimous, and I am the organ of its expression."[42] Members of the faculties of science worked to interest others in Schelling; through his followers in the philosophy of science, theologians and philosophers were drawn to the thought-world of Schelling's grandiose systems appearing each year.

In the next chapter we will see how the Romantic idealist's influence quickly grew as the pastoral theologian of southern Germany, J. M. Sailer, urged his circle at the University of Landshut to plunge into Schelling's post-Kantian thought. There one could find a transcendental modernity that was also a philosophy of religion, perhaps even a mysticism of life, nature and God.

2
First Disciples:
Bavaria and the Rhineland

SCHELLING HAD BEEN delighted by the honorary doctorate in medicine bestowed upon him by Landshut in 1802. The degree had been conferred by a professor of surgery. The academic celebration was joined to a festival of thanksgiving that Bavarian Landshut had been spared in the recent battles. The portal of the former Dominican church, now part of the university, was crowned with a representation of Pallas Athene; below it was the inscription *Fiat Lux*. The text for the sermon was taken from Proverbs, "Wisdom built her house. . . ." A pageant celebrated Max Joseph IV as the protector of tolerance. Two honorary doctorates were given: one to Schelling and the other to Cajetan Weiller. Weiller was the testy *Beckmesser* of the Munich Enlightenment; Schelling was the young genius of the new philosophy.[1]

From our perspective, this celebration was a symbol of change from the Enlightenment to Romanticism. The academic ritual celebrated the entrance of Schelling and his philosophy into Bavaria—that is, into Catholic Germany. The following pages will describe the result of this meeting: the first encounters between Roman Catholicism and Romantic idealism, the first attempts by Catholics in Bavaria to fashion theology out of Schelling's objective idealism, the first writings by the Rhinelander Görres on nature and myth.

The University at Landshut

The Bavarian University of Ingolstadt had had a long history. There Johannes Eck and after him the Society of Jesus had created an outpost of the Counter-Reformation facing north toward the country of Luther. Centuries later, in 1800, the venerable university was moved not far to

Landshut. In this move, the powerful minister, Maximilian Montgelas, furthered his policy of transforming Bavaria into a model modern state. Church, education, even the monarchy were instruments of this purpose.

Montgelas was born in Munich to a Savoy family in 1759. Ambitious and enlightened, he became advisor to the Palatine branch of the Bavarian royal family. Montgelas moved with Max Joseph to Munich at the beginning of 1799, when his master succeeded to the throne of Bavaria. Montgelas then began his patient and clever efforts to reorganize the government: a modern constitution, the liberalization of class structure and the reform of education particularly at higher levels.[2] The old schools at Altdorf, Dillingen and, eventually, Bamberg were suppressed; Protestant Erlangen continued, and Ingolstadt University would move to Landshut. Montgelas expanded his grand educational design. Opportunities were offered to leading philosophers and historians despite their Protestant origins or their Kantian-Fichtean tendencies. Among Roman Catholics, those sympathetic to the Enlightenment were to be preferred. Montgelas paradoxically had no inkling that what was for him "modern thinking" was in fact already in decline, and that at Landshut the Enlightenment was embattled by a newer school: Romantic idealism. Ironically, the minister consistently called on Romantic professors to support the Enlightenment.

Contemporary Thinking

Convinced that Germany was at the threshold of a new era being ushered in by earthquakes, electricity, poetry and Napoleon's battles, Landshut was frequently in a state of upheaval. The students brawled with the soldiers of various armies; the professors carried their classroom controversies into the taverns and restaurants. No longer was the division between scholastic Jesuits and followers of the Enlightenment but between professors who had sought to draw from Kant a rational, ethical Christianity and those who esteemed the first currents of Romanticism as the force for a renewed Catholicism. There were Catholic Kantians: some Benedictines and ex-Jesuits had found the Enlightenment and Immanuel Kant a healthy stimulus after the decline of baroque scholasticism. In terms of their orthodoxy, the Catholic Kantians ranged over a wide spectrum, but they all agreed that criticism of the process of knowing and willing should be taken seriously, and that Christianity was less a historical drama than a model for moral living.

Matthäus Fingerlos was typical of the Enlightenment. Professor of pastoral theology at the university and director of the electoral seminary (the Georgianum), he led the anti-Romantic, anti-Schelling camp. His theology was a typical mélange. He began pastoral theology with a Kantian critique of religion and concluded with an explanation of the essence of religion as a cultivated moral stance inspired by some New Testament aphorisms.

The malicious Jacob Salat was more significant. As a theology teacher in Augsburg he had been suspected of membership in excessive, theosophical movements. But Montgelas, who favored those mystical rationalists, made him a professor in Landshut. Salat openly denied traditional dogmas and admired all that was of the Enlightenment. He fought a propaganda battle not only against Schelling but against every hint of Romanticism. For Salat, God is subsistent reason and what is called revelation flows solely from reason's forms. Protestantism and Catholicism are two complementary branches of a Christianity whose essence is a morality suitable to a religious humanitarianism. Schelling observed en passant that Salat's numerous volumes were "of little merit."[3]

Professors at the beginning of the nineteenth century moved comfortably from natural science to philosophy, back to teaching medicine and then theology. Through this academic mobility Schelling's ideas spread. Some professors at Landshut, in either private or public lectures, offered students an introduction to objective idealism. Empty positions were filled by men sympathetic to the new thinking. Schelling's followers grew in numbers, splitting the university into two opposing camps:

> The conservative direction was represented by the old and new devotees of the Enlightenment in philosophy and theology, and by those sympathetic to them from other faculties, especially law. . . . On the other side was the new direction, the party of "monks, mystics and Schellingians." The members of the new party had the advantage: greater numbers and better minds. Moreover, their spirit was on the upsurge, on the move. The leader of the Enlightenment party was the government, and it had the misfortune that many of its measures served the opposition. The calling to Landshut of Sailer, Zimmer and Weber furthered precisely what the government wished to discourage, as did the intellectual stance of the new Protestant professors. A new time with a new spirit had broken through.[4]

"Church Father of Bavaria": J. M. Sailer

Some men and women influence history not through the originality of their thought or the productivity of their writings but through their personality. Their presence points a way into the future or clears a place for life and grace. They attract disciples who will multiply efforts for change, carry new ideas into different corridors of existence. They form a circle, a school whose members collectively excel their founder. Such a person was J.M. Sailer.

Sailer's writings today seem undistinguished and even uninteresting. He was born too late for the Enlightenment, which he disdained, and he held back from fully accepting Romanticism. He looked for a new era after 1775, and yet he was frightened by the freedom of Fichte, the absolute of Schelling, the politics of Görres.

Sailer has been called "the church father of Bavaria."[5] He was concerned with the practical side of religion—education, morality and the interior life. The systems he wrote were encyclopedias of pedagogy or morality, not philosophy or theology. He was, nonetheless, an important catalyst for the Catholic restoration of the early 1800s. Through him Catholicism moved from the emptiness of church life during the Enlightenment to a revitalization by Romanticism whose first philosophical inspiration was Schelling.

Sailer's life, reaching from 1751 to 1832, spanned the years of Enlightenment, *Sturm und Drang* and Romanticism. For over fifty years—years that reach from Kant's *Critique of Pure Reason* (1781) to Hegel's lectures on *The Philosophy of Religion* (1830)—he taught, wrote, inspired others. Sailer was a personal synthesis of many of the cultural and religious movements around him, not a person of speculation like Fichte, Schelling and so many others, but of praxis. The center of the world was for him the self, not the transcendental ego but the virtuous self discovering inward communion with God.

Through several revolutions, in the pain of seeing one age end and another being born, Sailer—priest, academic, bishop—remained a column of strength and support. In his diary he arranged his life around the rivers of Bavaria:

On the Isar in Munich I completed the years of education at the *Gymnasium*. In Landsberg on the Lech I was educated by the Jesuits in the science of the saints; this novitiate lasted two years. In Ingolstadt on the Danube I received my philosophical and theological education for five years. The position of teaching theology at the university there I held for four years. Then, after three years I moved to Dillingen, also on the Danube. Then on Pentecost 1800, I returned to Ingolstadt moving with the entire university to Landshut where I remained for twenty-two years, teaching pastoral theology, moral theology, pedagogics and philosophy of religion.[6]

Let us fill in some of the information that Sailer passed over in poetic brevity. He was born near Munich of a family that retained much of the piety of the Catholic baroque. At the end of his education in a Jesuit *Gymnasium*, he entered the Society of Jesus in 1771. His life as a Jesuit, however, came to an end through the suppression of the Society in 1773 by Clement XIV. He was ordained two years later and assigned to a professorship of the Bavarian university in Ingolstadt.

Sailer, young and energetic, was viewed there as a representative of the Enlightenment. During these first years of his life as a priest and teacher he encouraged the formation of movements for pastoral renewal and church reform. Drawn not only to ecclesial reform but to the interior life, he was suspected of belonging to the *Illuminati*, a recently founded, private sodality suspected of Freemasonry and pseudomysticism. A professor at Ingolstadt, Adam Weishaupt, had founded the group in 1776.[7] Resembling the Rosicrucians in theosophy and the Masons in brotherly bond, they planned for a future where mysticism would replace politics. Such groups of Catholic mystical pietists were, during the years of the Enlightenment, an alternative to the dominance of rationalism. With the dawn of Romanticism, their time seemed to have come. Sailer both opposed and supported such groups, seeing them as harbingers of the end of self-satisfied rationalism.

From his older colleague at the university, Benedikt Stattler, Sailer learned of possibilities for the modern thinking. Stattler was at the center of several controversies: one over educational reforms, another over positive relations with Protestants and, more significantly, one over Kant's philosophy. Stattler had set aside the fragments of Suarezian scholasticism. The appearance of Kant's critiques after 1781 filled that vacuum. Stattler handled Kant's views on religion roughly but he was not opposed to the examination of transcendental structures of knowing or to the establishment of revealed truths through rational analysis. Stattler belonged to a group of Catholic Kantians who in a general way contributed to the Catholic Enlightenment, but who also distanced themselves from that older approach. Kantian philosophy quickly conquered the universities, not only Protestant ones but Catholic schools such as Würzburg, Salzburg and Dillingen. It won followers, defenders . . . and professors.[8] Stattler led his promising student Sailer into a career of teaching and the dialogue with Kant.

Sailer's courses were popular, but his professorship soon became uncertain. In 1781 at Ingolstadt and again in 1784 at Dillingen, Sailer was relieved of his teaching position, actions that were part of the controversy over whether there could be a modern Roman Catholicism open to the ideals of the Enlightenment and the French Revolution, and to the ideas of Kant. At Dillingen members of movements such as the *Illuminati*, disciples of the mystic Louis Saint-Martin, Kantians and Wolffians sought converts. Sailer had friends among all these groups. He was also colleague and friend to Lutheran theologians, for he had come to the conclusion that contacts with Protestants should be normal and mutually enriching. A Danish disciple of Schelling, Henrik Steffens, recalled that when he talked to Sailer, the future Catholic bishop's positions seemed Protestant, and his views of Protestantism seemed Catholic.[9]

From Sailer's Dillingen circle came future professors, ministers, archbishops, men who themselves in Tübingen or Lucerne were at the center of a school. When Sailer was forced into retirement, two other professors, Joseph Weber and Patriz Zimmer, were compelled to leave with him. They had formed what was known as the "Dillingen trio" and will become important advocates of Schelling.

Just as the weak prince-bishop of Augsburg had yielded to the complaints of conservative ex-Jesuits and had dismissed Sailer and his friends, so the liberal prime minister, Montgelas, came to their rescue. He saw in Sailer a man of more than average importance for the construction of an educational system and church in Bavaria along enlightened, modern lines. To enhance the university, whose move to Landshut was a symbolic ritual of a move to modernity, a number of promising teachers including Sailer were offered positions. Sailer moved with the university from Ingolstadt to Landshut in 1800 and became a symbol and prophet of Catholic renewal for the next twenty years. Shortly after his arrival, the scientist Röschlaub joined him on the faculty and began to campaign for Schelling's philosophy.

Sailer and Schelling

In the first years of the nineteenth century Sailer was already fifty years old but he was no detached observer of the world around him. Sailer saw in the frequent series of cultural changes following the French Revolution hope for Roman Catholicism. To the clergy he wrote: "Our age is truly no copy of any other epoch. It is an original . . . , an original in the situation of the world and an original in the situation of religion."[10] Securely established in Landshut, he urged his students and disciples to attend Röschlaub's (and then Zimmer's) evening lectures on Schelling's thought. He himself studied thoroughly the more accessible of Schelling's works, especially the one that first treated explicitly of Christianity, the *Lectures on Academic Studies*. No doubt he was attracted by the young philosopher's view of a vibrant intellectual world where Christianity was revitalized by the new philosophy. Schelling's philosophy of identity, published in large works between 1799 and 1803, demanded more time, and the treatment of religion in those works was as spare as their description of the absolute was austere.

In January 1803, Sailer wrote that he was deep in the study of the writings of Schelling. In April, on a trip through the north of Germany, he met the young philosopher. "In Jena I visited Professor Schelling (I'll bet Zimmer is smiling) and found a countenance filled with spirit. He greets both of you."[11] The two whom Schelling greeted were Sailer's colleagues at Dillingen and now professors at Landshut: Zimmer and Weber. Zimmer was studying Schelling assiduously and feeling that here at last was the right philosophy for the times. He began public lectures on the new philosophy. This, however, displeased the government in Munich, which had hoped for their brand of discreet Enlightenment from modern faculty members and now saw Zimmer planting excessively emotional and mystical views in the heads of students. Romanticism and Schelling's idealism of nature and history were viewed by Enlightenment philosophers as a mystical enthusiasm devoid of rationality and science.

Sailer's interest was not philosophy but Christian life and culture. "We want the truth and we want to pass it on to the world in a more vital form," Sailer preached in a sermon.[12] And he continued to encourage the movement to Schelling in Landshut. "Schelling is now the rising sun," he wrote. "He who has looked through the situation in a thorough way may help to move the morning sun to midday."[13]

But then Sailer slowly became afraid that the overbearing claims of objective idealism would not further the Christian faith and a renewal of spirit. Consciousness and intuition, the absolute as an identity of nature and history—these were not Sailer's program or theology. Schelling's systems seemed too vast, too presumptuous, too solid in their metaphysics. Direct access to the divine and to the divine as self-revelatory cannot be the unique or normal position for a Christian philosophy. All forms of revelation are subject to the external, historical life of the incarnate Logos and his gracious presence.

Sailer's writings contain few explicit references to ideas from Schelling. Sailer used (but did not develop) the motifs of organic life and polar development from Schelling's philosophy of nature. Process and history, which attained more and more importance in Schelling's writings after 1798, escaped him.[14] History remained for Sailer little more than the line connecting examples of moral life. But in imagination, symbol, beauty—there Sailer rooted his worldview. Where there are similarities between Schelling and Sailer, they are best traced to a general influence from Romanticism and idealism.

Sailer's lectures on the philosophy of religion, published as *The Basic Teaching on Religion*, written after his study of Schelling, are very much a work of search, of transition from the Enlightenment to Romanticism. The reader sees terms such as "clarity," "wisdom" and "reason" yield to "life," "power" and "nature." Without mentioning Schelling by name, Sailer's treatment of "philosophy in our times" is clearly intended to meet the thought of Kant, Fichte and Schelling. The middle-aged Sailer cannot exchange Kant for Schelling. Nevertheless, his statement that the divine inscription in the temple of philosophy—"I am the moral order of the world"—has been replaced by "the One and the All, *hen kai pan*" (the motto of the Romantics at Jena) is significant.[15]

Sailer's course began with the dynamism of reason and nature; these were not only powers of subjectivity in life but a place of religion. Their revelation led not to an identity in the absolute but to a fuller revelation in Christ. Introductory questions on the nature of religion and science led to God, first as the beautiful and then as the existent. "It is hard for our contemporaries," Sailer observed, "to hold belief and science together."[16] The pastoral theologian's solution was to interiorize religion, to transform theodicy into spirituality, to make the struggles of philosophy into support for a devout life. "If it is the highest reason to believe in one God and to recognize him as the one God, so it is the highest reason to believe in the eternal being of the human spirit."[17] A philosophical principle such as this was not developed, however, and Sailer's approach soon became that of a handbook on Catholic spirituality.

If it is true that reason has an instinct to believe, a drive to prayer, this does not mean we can research or explain the eternal God. Nor is the perceptual element in faith a kind of lofty, epistemological intuition that penetrates to the divine absolute. Sailer's approach resembles that of the early Schleiermacher as he argues that philosophy leads to revelation:

> Philosophy is homesickness for the land of truth and holiness. . . . To philosophize is to mount up to eternal ideas and to descend from them to the world, to nature, to humanity and finitude, to the entire universe. An arrangement of all this as the totality of knowledge is a philosophical system."[18]

Sailer's volumes begin as a philosophy of religion but then move too easily into every area of systematic and moral theology. Although his emphasis upon the spirituality and ethics of the Christian's life is broad, he sketches Jesus Christ in the style of the Enlightenment, as teacher and model. A lengthy apologia on the teachings of the Roman Catholic Church brings the basic course in religion to an awkward conclusion. What is important is the open if modest attempt at mentioning the latest philosophy in works of pastoral and spiritual theology.

As much as Sailer longed for a more mystical, more personally intense world of spirituality, he never escaped the influence of Kantianism. Indeed, the philosopher with whom he continued to feel most comfortable was the Protestant Kantian, Friedrich Jacobi. Jacobi was an opponent of Schelling: for him motion toward the absolute implied an intuitive leap of faith. Sailer never lost his respect for Jacobi, the safest and the most religious of the post-Kantians and, like the Landshut professor, an intermediary between Enlightenment and Romanticism.

> Jacobi is a historically necessary intermediary between Kant and Fichte; philosopher of faith on behalf of reason, grasping God where the ideas of genius, emotion and piety flow together within a *logos* mysticism. . . . There is no Catholic theologian active between 1800 and 1830 who seriously studied the basic problem of theological knowledge without being influenced by Jacobi in a positive way . . . Drey, Möhler as well as Sailer.[19]

Jacobi came to Munich in 1804 to direct the Royal Academy of Science. More and more, the Catholic Kantians in the Bavarian capital accepted his transcendental philosophy of faith. Jacobi criticized infinite reason as the source of being, system and God. He moved the focus from reason to faith. The incipient movements of knowing God are indeed begun in the darkness of feeling and intimation, but they end not in the light of rational insight where finite and infinite self meet (as with Schelling) but in faith. Faith grounds and completes reason. The Protestant philosopher of faith and the Catholic pastor of the interior life agreed in opposing a common danger: an evolving system of nature and spirit that unfolds simultaneously in self and God. Paradoxically, the guide to spirituality for so many Catholics found the mystical philosophy of Romantic idealism unsettling and chose to remain in a broadly Kantian world.

Sailer's Circle

In Dillingen and in Landshut, Sailer was always surrounded by others: students, soldiers and teachers, colleagues and writers. For decades, through spiritual direction and friendship, he formed the spiritual climate of Bavaria. The three pioneers in Catholic idealist theology— Zimmer, Weber and Thanner—belonged to his Landshut circle. The students who moved in and out of his circle over the decades came to be men of significance: future bishops of the sees of Bavaria, professors at Munich, theologians such as J.B. Hirscher and Alois Gügler.

One particular group became the future counselors of Ludwig I, his agents for the Munich restoration. Eduard Schenck was the source of ideas for the future academic life of Bavaria; Johann Nepomuk Ringseis was the first rector of the University of Munich. Through Sailer they were introduced to a Romantic worldview, to a world in process whose future held great potentiality; and they were introduced to the new transcendental philosophy and to Schelling. In 1803 the crown prince, the future Ludwig I arrived. He had been directed to Sailer by his tutor, Joseph Sambuga, a gifted pedagogue and polymath. Sambuga was convinced that Sailer's ideas and circle represented the right kind of Catholicism, personal in approach with traces of transcendental and theosophical philosophy. The future king's ideas came from this circle, for ironically, as the church buildings of Bavaria were being dismantled by the secularization of 1803, the prince, who was to restore so much of what had been destroyed, met several times a week to be tutored by Sailer. The modernization begun by Montgelas under the rubric of the Enlightenment would be continued by Ludwig I, for when he ascended the throne the Landshut Romantic movement became the Munich restoration.

The discussions of the young men with Sailer turned into discoveries they made about their own lives and the hopes they had for a different future. Their interests have been summed up in this way: a sense of history, a belief in the reality of truth, attention to the impressions of their youth, a poetic feeling for the dignity of the Roman Catholic Church, a shift of attention from Graeco-Roman classical to the medieval, a hope for a future of freedom.[20] Without setting foot in Landshut, Schelling had established an influence he had not had in Jena. Dialogue between Roman Catholic thinkers and the new philosophy had begun, and in the change from a tense Catholic Enlightenment to a more comfortable Romanticism the significant role was played, unlike at Jena or Heidelberg, by theologians.

Patriz Benedikt Zimmer

Among the professors included in Sailer's circle was P.B. Zimmer. Zimmer is the clearest example of Schelling's influence upon this first generation of Catholic theologians and philosophers open to modern philosophy. His writings could draw upon the full range of the early Schelling. Zimmer thought through the philosophy of nature and the system of identity. His writings are the first attempt by a systematic theologian of the Roman Catholic tradition to accept idealism, Romanticism, the philosophy of historical consciousness and objectivity. Sailer and Zimmer and their comrade in Schelling studies, Joseph Weber,[21] were not the Catholic idealists of the greatest genius—their intellectual influence faded quickly—but they were the pioneers.

Zimmer was born near the Catholic educational center of Ellwangen in 1752. Educated by the Jesuits there and at the University of Dillingen, he was ordained to the priesthood the year Schelling was born. From 1777, he was at Dillingen with Sailer, instructor in various fields and, after 1784, professor of dogmatic theology. In his first writings he was searching for an alternative to Jesuit scholasticism. He, too, believed initially that he had found this in Benedikt Stattler's openness to Kant, in his tradition-supported critique of Kant's conclusions. Zimmer published in 1787 a theological system in Latin (as was the custom). In the conflict at Dillingen between the older professors and their colleagues studying Kant and Fichte, the prince-bishop of Augsburg removed the younger professors. In a short time, however, Minister Montgelas brought them to Ingolstadt (and then to Landshut) to assist in the transformation of the Bavarian university. Zimmer was professor of dogmatic theology and he lived in the same house with Sailer and Weber.

Zimmer's acquaintance with Fichte's publications showed him that

Kant had been only a beginning. It was important for Catholic theology to gain for itself the new perspectives to begin with the self, to find in subjectivity the spirit of the world. After reading Schelling, Zimmer wrote to a colleague: "Now we have the true philosophy."[22] In 1802 Zimmer began to publish a multivolume dogmatics, *Theologiae specialis et theoreticae*. The third volume, appearing in 1804, showed the influence of Schelling and included, daringly, long sections written in German rather than in Latin.

From Sailer's letter to Zimmer recounting a meeting with Schelling in Jena, we can conclude that he was studying Schelling by 1803. Röschlaub wrote to Schelling a few months later that Zimmer was making an extraordinary impact upon the students. "Zimmer lectures on and defends your system. He has received a decree forbidding the new edition of his theological handbook."[23] The supporters of the Enlightenment in Munich and Landshut had reached the Bavarian court and argued their case that the latest philosophy was a dangerous mysticism, a doctrine about a God disclosed neither by theodicy nor revelation. Ultimately the quarrel was not over the content of philosophies but over the popularity of schools and factions. For a while Zimmer had to cease lecturing on Schelling in public, although in private lectures he developed further a theology within the framework of objective idealism.

Zimmer: Subject and Revelation in Catholic Thought

From Schelling's systems of 1800, 1801 and the *Further Presentation of 1803*, Zimmer drew a framework for his *Philosophy of Religion: Doctrine on the Idea of the Absolute*. For Zimmer the focus was always religion, not philosophy. He followed Schelling's approach to the nature of philosophy, the possibility of absolute knowledge and intellectual insight, the real and the ideal, and the powers of nature. In the critique of Kant, in the terminology, in its content the book was derived from Schelling: "This entire book has been written in the closest dependence upon Schelling's *Further Presentation*. Zimmer took over the outline and the five basic principles as well as literal quotations. Zimmer had by then studied all the writings of Schelling's philosophy of identity."[24] Zimmer's work is the first Roman Catholic-authored philosophy of religion and Christianity based upon idealism.

The plan of the *Philosophy of Religion* foresaw two main sections.[25] The first described "absolute and esoteric philosophy" in its nature, in its exposition of "the idea of the absolute" and in its method. A second, "exoteric" section would treat the relationship of the absolute to the universe; there such areas as the eternal generation of ideas, the fall of the ideas, matter and creation would be examined. The second major part would treat the explicit religion—Christianity—by looking at God's being, the absolute revelation of God in reason, the objective revelation of God in the incarnation and the church: these last are "the historical construction of the objective revelation of God in reason." This second part was never published, and the first part reached only as far as the method.

Zimmer began his philosophical interpretation of all that concerned the topic of religion by stating that his pages would bring forth truth out of a confrontation of Kant with Schelling.[26] The Catholic theologian adopted completely the approach of idealist speculation where an analysis of knowing and its absolute ground led through a philosophy of religion to a discussion of the objective claims of Roman Catholic Christianity. To begin is to treat the subject, to treat all that is spiritual, all that pertains to intellect. The objective dimension need not be omitted, but the subjective presides. Beyond the dialectic of the real and the ideal is the identity of the absolute:

> The finite, the infinite and the eternal—we distinguish them as three forms in the absolute. These three realms (the polarity of the real and the ideal, a philosophical construction, and the three potencies of philosophy) belong to a teaching on the idea of the absolute. . . . The real gives us natural philosophy, the ideal gives us ideal philosophy, and the unity of both gives us theology. So in the real we have the potency of the finite, and in the ideal that of the infinite, and in the unity of both the potency of the eternal.[27]

All this is pure Schelling. Zimmer borrows the philosopher's language (and the weaknesses of his theodicy) as he affirms that the difference between the subjective and the objective, the absolute and the universe, is only "a quantitative difference." In God there is unity, absolute identity and fullest totality.[28]

The objective, theological parts of the system (the "theological construction") were not published but we have a hint of their content toward the end of the philosophy of the absolute. These seemingly inevitable tripartite forms, this discussion of three potencies in the absolute, suggest the trinitarian thought-forms that Zimmer calls "triotheism," which he identified with Christianity. The Catholic theologian implied that the close connection between the philosophy of identity and a triad of spiritual potencies in the absolute mind is prelude to the higher religion, Christianity. The dialectic of polytheism and monotheism must end in triotheism. The highest form of religion is that of absolute subjectivity where diversity and identity flow together in the knowing absolute.

By the end of the published first part, Zimmer was pursuing, he said, "a thorny path."[29] To construct a defense of Schelling's early philosophy of identity and to offer his own philosophy of religion, he has used Schelling's construction of the philosophy of the absolute as an apologetic for Christianity. This modern philosophy bestowed upon religion "its natural superiority over all, and gave theology its preferential place ahead of all the sciences."[30]

Zimmer's enthusiasm for Schelling was boundless and genuine: Schelling allowed religious life—like reality—to be concrete, organic, historical, universal. It is possible that Schelling visited Zimmer at his parish in Steinheim.[31] In 1806 Zimmer was forced to withdraw temporarily from teaching theology. During this retirement, brought on by the suspicion of being "a Schellingian," he and Schelling carried on a lengthy correspondence. From the sole surviving letter, we gather that they were accustomed to meet for philosophical discussion. Zimmer's vacant professorship was given to Ignaz Thanner. Thanner, however, soon became an equally firm follower of objective idealism.[32] The commitment to Schelling's thought grew at Landshut and a campaign was launched for him to be offered a position. In 1807 that movement failed; Friedrich Köppen, an Enlightenment Catholic, a student of Jacobi, received the professorship instead of Schelling and continued to publish his own polemical writings against Schelling.

We do not know what the young philosopher, successor to Fichte and mentor of Romanticism, thought of this enthusiastic employment of his thinking by men active within the spiritual corridors of Roman Catholicism. There is no reason to think he objected. After all, the issue for philosophers and theologians in the years surrounding the year 1800 was not exegesis or dogmatics but the philosophy of religion. And Schelling then viewed himself not as a Protestant but as a transcendent savior. Idealism, he claimed, was to play Beatrice to Christianity's Dante, in a reversal of roles. "Philosophy . . . restores the true meaning of religion . . . , gives rebirth to the gospel of the absolute."[33]

When Zimmer died, in 1820, Sailer said that Bavaria had lost its strongest theologian.[34] We know that he was not the greatest Catholic thinker or systematician of the early nineteenth century, but he was, among those of some lasting achievement in the dialogue with modern philosophy, the first.

Görres and the Rhineland

Like Bavaria, the Rhineland was a traditional center of Roman Catholic life, and a place destined to new vitality through the beneficial climate of the Romantic movement. The new philosophy and its application to religion and faith appeared, took hold and expanded there. As in Landshut and Munich, there was a Roman Catholic adaptation of the Enlightenment in Coblenz, Bonn and Mainz, cities on the Rhine.[35] Joseph Görres was typical of that time of revolution and anticlericalism, and of the subsequent move to the mystical metaphysics of theosophy, idealism and Romanticism. Görres was a figure of major importance for Catholic intellectual history during the nineteenth century; we have in him an example of a seminal, if limited, and lasting influence from Schelling's philosophy. Not as philosophical as Patriz Zimmer nor as devout as Sailer, the young Görres resembles Friedrich Schlegel in his early attempts to synthesize political history with the philosophy of natural science and Asian religion.

Johann Joseph Görres was born in 1775, the same year as Schelling, in Rhenish Coblenz, son of a German merchant and an Italian mother. Perhaps because his spirit was so tuned to the political movements after 1776, Görres died in the year when his era and his hopes ended, 1848.

Görres's energy and curiosity were inexhaustible. A sensitivity for the numinous joined with an inextinguishable drive for political progress. He thought broadly, he wrote well. His career was itself a dialectic of opposite interests. He began as a philosopher of science but ended writing a system whose format was mysticism. In 1804, as he worked meticulously on the structure of Asian and Teutonic myths, he was viewed by Prussia as a revolutionary. Politically radical in the Rhineland, he felt at home in the close monarchy of Catholic Munich. He was capable of research in natural science and Sanskrit but his journalistic pen made him famous as the founder of several periodicals of lasting impact: *Rheinischer Merkur, Der Katholik*. With only some exaggeration, Horst Fuhrmans writes: "Görres, often misunderstood, is seen now as *the* figure of Late Romanticism. Clearly he was the decisive figure in Heidelberg.

When we hear his voice we touch the real depth of later Romanticism."[36]

The *Gymnasium* at Coblenz attended by Görres was no longer in the hands of the calm, intellectual Jesuits. After the Society's suppression in 1773, diocesan priests came, and with them came new ideas. One teacher, Nicola, was a militant Kantian. By 1793, finished with that first level of his schooling, Görres was already secretary to a group whose ideas were those of the *Sturm und Drang*: freedom, German unity, suppression of secular and ecclesiastical aris-tocracy. He edited a journal, *The Red Page*, and published a book, *On Universal Freedom*, which described the papacy as the worst of all dictatorships.[37] Even during this turbulent, areligious period in his life, we can suspect that the subconscious of the young political activist was moving toward religion, through, as we will see, nature, myth and mysticism.

The Power of Schelling

The young Görres had intended to study medicine but his political exuberance interfered. When the fires of his revolutionary zeal faded, a position was available as professor of physics in a secondary school in Coblenz, and Görres accepted. He became a teacher of physics without having attended university, and he filled his spare time with studies in medicine and natural philosophy. As with many other thinkers throughout Germany, Schelling's writings on the philosophy of nature captivated Görres. They seemed in their transcendental format and in their quest for total system, in their fine, literary unfolding of a unified view of the new sciences, to be a leap forward into continents awaiting exploration. The latest and best philosophy of science was being written by the young philosopher at Jena.

Two qualities lifted Schelling's volumes published from 1797 to 1801 above the many writings on science and physics that appeared in the intellectual centers of Germany. First, he brought together the discoveries of Lavoisier and Galvani with the theories of Brown. Second, outstripping Herder, Kant and Goethe, he fashioned this new data into a system and so gave the pattern to natural philosophy, to "speculative physics," for an era. The Rhinelander had no personal contact with the philosopher of Romanticism; Schelling's publications linked them. Görres wrote not long after 1800: "Schelling's character always put me off, but his power and spirit attracted me."[38]

At the time of our theological history, cultured men and women liked to publish collections of aphorisms. Schelling employed this style for some of his presentations of natural philosophy, composing several sets of philosophico-scientific aphorisms on nature for the medical journal he edited. Görres's *Aphorisms on Art* was written while he was a teacher of physics in Coblenz; it was published in 1802. It was an introduction to the ensemble of natural science, a grounding of individual natural sciences in the framework of idealism. Schelling's influence upon Görres is first and fully manifest in these early sets of aphorisms: one on art, another on physics. "Görres sets himself the task of proving that polarity is the law of the universe. The philosophy of identity [Schelling] is present in a limited way as everything real strives toward the ideal."[39] In his *World-Soul*, Schelling had concluded: "The law of polarity is the general law of the world."[40] In his selection of polarity, in the elevation of the organic into an entire science, in his affirmation that intellectual intuition is the subject and way of philosophy, Görres accepted the modification of transcendental philosophy intended by the Romantic understanding of science.

One difference present from the beginning between Görres and Schelling was that Görres interested himself less in the transcendental subject with its free and creative subjectivity, less in nature's mirror image of transcendental forms, and more in the ways nature actually behaved. Even in this age of the birth of idealism, Görres was a philosopher of concrete empirical thinking, whereas Schelling remained longer with conceptual constructions. Schelling worked throughout his life outward into experience; Görres worked out of experience, although he, too, uses the forms of the idealists. In the aphorisms, intellectual insight embraces and organizes the unfolding of philosophy, physics, medicine (Brownianism is mentioned). There is already in this philosophy not only organism but cosmogenesis. One can detect in every organism the primal organism's becoming itself. And for Görres, too, the dual system of intellect and nature ends in art. Art gives the vision of the union of the real and the ideal. "The goal of our undertaking, discovering the highest level of the ideal in the ultimate art. . . . There is nothing beyond that; from there we can only look backwards."[41]

Görres published a second selection of aphorisms, not loosely connected and random sayings but prose segments arranged to show the tentative skeleton of a system. Beginning with a literary flourish, the *Aphorisms on the Organic* of 1803 compared Fichte to Michelangelo and Schelling to Raphael. "The second genius," Görres wrote, "had shown the absolute to be where the ideal and the real interpenetrated each other, where being and knowledge flow together. Living in an unreachable twilight and in its own self-intuition, the God-nature divides and crystalizes into space and universe where the ideas undulate and surge in the stream of time."[42] Gifted writer and master of the philosophy of science, Görres developed his own stance and he could look back upon the course of his recent thinking:

> Schelling's powerful nature excited me just as Plato stimulated him. But an individual is his own product, the product of his total past. I spoke Schelling's language because at that time that kind of language was widely used. My eccentric nature, however, has driven me out of this form. I must create my own forms.[43]

For German Romanticism the years after 1803 were a crisis. The happy circles in Jena could not sustain their enthusiasm. The works in progress of Schlegel and Hegel, the publications of Görres and Schelling, illustrate the shift in the times. Schelling was questioning the connection of the world to God, the phenomenon of religion and its history in Christianity. "The new religion," Schelling wrote in an article, "which had already announced itself in particular revelations, can be led back to the first mystery of Christianity whose fulfillment it is. It will be recognized in the rebirth of nature as the symbol of eternal unity . . . , the life of the newly emerging godhead."[44]

In the winter of 1804, Görres wrote "Three Revolutions" for a Romantic periodical in Munich. The three revolutions were those of "politics in France, philosophy in Kant, poetry in Romanticism." The next year, Görres interrupted his work on physics and mythology with a book whose title expressed the theme of the entire epoch, *Glauben und Wissen*, "to believe and to know." He described it to a friend:

> I am having a book published where I develop my system of philosophy based upon the idea of the godhead and developed along the line of the duality of the sexes. My principle is in contrast to Schelling and so are my results. The finite and the feminine which Schelling demeans are again honored. The godhead proceeds from its thought into the transcendentally sublime, and so reaches the primal idea. Schelling's philosophy appears as the masculine opposite to the feminine philosophy of Jacobi. Both of equal value, each one is only one side of philosophy, not necessarily hostile to the principles

which give full value to philosophy and to religion, principles toward which Schelling, although unconsciously, is [moving].[45]

Görres's approach in this, his first real system, did not resemble Schelling's attempts at a universal philosophy but went ahead, anticipating the outline and material of the next years. A total system for philosophy, Görres began, would begin with the godhead. No longer content with medicine or politics, Görres too would be a transcendental philosopher, a system-builder for all of thought and reality:

> From the transcendent, sublime, ineffable, the godhead emerges into being as it exercises the act of self-consciousness. From the ungrounded realm of its nature it goes forth into glory, revealing its power and fulfillment. In the godhead all existence is placed. . . , and all comes to existence. The act of divine self-consciousness is, therefore, the act of creation.[46]

But the motif for exposing this world-system, organic polarity, is metamorphosed into a surprising duality—namely, that of sexuality. Male and female serve as forms of powers and beings.

Belief and Knowledge is only a sketch of a system, but it includes, in an extraordinary originality, surprising elements: not only idealism and the new philosophy of nature but Christian mysticism and Asian mythologies. Writing not as a Christian believer but as a phenomenologist of religion, Görres contrasted oriental mythologies with the Christian apocalypse, deriving a higher philosophy from the latter. The images of mythical and apocalyptic writings describe a theogony, he explained, where a plurality of divine powers objectify themselves through the cosmos and through the night-side of existence, which is nothingness and evil. Görres then turned to world history, which has its own movement and ages. With the advent of Christianity, the old time of paganism ended and an adult humanity turned to the divine powers.[47] All of this anticipates by twenty years Schelling's positive philosophy of myth and revelation.

Heidelberg: The Medieval and the Oriental

With *Belief and Knowledge* in print, a brief but potent manifesto for the times, Görres moved from Coblenz to Heidelberg. Perhaps this move down the Rhine, from a center of the Rhenish Catholic Enlightenment, to

Heidelberg, one of the Romantic circles, was symbolic. He was now beyond the aesthetics and philosophies of nature so much a part of early Romanticism. The revolution, he knew, was incomplete; both philosophy and politics were glowing coals waiting to set the world on fire.

Heidelberg was alive with the activities of a Romantic circle, one with contacts in Jena but with its own interests. The Tiecks and Schelling's comrade, C.J. Windischmann, passed through often. An early friend, Clemens Brentano, who had studied in Jena, was at work with Achim von Arnim on the collection of medieval German myths, *Des Knaben Wunderhorn*. As a preparation for a possible lectureship for himself, Görres attended lectures at the university. In theology, there was Karl Daub, a young polymath who had been exploring Schelling as the framework for a new Protestant systematics. More important was the presence at Heidelberg of the pioneer researcher into Asian mythology and linguistics, F. Creuzer. Görres hoped to expand the horizons of philosophy with the history of religions. He learned Sanskrit. Because he did not hesitate to describe, as Schelling did at the time, Christianity as a myth system, he could only hope that light would be shed upon the plan for a philosophy of religion through the religions of India.

Görres began to lecture as a *Privatdozent* in Heidelberg. Among other distinctions, he was the first to treat German literature as an academic field.[48] His lectures expanded the themes of science and faith. Görres was becoming quite critical of Schelling's philosophy of identity; it was empty, a twilight, the vaporous worldview of a man who earlier had been a prophet. Schelling's systems displayed an obsession to do the impossible. Görres had advanced beyond transcendental metaphysics, filling in those forms with mythology, sexuality and political history. Schelling, outraged at his marginal treatment in Görres's writings, and not yet grasping the role myth would play in his own philosophy, wondered "how men like Creuzer and Daub could offer such a crazy coworker their protection."[49]

For two years Görres played his part in the Romantic circle at Heidelberg. If in Jena men and women had been concerned with the very essence of the new approach to literature, theater and philosophy, Heidelberg's circle focused upon medieval folk literature and German culture. Fables and myths were also a way for the voyage by Romantics toward religion. Mystical science and magical fable spotlighted the philosophy of nature, whether it was Schelling's or Görres's. Görres did not hesitate to exchange for a while the world of politics for the cosmos of the mysterious. He did not, however, attain a chair at the university and so retired back to Coblenz where he put the new discipline learned from Creuzer to good use: he wrote a two-volume study of Asian mythologies.

Even before Heidelberg, Görres showed traces—so congenial to idealism—of the potential union of mythology with the philosophy of the life of God. Görres's work with Asian mythologies led him to view God as present in all religions; it was not the specificity of religion that was important but its development. "While the godhead remains at rest, thousands of forms of religion unfold and act out their histories."[50] The message of all revelatory religion is the same: the presence of God in the world, the presentation of God in a panoply of forms. Görres's books *Growth in History* and *History of Asian Myths* explained how myth is the history of the developing personality of the universe. The eternal circle of things displays a law which we perceive as a myth: in birth becoming begins, and in death dying ends. Metamorphosis and polarity are spheres of development and Görres uses them to explain ontology and history as his curiosity roamed through Greek, Roman and Germanic history, and then on to all that could be known of China and India. He concluded: "Religion works in all, drives all forward . . . just as the godhead lives in all of life."[51]

All the elements for Görres's career, for his innumerable articles and books are now present: an approach from subjectivity toward system, a philosophy of nature that is organic, a growing appreciation of mysticism and religion, revolutionary political experience, a knowledge of myth. The physics of Schelling has been absorbed and surpassed. The Jena philosopher's idealism of the absolute and organic had been seminal for Görres but in the area of religion and myth (paralleling Friedrich Schlegel) Görres has gone ahead of Schelling. Before the two men became colleagues in Munich after 1827, there would be more political controversy than philosophical system for Görres. After his return to Roman Catholicism, Görres will pursue the ultimate science. He and his colleague Schelling together in Munich after 1827 will agree on the general style and outline of the last system, one capable of presenting all of history, science and religion.

3
Würzburg and the
Catholic Enlightenment

As ROMAN CATHOLICS were first turning to Schelling, he was at the youthful height of his powers. New ideas for books came quickly and the respected monographs and systems were easily written. Yet by 1803 he wanted to leave Jena: no chair of philosophy had been offered him by its university. The once exciting soirees and projects of Weimar and Jena were less frequent. Fichte had gone to Berlin; the Schlegel brothers were geographically as well as personally distant in Paris. Caroline Schlegel had received her divorce from August and she was free to marry Schelling. The couple quickly left Jena; perhaps they would continue medical studies in Vienna, perhaps they would sojourn through the galleries of Italy. Schiller wrote: "With Schelling's departure, philosophy itself has departed."[1] But threats of new Napoleonic wars made foreign travel inopportune. And so, not yet thirty, Schelling, the philosopher of both the new science and the new literature, found himself, without a position, back in Württemberg from where, seven years before, he had departed with such bright hopes.

Schelling and Würzburg

As a result of Napoleon's stunning victories over Austria in 1802, the domain of Würzburg became part of an expanding Bavaria, Napoleon's ally; its prince-bishop remained only a bishop. The authorities at the Munich court selected Würzburg to be, next to Landshut, the site of the second Bavarian university. This change in status for the quite Catholic and traditional *Julius-Universität* provided another opportunity for Montgelas to introduce the ideas of the Enlightenment. The various faculties would be filled with the modern spirit by attracting scholars— Protestant as well as Catholic—of the new philosophy. Instead of introducing a double faculty (as Tübingen would do later) the equality of Christian confessions before the modern state was encouraged and symbolized by having a single theological faculty of Protestant and Catholic professors. Montgelas was replacing the suppressed monasteries with universities lacking a confessional stance. Again the minister mistook his foes for his friends, bringing in enemies of the outdated Enlightenment and so encouraging Romanticism.

Among the many professors who were enthusiastic about Schelling's philosophy of nature none, we have seen, was more loyal than Adalbert Marcus at Bamberg. Through his favor with the Munich regime, he worked to secure a professorship in Bavaria for Schelling. The court and the curatorium of the universities were interested. In September 1803 Schelling went to Munich, impressed Montgelas, and accepted his first ordinary professorship: in philosophy, at Würzburg. Meanwhile in Würzburg many looked upon these changes in organization and personnel with fear. Munich hastened to reassure the incumbent professors that they would remain. Yet, "among the new professors Professor Schelling has accepted a position and will teach in Würzburg the next semester as *ordinarius* in philosophy. The name of this great professor needs only to be mentioned to indicate that the active wishes of the government for the flowering of science are quite real."[2]

Several of Schelling's acquaintances came to Würzburg with him— for instance, H.E.C. Paulus. Paulus had encouraged the young Schelling by publishing in his theological journal Schelling's Tübingen thesis on myth. Paulus attained a certain notoriety with his New Testament studies and their naturalistic explanation of the miracles of Jesus. The circle of Protestant intellectuals (the Schellings and Pauluses shared lodgings) was looked upon with little pleasure by the Catholic establishment.[3] Schleiermacher too had received an invitation from Montgelas to Würzburg, to a professorship in pastoral theology. What a difference in the history of theology a move by him to the south might have made! But he was loathe to enter the Catholic south, reluctant to come into too close association with Schelling, whom he found cool and distant. Schleiermacher's straitened circumstances at Stolp would have forced an acceptance of the Bavarian offer had not the Prussian regime stepped in and offered him a position at Halle.[4]

In Würzburg, Schelling developed a new, less turbulent circle of friends, mostly physicians and scientists. From 1805 to 1808, he and Marcus edited the *Jahrbücher der Medizin als Wissenschaft*. Ignaz Döllinger, the father of the famous church historian, was one among his supporters in the Würzburg faculties of medicine and science. Now great years seemed to lie before Schelling. He was recognized in Germany as the leader of the new philosophy; his writings were sought after; he was united with the woman he loved. In favor with the regime, he was professor and member of the university senate.

Würzburg, however, would not offer him the place of rest and the fame he wished, and his time there would be short. He would find himself embattled by Catholics and by Protestants, by *Aufklärer* and *Romantiker*. Würzburg would emerge as transition, as a place and time of passage to Munich. This brief period was important because it brought a renewed interest by Schelling in philosophical issues posed by religion. Not only his critics but the inner dynamic of his system demanded a reexamination of religion. Equally important was the wider catalytic role exercised by Schelling among Catholic intellectuals. While his disciples at Landshut continued to write tomes inspired by Schelling's first systems, an attack upon him by other Catholics began.

Although it had been the domain of a prince-bishop for close to a millenium, picturesque Würzburg had known modernity as well as tradition, theological creativity as well as episcopal firmness. The city had experienced a gilt interplay of rococo and classicism as the new urban residence of the prince rose after the middle of the eighteenth century, displaying in its stones a synthesis of old and new styles. Prince-Bishop Karl Friedrich von Schönborn, who called Balthasar Neumann to direct the design of his *Residenz*, was a promoter of the Enlightenment's philosophy and theology; after 1735 disciples of Christian Wolff taught there.

In 1780, Würzburg was a model for Catholic universities in the Enlightenment style, but by 1800 its spirit had declined and the *Julius-Maximilians-Universität* lived in a more conservative atmosphere than did Landshut. The bishop during Schelling's years in Würzburg, Georg Carl von Fechenbach, had seen the secularization of his world coming. He spent his episcopal energies helping his realm to recover from Napoleonic occupation and from a secularization of ecclesiastical properties in 1802. All of this change brought a certain fear: not only of political but of theological upheaval.

Lectures on Religion

The lectures given by Schelling during his first semester at Würzburg were drawn from his book on academic studies, and from his latest system of transcendental philosophy realized in nature and art:

> In his first semester he had the extraordinarily high number of ninety-five hearers, so strong was the attraction of his name. This fired Schelling's ego and in the first lecture he got rather carried away. He had come, he said, at the command of the prince to bring light into the darkness of southern Germany. . . . At the same time he complimented Catholicism: the Christian religion, and the Catholic faith particularly, was to the greatest extent poetry. Of his own philosophy Schelling said it could not be defined, for it is the philosophy above all philosophy.[5]

Success quickly surrounded Schelling's lectures. Their language was as dazzling in poetic allusions as it was austere in its philosophy of absolute identity behind all that was ideal in spirit and real in nature. The gossipy critic Jacob Salat described the aura surrounding a lecture by Schelling: "A solemn hush falls as the hour nears; two or three silver candelabra on either side throw light on the lectern; the professor enters with a small entourage."[6]

At this period, when all pursued *Wissenschaft*, it was very much the fashion to offer plans for academic studies, for renewing university life and curriculum.[7] Schelling, first in lectures and then in a book, surveyed all the faculties of a German university and he gave theology and Christianity a great deal of attention. There is little trace of the earlier sarcasm evident in his attitude toward Christian faith in Jena; perhaps Schleiermacher's *Reden* had impressed him to the extent that he intended to take not only the general religious dimension of philosophy seriously but also the religion of Christianity. The doctrines of Christianity, Schelling asserted in the *Lectures on Academic Studies* delivered at Würzburg, are now so embattled because they are interpreted only in an "empirical sense" and not within the framework of a higher knowledge. Religion must be concerned directly with the infinite and not merely with its symbols. With the end of the Enlightenment, Christianity can accomplish this, for Christianity, and all religion, lives not from nature but from history, the realm where the ideal is disclosed in the real. Schelling's philosophy is the true organ of theology, because it is the guide to the expression of the identity of the ideal and the real. Religion, with art and history, expresses what philosophy reveals and organizes. "(In philosophy) the highest ideas of the Divine Being—of nature as its instrument and of history as the revelation of God—become objective."[8]

The Enlightenment was the villain: its rational distillation of Christianity is inadequate, for it holds religion to be a science of objects and merely replaces dogmatic entities with moral imperatives. "One of the operations of the modern pseudoenlightenment—which, with respect to Christianity, might rather be called a disenlightenment—is the attempt to restore [Christianity] to its original meaning."[9]

The modern restoration, however, comes not from forms of rationalism or from the critical methods of exegetes but from a philosophy of religion where the idea of Christianity can emerge from history and disclose history itself as revelatory. Religion and philosophy are distinct, as faith and reason have been, but both proclaim the absolute, which they reach independently. Indeed, all iaaeas are expressions of the absolute, and as such are religious and revelatory. "The modern world . . . wills the eternal idea itself . . . a rebirth of esoteric Christianity and of the gospel of the Absolute."[10]

Schelling emphasized the historical nature of Christianity. This does not mean that he saw history as a Judaeo-Christian salvation history where a chosen people acted out special events. Rather, the historical nature of Christianity fits in well with an absolute whose very being is consciousness-in-history. Schelling referred to the Catholic Church as an advocate of Christianity conceived as "a living religion, not something from the past but an everlasting present." Protestantism, he observed, has been too linked to books. The idea of Christianity, however, exists independently of them: it is more loudly proclaimed by the history of the modern world than by the history of the ancient world where the idea was still in a rudimentary stage of development.[11] Schleiermacher in a review said that the *Lectures on Academic Studies* were the esoteric presentation of Schelling's more speculative systems.[12]

Schelling's second course of lectures at Würzburg presented another systematic form of the writings of the previous three years but, of course, reworked anew. The Würzburg lectures (published only posthumously) possess one significant difference between them and the previous systems. While all began with the quest for an absolute in the realm of spirit, resolving in identity the real and the ideal, the precise relationship of absolute identity to finite world was still left unclear. For instance, in the *Presentation of My System of Philosophy* Schelling concluded:

> The absolute identity is not the cause of the universe but the universe itself. . . . We can rightly say, "The absolute identity itself is the universe." But we can affirm only with qualification the opposite,

"The universe is absolute identity." The universe is the absolute identity viewed according to its essence and in the form of its being.[13]

In the Würzburg lectures, however, Schelling was not so reluctant to speak of "God" rather than the absolute, or to find ways to disentangle God from the eternally copresent world. What is one in God and one with God is distinguishable in the world as various things and forms. Schelling objected to the traditional philosophical illation of positing the creator from creation by cause and effect. Then God would be merely the highest reality, something far less than the absolute-as-idea. Rather, he said, we must search for God in consciousness and find there not a temporal causality of the world but a moment of an ongoing process that is deeper and richer than the distinction between subject and object. When God affirms himself he affirms both the objectivity and the subjectivity he is beyond. God's self-affirmation contains the idea of the world in its coming to be.[14]

The charge of pantheism against Schelling was considerably more audible in Würzburg than in Jena. Schelling denied it; he had insisted that the finite is fully separate from the absolute. The self is not the absolute but the point of differentiation of the real from the infinite. What mediates, and separates, the material universe from God is God's idea of the universe.[15]

The final lectures of the Würzburg system presented the religious nature of culture and history. Art, morality, politics and religion are realms where the real becomes the ideal. History is not a segment of the universe's destiny but its symbol of realization. Art and religion mirror God. Religion, Schelling argued, is more than devotion or feeling, more even than faith. It is the serene and free unity of knowing and acting; it is a lordly insight into spirit in the world. Echoing Schlegel, Schelling ended his course at Würzburg with a call for "a rebirth of mythology," the contemporary expression for a religion that is "insight into the symbolism of the mystical present in nature."[16]

The Religious Problem

Schelling's more explicit treatment of some themes of religion was important not only because of its place in Schelling's career but because his expansion of the religious dimension made him more interesting to theologians, at least to Roman Catholics. The *Lectures on Academic Studies* was endlessly fascinating to Catholic philosophers and theologians in its treatment of Christianity. Moreover, during the Würzburg lectures, Schelling was writing his first philosophical treatment of distinctly theologial issues.

C.A. Eschenmayer, physician and author of treatises in the natural sciences, was a friend of Schelling. In a small book, *Philosophy in Its Transition to Nonphilosophy*, Eschenmayer asked respectfully whether Schelling had dealt successfully with the reality of God. Schelling usually reacted poorly to criticism, exaggerating it, yielding to anger, but in this case he reacted calmly and set to work to respond to his colleague. Eschenmayer used his term "nonphilosophy" not pejoratively but to mean "theology purified from the purely speculative."[17] Religious thought needed to go beyond Schelling's highest identity to find a deity worthy of our reverence. "The last step of philosophy is the first step to faith or to nonphilosophy." At the limit of the idealist system is faith, and God is at the limit of faith. Eschenmayer employed the language of Romanticism—potencies, symbols, insight, interior light, divine ideas—but concluded, as Friedrich Jacobi did, with faith. "Faith thrones over the ideas as religion does over philosophy; the visible world is enclosed by an invisible one that sends out the light of revelation. Faith is at the end of all speculation, as Schelling has said on many occasions in his writings."[18]

Schelling replied with *Philosophy and Religion*, written and published within his first academic year in Würzburg. In an opening that recalled the Hellenism of the *Sturm und Drang*, the work began with Greece and its mysteries; there a primal unity of philosophy and religion had once governed all. Religion stole away the matter of philosophy but now philosophy is regaining possession of the absolute and the eternal birth of things. In the harmony of free, detached knowing, happiness and revelation appear. This is religion, Schelling wrote; an interior touch of God in the soul is not enough. Passing emotions in the self might qualify as a general faith but they do not do justice to a precarious absolute spirit at work in the universe. Schelling disagreed that there was another God, above his absolute, accessible to religion. Eschenmayer was mistaken to begin with finite experience, just as he was mistaken to resolve the power of the mind in faith.

Schelling next turned to the issue of religion still posited (as it had been for centuries) in the relationship of the finite to the absolute. "In one word, from the absolute to the real there is no constant passage; the origin of the sense world is thinkable only as a complete breaking off from the absolute, through a leap. . . . It can lie only in a distancing, in a fall from the absolute."

This fall was Schelling's creative answer to the issue of the distinction, the relation, between finite and infinite. Fall is an alternative to creation, to emanation, to causality. This primal, eternal fall is a facet of the necessary and free self-objectification of the absolute. "The basis [*Grund*] for the possible fall of the universe into reality lies in God, but the reality itself lies in what has fallen into existence."[19] Schelling brought into his thought both process in God and fallen existence. He bracketed the Christian overtones of the fall and, although setting aside divine emanation, his concept does not escape all overtones of Neoplatonism. The fall is atemporal and ontological, not moral or sinful; it emerges from limitation, hovers at the edge of nonbeing, explains distinction and existence. The fall is not explained by Schelling but is asserted as a necessary moment in a wider explanation of God and the world. J.F. Marquet's observation of this important turn in Schelling's idealism is worth noting: "As the vocabulary of theology enters Schelling's idealist systems, little by little his thought takes on the overtones of a sacred drama that will be seen to be quite explicit in the later periods of his thinking."[20]

The Catholic Enlightenment

By 1750 Catholic theology according to the content and format of scholasticism had quietly faded away. It had perdured as the normative approach for Catholic intellectuals for a long time. Trent had reacted to Luther's anger at scholastic dictatorship and to his call for a return to biblical language by reasserting the scholastic approach. At the time of Luther's return to Paul and Augustine, the baroque neoscholastic renaissance was already underway with Cardinal Cajetan and others in Italy, and with a number of Spanish universities and scholars. The unhappy finale to this scholastic revival, perhaps too narrow and heated in its Counter-Reformation mission, came in the tense disputes between the Dominicans and Jesuits over the nature of grace and free will.

"Baroque scholasticism," "Catholic Enlightenment," "Romantic idealism"—we lack historical studies for all these periods of Roman Catholic theology from Luther to Nietzsche and Freud. Baroque scholasticism favored not the *summa* but the textbook. The commentaries and compendia written during the centuries before and after 1625 presented an elaborate arrangement of definitions, divisions and elaborations of the metaphysical theology of the Middle Ages. With the eighteenth century a certain positivism entered; limited historical research suggested collections and encyclopedias. Nevertheless, the mentality of much of dogmatic, moral and canonical theology remained scholastic. The custodianship of German scholasticism had fallen to the Benedictines: in the Black Forest at the Abbey of St. Blase, and in Salzburg at St. Peter's. By the middle of the eighteenth century, however, their work too had slackened. The suppression of the Society of Jesus in 1773, whose numerous faculties were committed to baroque scholasticism, further weakened the force of that philosophical and theological approach.

Würzburg was an exception to the law of scholastic dominance. From 1766 to 1777 a group of Jesuits had put together an alternative theological plan. The *Theologia Wirceburgensis*, in fourteen volumes, followed a pedagogical and positivist arrangement, even if many of its segments were scholasticism repeated. The collection of volumes was not an imposing or particularly creative theology but it, too, marked the disappearance north of the Alps of neoscholasticism for almost a century after 1750. It pointed to a void into which the thought of Kant, enthusiastically advocated in southern Germany by Catholic supporters, would enter.

Excitement about Kant brought some remedy for a state that had become intellectual dillettantism. Discontent with Descartes, with Leibniz, with Wolff had been mounting after 1775. Kant's critical philosophy became known quickly to the Catholic universities of southern Germany after 1780. It seemd a crown for a structure of Enlightenment ideas already in place.[21] Not only the *Theologia Wirceburgensis* but the school of Christian Wolff, brought to Würzburg by the prince-bishop in 1713, prepared for Enlightenment and Kantianism. And so, like Dillingen, Landshut and Munich, Würzburg and its university had a circle of Enlightenment Catholics. Because the prince-bishops had introduced measures such as obligatory education for certain social groups and special colleges for teachers and a general university reform in 1782, Würzburg was recognized as the model school of Catholic Germany, an educational institution fully fashioned along the principles of the Enlightenment.[22]

The rationalism of the Enlightenment led Catholic theologians to pursue those introductory speculative questions concerning the foundations of science and faith, and the critique of method and epistemological structures. At the same time, the Kantian view that the moral dimension of human life was the revealer of religion was accepted. Enlightened society preferred fideism and voluntarism; the New Testament was interpreted as a text for moral behavior, and the kingdom of God was not a supernatural reality existing in the church or at the end of time but a universal human covenant of morality and freedom realizable in contemporary society. The reforming spirit of the Enlightenment entered the church, encouraging liturgical and educational renewal, and it worked toward an administrative organization that might effect in the small German state an exemplary synthesis of the ecclesiastical and ducal spheres of the spirit.[23]

From the South Tyrol north to Bamberg and Würzburg there were devotees of Kant in philosophy, theology and science. Benedikt Stattler and Sebastian Mutschele were Roman Catholic Kantians. They were figures who lived in the Catholic intellectual world immediately prior to the advent of Romanticism and idealism. They cultivated what the followers of Schelling, in a spirit of further revolutionary excitement ignited by Romanticism, will eventually cast off.

Benedikt Stattler left the Jesuits at the time of their suppression but was able, as a diocesan priest, to continue as professor of dogmatics at Ingolstadt. Stattler agreed that the critical and rational philosophy of Kant was the correct tool for apologetic and theological thinking, but he devoted volumes to evaluating and criticizing Kant's method. Stattler was concerned with the current method in university disciplines and in the sciences that attacked belief as unenlightened, unscientific.

Accepting a Christianity at least in form traditional and supernatural, Stattler wished to show the originality and the limits of the new Kantianism. At the same time he had definitively set aside the alternatives to the new philosophy: scholasticism or Spinoza. Rome censored his *De locis theologicis*; despite an *Anti-Kant* published in 1788, his views seemed too modern. The novel idea that Kant might be Rome's ally against the deists was hardly acceptable. Stattler's rationalist and critical view of the time of the Reformation led his thinking to an original plan for the reunion of the churches. This preliminary ecumenism was something congenial to the universal humanism of the Enlightenment, just as it would be to the theory of developmental and collective life in Romanticism. Stattler's clarity and energy made him a leader among Catholic Kantians, and his spirit perdured, as we saw, in the vitality of his protégé Sailer.

In contrast to Stattler, Sebastian Mutschele was thoroughly a son of the Enlightenment and then of Kant. Less productive in publications (he died in 1800 at the age of thirty-five), Mutschele saw no problem in accepting Kant's critique of Christian orthodoxy, Catholic as well as Protestant. He argued that Kant's philosophy of categories—the reduction of time and space to mental horizons—was tenable. Beginning with this epistemological foundation he wanted to transform Christianity into a religion of a free fellowship committed to morality and fired by the teachings of Jesus of Nazareth. As the eighteenth century approached its end, the Catholic Kantians saw no need for a "new philosophy," a transcendental thought objectified in nature and in history such as Schelling proposed. Its mystery and dynamism seemed too mystical, too arational, when compared with the lucidity of Kant.

The Catholic Enlightenment was not an important period in Catholic theology, although its very existence is surprising. A culture into which the baroque had entered so fully in music, architecture and worship still lay beneath the ripples of critical rationalism. The Catholic spirit longed to find in Romantic idealism something richer than the Enlightenment. For *Aufklärung* was inevitably alien to the incarnational and mystical dynamic of Roman Catholicism.

Jacobi, Fries and then Schleiermacher, true to the tradition of Luther, found a completion for the subjectivity of Kant in faith. Faith was their future for religious philosophy, the fulfilling response to the Kantian critique of theological words. But faith and word were not nearly so attractive to Roman Catholics as were intuition and nature. Schelling's objective idealism, with early and clear overtones of the mystical, was not foreign to the contemplative, spiritual and sacramental nature of Catholicism. Consequently, the void in the cultural life of Catholics, which the decline of scholasticism had caused and the Enlightenment could not fill, became something positive as the turn of the century approached. The void, through the winds of Romanticism, became an atmosphere where not only Schelling but Schlegel, Görres, Sailer and others now felt at home.

Schelling's Catholic Critics

Word of Schelling's lectures on the inner life of God, during which he explained the Trinity as three potencies realizing the ideal in the world and advocated a metaphysical original sin, spread quickly through Würzburg. Within a few months of the philosopher's inaugural lecture, the bishop had forbade Catholic attendance at the lectures under threat of excommunication (for laity) and withheld ordination (for clerics).[25] The bishop's decree was only a firecracker compared to the cannonade soon fired at Schelling. The Catholic Kantians in Landshut and Munich joined with the older Würzburg clergy and academicians. Schelling was surprised at the strength of the Catholic Enlightenment. His introduction of a primal fall into philosophy antagonized the Enlightenment Catholics who ignored original sin and who saw Christian existence to be a universal morality of balanced virtue. Schelling's view of revelation as an intuited realization of the absolute in history did not appear any more attractive.

Franz Berg was representative of the anti-Schelling feeling among the Catholic theologians and churchmen in Würzburg. Berg had cultivated the philosophers of the Enlightenment even during his seminary days. The study of Kant, Hume, the English Deists and the French Encyclopedists had left him with a Christianity almost devoid of supernatural content. His sermons in 1785 attracted the attention of Prince-Bishop von Erthal, who placed him among the new professors commissioned to resurrect in an enlightened way the declining university.

Berg, in his fields of patrology and church history, focused upon a rationally probative apologia for Christianity. For a natural morality, proof-texts were mustered from the fathers of the church. Berg's knowledge of patristic literature allowed him to explain the supernatural dimension in Christianity as the influence of Platonism. His attitude toward revealed religion was always flexible; at the behest of church authorities he could either defend or attack Kant. His *Epikritik* is free of traditional dogma; it synthesizes Kantian approaches and Christian deism and morality.

Berg's first salvo at Schelling, the sarcastic *In Praise of the Latest Philosophy*, appeared anonymously, before Schelling's arrival. Here Berg resembled Fichte or Jacobi. The ground of all was a mysterious "thinking-willing." Philosophy's task, he maintained, was to analyze human experience and mental activities, but ultimately it remained contentless. Clearly unacceptable was Schelling's system, where a vital nature and history fleshed out spirit. Schelling's claim to surpass Kant, to present *the* philosophy of science, to do this in a garb that at times seemed a return to the religious dimension Kant had critiqued, could find only rejection. Friends of Schelling published in 1802 a similarly anonymous *In Praise of "Kranicopie,"* ridiculing Berg.

The Kantian patrologist did not hesitate to attack the new philosophy in the name of the bishop, in the name of Catholic orthodoxy. This took the form of a dialogue: *Sextus or On Schelling's Absolute Knowledge*.[25] Sextus and Plotinus, the skeptic and the mystic engaging in philosophical conversation—these are Berg and Schelling. The level of philosophical discourse is not high; one interesting point is the recognition of the influence of Plotinus upon Schelling. By using terms such as "fall" to describe creation, Schelling seemed to have embraced Neoplatonism. The objection of the Catholic critic, however, is not that Schelling's sources are pagan rather than Christian, but that they are mystical rather than critico-rational. Schelling complained that one day he was called a Catholic mystic, the next day an atheist.[26]

The Munich Critics

Not all the Roman Catholics outside Landshut were against Schelling. The court physician at Aschaffenburg, not far from Würzburg, was devoted to the philosopher of objective idealism whose writings showed a course that had already gone beyond the philosophies of nature and transcendental identity. Carl Josef Windischmann was from a Rhenish family; he was a doctor in the new medicine. He had left the church for modern politics and philosophy. (Later, influenced by Görres and Friedrich Schlegel, he would return to Catholicism and, in Bonn after 1818, be a leader of the movement against the Catholic Kantian, Hermes.) He dedicated his translation of Plato's *Timaeus* to Schelling. Windischmann took Schelling's side in a sharp review of *Sextus*, although he too had reservations about the introduction into modern philosophy of a primal fall.[27]

Schelling wrote to Windischmann in early 1804: "The situation here I suppose you can imagine. The clerical party abhors me and the young clerics who attend my lectures . . . are threatened with excommunication. All that makes no difference to me, although I should like to find as much peace and harmony here as possible."[28] Attacks came not only from the Würzburg clerics but from contributors to Bavarian and Austrian periodicals whose columns after 1803 planted in Schelling's mind thoughts of possible suits for libel. Articles called him a pantheist, an atheist, a thinker without ethics, a mystic.

Friedrich Köppen wrote a harsh critique in 1803.[29] A former student of Fichte in Jena, he too was a disciple of Jacobi who would help procure for him in 1807 the professorship in Landshut that might have been Schelling's.

Cajetan Weiller, "the schoolmaster of Munich," coordinated the overall attack. Weiller was born in Munich and educated by the Benedictines. A priest, he soon became professor of philosophy and rector at the Munich lyceum, a center of the Catholic Enlightenment. He had been Schelling's corecipient of the honorary degrees at Landshut. His attachment was to Kant; his faith was from Jacobi. Jacob Salat was his follower, an indefatigable apologete and journalist for Enlightenment Catholicism.

Weiller's special interest was pedagogical; there he could employ with ease the Kantian reduction of Christianity to moral humanism. He minimalized grace and sin, and found Schelling's dialectic of fall and organic growth unattractive. In 1803 he and Salat published *The Spirit of the Latest Philosophy of Schelling, Hegel and Company*. The next year saw more books by both men. These writings are of little philosophical significance and make no attempt to understand the Schelling they cite. The issue was the birth of a new way of thinking: Romantic idealism. In Munich the charge was not "pantheism" (as in Würzburg) but "mysticism" and "system." Mocking the students of Würzburg and their enthusiasm, Salat wrote, "Many of these young heroes assert that St. Francis Assisi was one of the great philosophers in Schelling's pantheon."[30]

In April 1804, Schelling received an explicit warning from a minister, Count Thürheim, to avoid further controversy. But that summer, in the face of irresponsible attacks from Munich, Schelling decided he could remain silent no longer. Government measures had shown that the electoral court was distancing itself from him; a new school plan based upon two volumes by Cajetan Weiller forced education into a Kantian pedagogics and forbade the new philosophy to be taught in the *Gymnasium*.[31] When Schelling's followers presented their case to Montgelas—their freedom of discussion was being prohibited in an enlightened land—he explained that the new philosophical systems could be discussed but only as part of the history of philosophy or as material for critiques.

The literary attacks of his opponents enraged Schelling more than the cautions of the court intimidated him. At the end of March 1805, he published an open letter to the public. In an elegant if volatile style he denied the many calumnies of the "toadies of the ever darkening Enlightenment." He ridiculed the accusations that he was both too scientific and too mystical, that he led students in one lecture to Catholicism, in the next to atheism. He quickly explained his own position vis-à-vis philosophical schools and Christian confessions. He ended with threats of lawsuits but also with a hopeful metaphor: "The seed of a new creation that the always praiseworthy government of Bavaria has sown in southern Germany will bloom and bear fruit a thousandfold."[32] There could be no doubt—the seed was Schelling himself.

Political events took control of philosophical disputes. Napoleon declared war against England, Russia and Austria; Bavaria remained his ally. Many students left the university for the army. At the end of 1805, after the battle of Austerlitz, the peace negotiations of Pressburg declared that Würzburg would no longer remain with Bavaria (now a kingdom) but would be given as reparation for Salzburg to Ferdinand of Tuscany. Würzburg passed to Ferdinand in February 1806. Schelling and his companions knew at once that the new authorities would not patronize the Protestant, non-Bavarian professors of post-Kantian thought brought in by Montgelas. The controversy with the Catholic Enlightenment and some decline in favor with the Munich court helped Schelling to accept what had been decided by the events of war and peace: to leave his present professorship. Heidelberg was a possibility for a call; with a tone of hope, Schelling wrote to Goethe about a return to Jena.[33] But no firm offers came.

A New Spiritual Space

And so in the winter of 1805/1806, Schelling again needed a position. No doubt it was difficult for him to turn to the government in Munich for assistance. Although educational positions were found for other professors such as Paulus and Niethammer, for Schelling nothing seemed suitable. Finally it was suggested that he become a member of the Academy of Science in Munich. The purpose of the academy had been to offer the capital (which then had no university) the fruits of science. The academy had had an insignificant existence, and Friedrich Jacobi, no friend to Schelling, had been called to Munich to give it life.

Schelling accepted. He went to Munich hardly realizing that there his thinking would receive a third cluster of major stimuli: mysticism, myth and Christianity. When Schelling had first seen Bavaria in the summers of 1800 and 1803, he was the young genius of idealism, the philosopher of Romanticism. Now over thirty, he appeared to be a professor without a worthy position, a man who had lost important friends, a public figure who could not avoid controversy. And to his eyes Munich appeared unexciting; it was in the hands of his enemies, the Enlightenment; it seemed rationalist, clerical.

If Schelling had returned to the north of Goethe, Hegel and Schleiermacher, his thought would surely have followed other directions. A meeting with a new world took place in 1806 as he moved to Munich. Schelling entered a new cultural and spiritual landscape. Munich with Franz von Baader opened the passage from bright, transcendental systems to unexplored, mystical abysses. Jakob Boehme's descent into the irrational ground of the universe awaited exploration, as did Tauler and Eckhart, the mystics of the Middle Ages, and the mythology of the East. At the same time, by remaining in the south of Germany, he guaranteed that his future philosophy would play a central role in the renewed cultural world of Catholicism.

In the move from Jena to Bavaria, from Würzburg to Munich, Schelling's mind was traveling forward, often unconsciously, on his personal odyssey, leaving the port of the philosophy of identity where ego and nature melded into the absolute. He was setting sail for the godhead, for a turbulent abyss of divine will. A new geography meant a new philosophical world. A few months before he left Würzburg for Munich, in April 1806, Schelling wrote to his friend Windischmann: "In my seclusion in Jena I meditated constantly and vitally on nature, less so on life. Since then I have learned to see that religion, public faith and life in the state form the point around which everything else revolves."[34]

PART TWO

God and the World Becoming
1806 to 1821

4

A Dark Romanticism and a
Subterranean Man

BAVARIA WAS CAUGHT UP in the ebb and flow of the armies fighting
Napoleon's wars. Munich, the capital, was filled with political intrigue as
Bavaria sided with France against its neighbor Austria. Nevertheless,
culturally Munich remained a crossroads for thinkers and artists, a city
possessing enough magnetism to draw two of the great philosophers of the
post-Kantian era, Jacobi and Schelling.

In his first months in Munich, Schelling feared he had gone too
deeply into the corridors and chanceries of the Roman Catholic south. He
described the atmosphere in a letter as "ultraclerical" and, drawing on the
Psalms for a metaphor, he spoke of how "Sion's watchmen" guarded
orthodoxy.[1] Friedrich Jacobi had recently arrived in Munich to head the
Academy of Sciences. As we have seen, his philosophy drew Kantianism
to a climax in faith and reminded some of Schleiermacher. Jacobi along
with Catholic disciples such as Köppen had long been opposing Schelling. Consequently the philosophers' relationships were cool if polite.
After reading Schelling's new writings where each page explored mystically and theosophically God's freedom and will, Jacobi attacked—not
because Schelling neglected God but because he described him. Schelling's reply was lengthy, ponderous and bitter.

Schelling's expanding vision of the powers of mind and insight was
looking for a new world and it gained energy not from Jacobi's faith but
from the mystics' insight, from Tauler and Boehme. Schelling did not
want to let disappear the admittedly vague absolute of Fichte and
Spinoza. The Rhenish and Silesian mystics guided him toward new horizons extending forward into the reality of the godhead. Schelling also was
contemplating the religious absolute in an objective as well as subjective
manner; the absolute was not Fichte's extension of the knowing self but
the mysterious life of a godhead beyond God.

For the name day of the Bavarian king in October 1807, Schelling delivered an address that enhanced his standing. The theme was a discussion of the relationship of the fine arts to the philosophy of the natural sciences resolved in *Geist*. This address made him a personage in Bavaria: the king knighted him and created for him the general secretariat of a new academy, the Academy of the Fine Arts.[2] After 1806, Munich could not be refused the glory of being a major center for German Romanticism. August Schlegel and Tieck passed through; J. Ritter, the inventor and scientist, moved there from Jena; C.F. von Savigny, the Romantic philosopher and historian of law, was not far away in Landshut. German Romanticism found a special form after 1806 in Munich.

> Munich, more than Jena, became Schelling's city of destiny. An encounter with a new world took place in 1806. Certainly it is no chance that this greatest among Schelling's moves is linked to his arrival in Munich. For that arrival meant concretely that Schelling had entered a new *intellectual-spiritual space*, a space which is specifically Christian. . . . In Jena, Schelling was the leader; now he will be led.[3]

Dark Romanticism

In the years after 1806 German Romanticism passed through a crisis. A period of proud revolutions and excited syntheses in many areas of culture had produced a new age: *Sturm und Drang* became *Romantik*. And yet the impulse for comprehending mystically or intuitively process and the infinite was far from being spent. Less hypnotized by a formless and unlocatable absolute, drawn to religion and to Christianity, slightly uncertain of the hour of the coming utopia's dawn, Schelling both followed and led as Romanticism moved into new tones, new shades of darkness.

Horizons of thought change through creative rearrangement and yet they maintain their deeper identity; both destruction and production bring something new. Schelling's own philosophy, always receptive to new impulses, changed considerably during this decade. His thought was moving from a confident, all-encompassing construction drawn from the absolute source of all that was knowing and known to an exploration of depths that were of the will as much as of reason. He had been at the center of early Romanticism, and then idealism found an easy marriage with what went under the title of Romantic. Both—the Romantic and the idealist spirit—dreamt of a reconciliation of, a unity among, opposites. Inevitably this led to a crisis: a breakdown of the optimism of the Romantic, a breakthrough by philosophy into a new realism. Here too, Schelling's philosophy was being formed by and forming culture.[4]

Dark Romanticism had its roots in Novalis's *Hymns to the Night* of 1800 and in Goethe's *Faust I*, finished in 1808. What was begun in Jena was furthered but changed when Franz von Baader introduced Schelling in Munich to the writings of the Protestant and Catholic mystics, especially to Jacob Boehme:

> It is certainly true that Schelling's change of stance around 1809 was almost a break. In fact, this was a move from a bright world into a world full of darkness and abysses. Yet, it was an embraced darkness, the dark realm of late Romanticism and of theosophy.[5]

The system of Schelling's middle years studied not human but divine freedom and concluded not with absolute spirit but with an undetermined ocean of the will in the godhead. The primal being was not bright reason but dark volition.

Schelling's writings of this period show the altered personal and cultural circumstances in his career. The Würzburg medical journal was continued for a while as he published occasional addresses on works of art or on experiments in the natural sciences that interested him. Four works in philosophy come from this period of Schelling's life, reaching from 1806 to 1821. There is a published critique of Jacobi, an unpublished set of lectures delivered at Stuttgart, which treat more explicitly of revelation and eschatology, the new but little developed and unpublished system *The Ages of the World*, and finally the *Essay on Freedom*. The last-named, a most radical and lastingly significant work, moved from system to mysticism, from understanding to will. It reflected the newness of this next stage of Romanticism. It was written in conversation not with Kant and Spinoza but with the mystics and their guardian Franz von Baader.

Franz von Baader

Before he was thirty years old, Friedrich Schelling had influenced the lives of many: the scientists Schubert and Steffens, in Jena; the theologians Zimmer and Sailer, at Landshut; the physicians Röschlaub and Döllinger, at Würzburg; on the Rhine, Friedrich Schlegel and Joseph

Görres. Only the truly great, however, would influence him: Goethe, Fichte, Hegel. When we look at Schelling's dialogue with Roman Catholic intellectual life, we see dozens of thinkers over a period of three decades who were touched by him, but only one who exercised a deep influence upon him: Franz Xaver von Baader.

Schelling met Baader shortly after his arrival in Munich. Baader was an extraordinary personality whose profession was mining, whose obsessions were mysticism and philosophy, and whose writings anticipated by decades movements that would later be called "ecumenism," "nihilism," "socialism." Baader was one of the remarkable figures of the nineteenth century. Hans Urs von Balthasar describes him as "the Titan" of German idealism.[6]

Baader was born in Munich, March 27, 1765, the third son of the physician to the elector of Bavaria. As a student at Ingolstadt from 1781 to 1783, he imbibed the atmosphere and ideals of Sailer as he pursued reluctantly a degree in medicine. This was an intensely mystical period in Sailer's life and under his direction Baader came to learn of the revival movements then sweeping the Catholic south. Their life and mystique offset his dissatisfaction with the institutional church. Sailer showed him the church as a community nourished by spiritual teaching and called to sum up the oneness of the human race. A voracious reader, Baader plunged into Goethe, Kant and Fichte and kept diaries of his own spiritual journey, diaries marked by unusual self-analysis. As with Hegel, Schelling and the two Schlegels, the ferment of the times after 1795 led Baader to a decision to reject the Enlightenment and to search out a new way of thinking and living.

Baader went to Great Britain to study for a change in profession; engineering was exchanged for medicine. Those years acquainted him with British empirical philosophy and with democratic politics. At the same time he came across the mystical writings of Louis Saint-Martin, a theosophic transmitter of Boehme and the Cabala, who lived until 1803. By the turn of the century, Baader was publishing new ideas about European unity, uncovering texts by medieval mystics such as Tauler, composing systems for the natural sciences and transcendental philosophy. These wide horizons of intellectual activity expanded to include negotiations with Czarist Russia over politics and church unity, and memoranda to Catholic Rome over the papacy. Franz von Baader coined the word "proletariat," he introduced into Germany the description of the coming times as "nihilism," he began theological conversation with feminism and sexuality. He worked for an ecumenical union of the Catholic, Lutheran and Orthodox churches, stimulated the Holy Alliance into existence, and, with only slight exaggeration, guided the spiritual life of personages as diverse as Czar Alexander I and Hegel. He corresponded in France with de Maistre, Bonald and Bautain, and wrote articles for de Lamennais's *L'avenir*.

> Philosopher of religion in Munich, friend of Hegel, colleague of Schelling, Baader seems to us today to have been more and more *the* personality in the history of philosophy in the nineteenth century. In a prophetic way he sketched the metaphysical background for the great European crisis of culture which began with the French Revolution, moved through the flowering of German idealism, and burst into the open with the transformation of Hegelian philosophy into dialectical materialism. Baader not only announced in advance the dangers which were coming, but he pointed out ways to overcome them.[7]

In the conversation between modern philosophy and Roman Catholicism, Baader was not a disciple of Schelling but an independent personality, a man who on his own channeled the new sciences in order to express the Catholic tradition anew, and who out of his own creativity suggested ideas to Schelling.

Baader's writings do not fall easily into precise categories: he wrote not only idealist and theosophic monographs but essays in mysticism and politics. He never succeeded in completing a single volume that would sum up his career of speculation. In 1786, he was already publishing treatises on the natural sciences, and at the age of sixty, with an address on intellectual freedom, he helped to inaugurate the new University of Munich. At his death in 1841, he was assembling a collection of material from the biblical commentaries of Aquinas and laboring over a first edition of another discovery, Meister Eckhart.

Baader's style is metaphorical and formless, his format open-ended. His interests move between the poles of the dynamic ground and process of reality, and the relationship of God and creatures. Subjectivity before objects, the harmony of the structure of thought with being, the parallel of spirit to nature, the dialectic of cosmos and humanity—these are metamorphosed by his talent into theosophy, the history of Christian theology, and political theory.

Baader and Schelling: Early Contacts

Prior to the year of Schelling's first publication, 1794, Baader had already moved from *Sturm und Drang* to early Romanticism and idealism. He began a friendship with Jacobi in 1796. What distinguished Baader from Schelling in their first writings was precisely the mystical tone. Baader, too, was preoccupied with the employment of the new subject-oriented philosophy of science, but his Catholicism had accelerated the Romantics' journey toward the castle of the mystical. Baader's early writings were a creative attempt to combine the new philosophy of natural science with mysticism. His dissertation on chemistry displayed that approach to natural science; he felt, as did so many others, that these intellectual movements had placed him "at the entrance to the temple of esoteric wisdom."[8]

Through acquaintances of Sailer, Matthias Claudius among others, Baader first came upon the writings of the mystics that were to prove such a rich lode for his work. Claudius offered after 1782 translations into German of the pages of Saint-Martin. Returning from England, Baader met Claudius and Jacobi in Hamburg. Jacobi gave him the idea of producing post-Enlightenment philosophy that would culminate in faith, and he introduced him to Schelling's books. Baader began a thorough study of the German mystics: not only Boehme and Oetinger but Eckhart, Tauler, Ruysbroeck, Angelus Silesius. Baader was also struck by the recently discovered John Scotus Erigena, whose thought later found exposition in a first book by the Tübingen theologian F.A. Staudenmaier, pupil of Drey and enthusiast of Schelling. Erigena showed how Christ could remain at the center of a Platonic system of developmental being and thinking. "Erigena," Baader wrote thinking of Fichte and Kant, "stands way beyond our newer critical philosophy."[9]

Baader quickly saw how much he and Schelling had in common and this spelled for him the end of Fichte's hegemony over the new culture. As Baader was reading Schelling's philosophies of nature published after 1797 he, too, had completed much of a systemic fragment uniting physics, mysticism and transcendental philosophy: *On the Pythagorean Ternary*. Its pages were similar to Schelling's philosophy of natural forces and praised Schelling's *On the World-Soul* as its model, "the spring of a new age." In fact, Baader was too modest: his work was finished before contact with Schelling took place. Prior to 1805, the two thinkers' works were parallel and similar but independently conceived. Schelling quoted Baader favorably in the *World-Soul* as a theoretician of organic principles for life and ontology.[10]

There were, however, contrasts between the two men. Baader was less interested in the idealist framework of a system and more preoccupied with the material from physics and chemistry needed for its furnishing. Before 1805, while Baader was moving into mysticism, Schelling was concluding his philosophy with aesthetics. Baader, although a mystic, abhorred any spiritualism without natural reality behind it or any static materialism without spirit—both were too reminiscent of the Enlightenment. In the parallel processes of nature and spirit, each moving organically and developmentally toward a fuller manifestation of its polar opposite, Schelling and Baader were one.

Munich and Boehme

Baader had come back to Munich in 1796 to enter the service of the state and he spent the rest of his life in the Bavarian capital. In 1806, when Schelling arrived in Munich, which he feared would be a dull, clerical keep, he was surprised by Baader. He soon wrote to his father of "my friend Baader, a great lover of mystical writings and theosophy."[11] Schelling's wife Caroline described the director of mines as caught up in a frantic round of letter-writing, visits, publications, lectures and yet "owning one of the most exciting minds in the world."[12] Baader wrote for Schelling's journal of medical studies.

In retrospect it seemed as if Baader were waiting until that mysterious flow that determines the history of ideas would send Schelling to him. The austere absolute of the system of identity, both the *Vernunft* and the *Verstand* of modern philosophy, were to be challenged by . . . mystics. In Baader, Schelling met at the right moment a kindred spirit who led him beyond the philosophy of nature, beyond an aesthetic Romanticism and the transcendental analysis of intellect. Beyond Fichte and Spinoza waited another kind of absolute: a dark, turbulent ground. Baader was the fulfillment of Novalis, for the young poet had earlier forecasted the move from epistemology to religion, from day to night, from Christian orthodoxies to world church.

In Schelling's farewell to Fichteanism written in 1806 he wrote an emotional confession that the ultimate philosophy was mystical, and that he was not afraid to be recognized publicly as one standing in the "company of mystics."[13] Schelling confessed his admiration for Baader in a clear if cryptographic paean:

> I know a man who is by nature a subterranean man: in whom knowing has become solid reality; in whom knowing has become being, just as in metals sound and light receive mass. He does not know, but rather he is a living, constantly altering, complete personality of knowing.[14]

If Schelling had already seen Boehme's writings at Jena, still it was through Baader that they altered his thought.

Baader never hesitated to boast that he had brought the German mystics, Protestant and Catholic, medieval and baroque, to light. He prided himself on having made Boehme and Eckhart known to Hegel, and to Schelling; he laughed that he had shocked the intellectuals with his "cobbler, Boehme."[15] In 1812 Baader began to work on an edition of Tauler. Schelling asked his father to send him from Swabia a fine edition of Oetinger, the eschatological pietist, which he presented to Baader in 1809.[16]

German Romanticism had entered a new phase and Baader was a prophet for this period of German cultural life. Through the motifs of mysticism and process applied to the levels of the subconscious as well as to history, he influenced not only the Roman Catholic Church but the intellectual life of Europe. During these years, however, Baader wrote little, for he was distracted by a flood of ideas, projects, persons. Friedrich Schlegel wrote: "If only he knew how to write the way he knows how to speak, people would not be talking about Schelling and Fichte for very long. . . . The most intelligent, the deepest man I have met in a long time is Baader."[17]

The Essay on Freedom

The *Philosophical Investigations concerning Human Freedom* was published in 1809, and for Schelling this work was an end and a beginning. The richness and variety of events that took place during that year illustrate the vitality and creativity of that age. Napoleon dominated from Spain to Prussia. Urged on by Fichte and Schleiermacher, the Prussian minister of culture, Wilhelm von Humboldt, planned a new university for Berlin. With the first part of *Faust* in print, Goethe mixed the new science of chemistry with the new attitude toward love and marriage in his novel *Elective Affinities*. Jean Paul and August Schlegel published important literary works of later Romanticism, while Hegel followed the *Phenomenology of the Spirit* with *Philosophical Propaedeutic*. Haydn died in 1809 after a burst of creativity in the late masses and in the two great choral works *Creation* and *The Seasons*. In the same year Beethoven composed the *Emperor* piano concerto and the sonata *Les Adieux*. Franz Schubert is twelve years old and is beginning to compose. Robert Schumann would be born the next year. Caspar David Friedrich, a kind of Schelling of nordic painting, had met the philosopher's loyal disciple Gotthilf Schubert and was completing his Romantic studies of the solitary in nature *Monk by the Sea* and *Abbey in Eichwald*. With these examples of the cultural milieu we glimpse the style of the early nineteenth century. At the same time, the addresses of Schelling and Baader, the experiments and articles of the electrophysicist Ritter, show a new version of the Romantic triad of natural science, art and religion that we met first in Jena.

Despite the title, Schelling's book on freedom was primarily about God's freedom, not human freedom, and about the relationship of necessity and freedom in the absolute. We have here an old theme but in a new philosophy. The absolute is not described as pure reason but as spirit and life, while the realms of mysterious nature and revelatory history look to a further ground. Into this world entered theosophy, mysticism, Christianity. Boehme led Schelling into the abyss where the irrational, the powers of the will, preformed the universe. All of this did suggest a metaphysics that drew on aspects of Christianity such as fall, sin, redemption and eschatology. The *Essay on Freedom* was written totally from the perspective of Boehme; and Baader, we might say, was the curator of Boehme's writings.

The essay itself—a fragment of a planned system—circles around freedom through three areas of interest: pantheism, evil, God. Pantheism may exclude freedom in the creature and in God; any monistic unity of the two, of which Schelling had annoyingly been accused, would seem to drive freedom away from each. Secondly, freedom implies the possibility of evil, but evil has normally been excluded from God. After these questions on pantheism and evil, linking the finite and the infinite, Schelling chose to turn not to human nature but to God.

To explain the close relationship between the absolute and all finite beings, Schelling criticized popular misunderstandings of pantheism, defended a legitimate understanding of Spinoza, and explained the difference between God and beings in the universe. Every reasonable philosophy, he asserted, holds that things are immanent in God, and philosophy may not reject the dependent, intrinsic transparency of the finite to the absolute. God exists in himself and the idea of God is conceived solely through itself, but that which is finite lacks necessity in existence and concept. God is always more than, and not the sum of, individual beings.

There seems to be freedom, Schelling continued, only where there is evil, at least where there is the potentiality for evil. "A real and vital conception of freedom asserts that it is a possibility of good and evil,"[18] and so the main philosophical problem in the area of freedom is not choice but evil. The question awaiting a response is whether freedom for evil can be included in an idealist system, whether the absolute spirit can own limitations of nature. Schelling praised Baader's "concrete conception of evil" shown in his writings through "penetrating analogies."[19] Evil is something positive, a tension among powers. Moreover, evil belongs to the will, and in the finite will it results from irrational, undefined moves in the ground of life and selfhood. Inasmuch as Schelling did not exempt the absolute from the dialectic of freedom and necessity, he did not avoid locating, even in God, that which our experience shows to be a necessary component of choice and freedom: evil.

To explain this new view of the existing absolute, God, and to resolve the problem of evil and freedom in the ground of all, Schelling drew upon Boehme's ideas. The absolute is not a pure simplicity, but it contains a ground of its own existence. Out of the ground but within God flow necessity and evil and therein freedon:

> God as spirit is the purest love; in love there can never be a will to evil, much less in the ideal principle. But God himself, so that he can be, can need a ground, a ground not outside of himself but in him. And God has in himself a nature, which, although belonging to him, is different from him. The will of love and the will of the ground are two different wills, each existing for itself. But the will to love cannot withstand the will of the ground nor absorb it, because otherwise it would be withstanding itself. The ground must work so that love can be, and it must work independently from it so love can truly exist. . . . The ground is a will to revelation, and as such it must call forth individuality and opposition.[20]

This dialectic within the absolute is mirrored in the creature. The active, plural world of divine freedom grounds the life of the finite being. Into

God's being, religions and philosophies have placed actions and characteristics that are reconcilable only in a process of becoming. Within and behind this God is a further, primal ground—Boehme's *Ungrund*. There the deity both rests and seethes like a geyser.

Schelling fills in this preliminary portrait of God with many of Boehme's favorite categories and descriptive phrases. The ground of God's existence is a longing *(Sehnsucht)* and a desire *(Begierde)* to give·birth to itself, to become a determinate unity. . . . The first stage in the process whereby the being of God is produced from the ground corresponds to the point in Boehme's thought at which the *Ungrund* (primal ground) produces from itself a mirror in which it foresees what it might become.[21]

Schelling describes the absolute as an infinite, undulating sea, dark and uncertain with unformed potential. Its desire "begets in God an inner, reflex conceptualization . . . through which, since it can have no other object, God looks at himself in an image."[22]

In a move filled with consequences for Western culture, Schelling has drawn forth a mystical content and language from Boehme (and perhaps also from Tauler and Eckhart) for whom the silent desert of the godhead is distinguished from God. "All birth is from darkness to light. The seed must die in the earth in darkness so that the shimmering shaft of light can call it forth."[23] The absolute is no longer Kant's reason—but will. The ultimate is not bright intellection but "an undulating, seething ocean"[24] of drives and desires, undetermined and arational. Schelling began the nineteenth century with a system whose repeated leitmotif was *Bewusstsein*, "consciousness;" the composer Richard Wagner will end that epoch with Tristan and Isolde longing to be *unbewusst*, "unconscious."

Moving away from the abstract, diaphanous world of the absolute, Schelling offered a new idea of God. The *Essay on Freedom* of 1809 presented a metaphysics of a God developing, of a philosophy of will, of a disconcerting realm of freedom where neither the human being nor God is fully in control.

After completing this work, Schelling was embroiled in controversy with Jacobi, whose appeal was always strong among Roman Catholics, from Sailer in Landshut to Drey in Tübingen. Baader had hoped to be a link of reconciliation between the young Schelling and the older Jacobi, but this proved impossible when Jacobi attacked Schelling's use of Baader and Boehme. Jacobi raised the spectre of atheism and pantheism.

An enraged Schelling replied that it was Jacobi's thought, so respected by theologians, Protestant and Catholic, that was atheist, because it culminated in an escapist faith and avoided the problem of how a real God grounded the world's life. By attacking Jacobi, Schelling hurled himself against the remaining bulwarks of the Enlightenment. Although he perceived this only dimly, he was rejecting religion without reality, an airy faith without content. God must include our life in his.[25] This affirmation of an objectivity for the transcendental system that treats religion, no matter what diverse forms it might take, brought Schelling and Baader together.

Although Baader agreed with Schelling in the insertion of organic development into the cosmos, they would differ over the development of a Christian anthropology. For Schelling, the process is God's; for Baader humankind is called from above to grow beyond the all too clear structures of his fallenness. Unredeemed nature is the chaos of the world. Freedom exists not for God to become himself but so that in temporality the human person can develop. Baader felt that Schelling in his search for the absolute was confusing the human spirit with the divine. What brought the two thinkers together was the problem facing Romantic idealism: the rejection of the science and religion of the Enlightenment, the pursuit of unity between nature and the inner spirit.

In 1813 Baader's lectures before Maximilian I transformed the Romantic approach to science into a Christian theology. His examples for uniting nature and spirit were the incarnation and the Eucharist, and the organic, corporate evolution of the human race toward the Body of Christ.[26] So far into Christianity (for Baader a kind of divine materialism) Schelling would not go.

Enmity

In his lectures as well as in this, his last published system, Schelling never tired of praising Baader. Baader, however, in 1809 uttered a first word of warning about too radical an appropriation of Boehme's views on God and spirit: "The human person does not need to give up his individuality, existence and personhood as a sacrifice to God as if this being a creature were a sin."[27] What kind of ungod in anger or love spewed forth and consumed creatures? What had Schelling meant by evil in God? Was it moral evil, ontological finitude or struggle? In the second decade of the century, Baader found himself less occupied with science and philosophy and more concerned with politics and church unity. He was advising Czar Alexander, the surprised conqueror of Napoleon, whom the events of 1812 had sent into mystical exaltation. Baader may have sensed that Schelling, too, sought the concrete now that the ideal was fully treated—sought it in the mythologies of the East (as Schlegel and Görres had suggested)—whereas he, Baader, was very clear about the eternity and perfection of God prior to the emergence of the world and about the centrality of the Word who is Christ.

Baader's absence from Munich intensified a growing personal gulf between the two thinkers. At great expense of energy and money he undertook a trip to Russia, hoping to persuade the czar to approve his plans for the reunion of the three great branches of Christianity. Meanwhile Baader's supporters at the Russian court lost power and he never gained admission into the country; he returned to Munich bitterly disappointed.

Baader's ecumenical and Russian enterprises annoyed Schelling; he wrote to Baader complaining that he had taken upon himself the role of "an avenging prophet opposed to all modern philosophy."[28] Baader reacted sharply to this detraction. Schelling, never easily drawn to reconciliation, dropped the relationship.

Baader was drawn more and more to Hegel, who had thought of accompanying him on the trip to Russia. En route to Russia, Baader had excited Hegel with Meister Eckhart. "I was often with Hegel in Berlin," he wrote. "Once I read to him from the works of Meister Eckhart, whom he knew only by name. He was so enthusiastic that the next day he held an entire lecture on Eckhart and at the end said: 'There we have it—just what we wanted.' "[29] Of Schelling, Baader wrote to Hegel: "Schelling cannot free himself from his old philosophy, cannot move forward. His early philosophy of nature was a generous, tasty steak but now he just cooks up a ragout with Christian spices."[30] Despite this collapse of the friendship and time away from Munich, both would meet again as colleagues in the first faculty for the new University of Munich.

Unfinished System: "Ages of the World"

After a burst of productivity in the essay on freedom and the response to Jacobi's attack, Schelling began to write works that he would subsequently withhold from publication. Due to personal tragedy and professional pressure, an inability to publish, to place his ideas in public view, came to the fore in a writer who had published so much so early. This compulsion to revise, to leave unpublished, will little by little imprison Schelling's works of this and the next, final period of his philosophy.

The system to rival Hegel, *The Ages of the World*, was never published. With phrases reminiscent of Meister Eckhart, the system describes not only the origin of the universe and the structure of consciousness and temporality but the development of God. We have here already the later, Christian philosophy, for the theme of the work is God rather than self, the history of God rather than the categories of human intellection, existence rather than reason. God not only is the absolute of the mind, he exists sovereignly; he steps out into further existence through creation.[31]

Schelling and the Roman Catholic Church

Schelling's move to Munich was a move deeper into the geographical and spiritual world not only of religion but of Roman Catholicism. When it was known that the philosopher, just thirty, numbered himself among the mystics and focused his philosophy not on the transcendental self but upon the mysterious godhead, rumor (after 1806) spread the question, Had Schelling become a Roman Catholic?

The world of the Romantics was a world of quick personal decisions where aesthetic and religious motivations ran together. It was in a limited way an age of conversions. After centuries of being condemned by the reformed and enlightened of Europe, in some fields the leading Christian approach was Roman Catholic or at least congenial to the Catholic mind. Goethe and Schiller at Weimar, and Schleiermacher and Hegel in Berlin were shocked by the famous men and women who found a home in medieval Christianity, a move epitomized in Friedrich Schlegel's conversion.

Schelling was being considered in 1816 for a second time by the academic administration of the University of Jena. Goethe was still minister at Weimar and influential in the choice of professors for the nearby faculty. He raised doubts that crippled Schelling's chances. As the following lines show, Goethe in a letter to the minister of education argued vigorously against calling Schelling:

> Does one know if he is *Catholic*? If he were such and declared it only
> after he had accepted the position, could one allow a Catholic

philosopher to dogmatize about religion? If he accepted the professorship as a Protestant and then converted to Catholicism, what could we do? And if he started proselytizing, could we drive him out into the night as Czar Alexander did with the Jesuits?

It strikes me as strange that we, on the occasion of the celebration of the third centenary of our truly great, Protestant accomplishment, permit that old outdated stuff to enter under a new, mystical-pantheistical, abstruse philosophical (although in its style far from contemptible) form.[32]

About the same time, Schelling asked his publisher Cotta to demand a retraction from a Hamburg journal that was circulating the rumor of his conversion to the Roman Catholic Church.

Schelling did not confuse his privileged position in Bavaria, his professional freedom outside the church, with a public life as a Roman Catholic committed to one tradition and responsible to the Catholic hierarchy. When he returned to Munich in 1827, he professed that his philosophy was not not only "positive" but "Christian." The rumor circulated that his reception among the Catholics was so boisterous that Schelling "expected that the Catholic Church would recognize his new philosophy as canonical."[33] It is worth noting that the two great idealists had very different views about the reality and destiny of Protestant and Catholic Christianity. Hegel lectured in Berlin that Protestantism caused and included all that was German, all that was progressive.[34] Schelling summed up well his attitude, positive and negative, toward Catholicism in an observation delivered during lectures on a future, ecumenical, idealist church:

> The defenders of the Catholic principle will have a considerable number of reasons for opposing this philosophy. Since, however, I have been accused by my coreligionists of an inclination to Catholicity (in which accusation they do not err, if they understand Catholicism from the point of view of essential content but not from the point of view of a principle) . . . , I have treated Catholicism without haste, with esteem and equity. I expect the same treatment for my views.[35]

Schelling never thought of entering the Roman Catholic Church. He had grown up in both academic and pietist Lutheranism. In an irenicism remarkable for his sensitive personality and anticipatory of later ecumenism, he showed an openness to Roman Catholics and a sympathy for Catholicism's penchant for the mystical and the panentheistic. Nevertheless, he remained Protestant—that is, Lutheran. The style of the academician, free for religious speculation and free of church, suited him fully. By uniting this Protestant role with Roman Catholic Bavaria he enjoyed maximum freedom, more perhaps than he would have found in Prussian territory. At a deeper level we can see the constant influence of Lutheran thought-forms: the tension of *simul justus et peccator*, the duality and polarity of law and gospel, of two kingdoms, the rooting of objectivity in an inner experience of freedom and consciousness that might be seen as a counterpart to Luther's "faith." It is not simply coincidence that Schelling's christology is one of the cross, and that his ecclesiology is one of critique and radical reformation of all existing churches, Protestant, Catholic and Orthodox. Just as scholars have shown the lasting impact upon his thinking up to the final system exercised by the Württemberg, Lutheran pietists such as Bengel and Oetinger, so one could discern there the lasting structures of Luther's spirit.

Schelling remained Schelling. Confessionalism was beneath him. The Christian traditions, indeed Christianity, Judaism and the religions of the world, were evaluated as they manifested the ages of God and his world. Idealism enlivened, explained Christianity: from that principle enunciated in 1802 and repeated in 1827, Schelling never swerved. As the years of the nineteenth century progressed, Schelling thought through Christianity anew and appropriated a few of its central forms. This happened not because he had undergone a conversion but because his idealism needed the mystical, the concrete. In his own way, along with F. Schlegel and J.S. Drey, he was moving toward history, and toward the blood of history: revelation. From the point of view of Schelling's dialogue with Roman Catholic thinkers in this period (the first "Munich period"), from 1806 to 1821, we find three levels of exchange. For the first time there was influence upon Schelling by Catholics: exposure to new sources, suggestions for systems. This came from Franz von Baader and from Eckhart, Tauler and Boehme, his medieval discoveries.

Secondly, it was during these years that the important influence by Schelling upon J.S. Drey began. Drey was the founder of the Tübingen University's Roman Catholic faculty, the father of the Catholic Tübingen school. He represents the second generation of Catholic thinkers under Schelling's influence, and his thought forms a stage between Zimmer and Sailer, and F.A. Staudenmaier and J.A. Möhler. There was no more important figure than Drey in the history of Schelling's influence upon Catholic intellectual life.

Thirdly, there was the presence of Schelling in Munich. The Bavarian capital was a crossroads where an Enlightenment administration, a Kantian Catholicism, a popular piety, and the artists and philosophers of the new Romantic culture all met.

5
Founder at Tübingen:
Johann Sebastian Drey

IT MAY BE DESTINY or it may be the narrowness of our perspective that suggests that Germans born around 1775 were destined to great, or at least to large, deeds. Beethoven and Hegel were born in 1770; Schelling in 1775; Joseph Görres in 1776; Friedrich Schlegel in 1772. Johann Sebastian Drey's achievement was not a book but a school, not a system but a movement. Born in 1777, he did not have the precocity of a Schelling or a Schlegel. Like Zimmer and Thanner, in the years around 1800, he looked beyond the Enlightenment toward Romanticism for a new perspective for Catholicism. By age, Drey might have belonged to that first generation of Roman Catholic Romantic idealists, but maturity came late to his theological talent. So he drew not quickly written tomes but a few catalytic ideas from the productive years of Schelling's philosophy published between 1798 and 1806. These ideas used by Drey in his own theology after 1812, precisely when Schelling ceased to finish any books in progress, exercised a considerable influence upon one group of modern, Catholic theologians.

The Catholic Tübingen school was a modern, theological school. It was a school in the sense of Origen at Alexandria, of Abelard outside Paris, of Albertus Magnus in Cologne—a gathering and place where culture and faith produced a number of vital theologians with a common perspective. As Tübingen founder, J.S. Drey exerted a significant influence; he cleared a crossroads for Catholic intellectuals, opened perspective upon figures such as Schelling and Schleiermacher. Because of his influence, as well as his theological originality, he ranks in our history with Sailer and Baader. Drey was not the systematician that Staudenmaier was; he had not the genius of Görres. But with a sure instinct he revitalized (beyond what Sailer could have fashioned) Roman Catholic theology.

Born and raised in the environs of the Catholic educational center of Ellwangen, Drey attended the *Gymnasium* there and found his attention drawn to both theology and the natural sciences. After seminary years in Augsburg, he was ordained a priest in 1801. For the next five years he worked in the pastoral ministry, enjoying some leisure to study the new philosophers and theologians of the time. In 1806 his teaching career began at the lyceum of Rottweil as instructor in physics and the philosophy of religion; in 1812 he returned to Ellwangen, to teach dogmatic theology, the history of dogma and apologetics.

Between 1803 and 1806, Napoleon rearranged the borders of the German principalities of the south. Just as this political action expanded Bavaria, so too it brought many Catholics into the new Kingdom of Württemberg. Ellwangen became a seminary of university status to provide for the education of the clergy. In 1817, to general delight, this small band of scholars was moved to Tübingen to become part of the ducal, Protestant university, which from that time on possessed two theological faculties, one Protestant and one Catholic.[1] Drey moved with the university and became professor of systematic and historical theology and apologetics. At forty, Drey had a clear idea of which direction he believed Catholic intellectual life should follow: out of the sterility of the Enlightenment and the false heroics of French adventures, beyond the unfulfilled pastoral plans of Sailer and the piety and mysticism latent in southern Germany. Transcendental philosophy and Romantic aesthetics formed the background for something new.

Drey's life, 1777 to 1853, encompassed the time of Catholic theological renewal. In 1819 he helped to found the *Tübingen Theologische Quartalschrift*. His reviews in that periodical surveyed European theology for decades. Programs for theological renewal flowed easily from his pen: a pastoral conference on the revision of theological studies (1812); an overview of the essence and idea of Catholicism, "On the Spirit and Nature of Catholicism" (1819); a *Short Introduction to the Study of Theology* (1819). In 1820, J.A. Möhler was studying with Drey; in 1825, J.E. Kuhn was his pupil. Drey was professor at Tübingen until 1846 when, at the age of sixty-nine, he retired. Hegel had been dead for more than a decade, and Schelling had given up lecturing in Berlin. Drey died in 1853 when Schelling had less than a year to live.

The Influence of Schelling

The young professor at Ellwangen found in Schelling's system the right combination; on the one hand, the systems from 1800 to 1804 had expanded the Kantian centrality of consciousness; on the other, they searched for an alternative. That lay with an intuitive idealism that seemed not far from religious mysticism and dwelt between rationalism and an excessive supranaturalism. Two of Schelling's insights were of lasting import for Drey: first, science's efforts constructing a system that unfolded from key ideas in a particular discipline; second, organic growth in all dimensions of the universe. This motif Zimmer and other early Catholic followers of Schelling had overlooked, preferring the writings on transcendental philosophy to those on natural science. With these approaches Roman Catholic theologians were going to work out not only a philosophy of religion and revelation but one of church and tradition.

In 1812, Drey addressed his colleagues in the priestly ministry on the condition of theological studies. He began by observing how valuable it would be to observe closely the parallels between the history of German culture and the history of theology. Scholasticism no longer exerted any influence, and the Enlightenment—a Protestant creation—was recognized as impotent.[2] It had been a mistake to try to eliminate all that was historical, symbolic and mystical from Christianity.

Six years later Drey was able to present the positive side of the mission and nature of theological studies. His first publications were examples of the widely cultivated genre of critiques and plans for university curriculum. Ignaz Thanner, the senior Döllinger, and others had preceded Drey, and of course the most successful example was Schelling's *Lectures on Academic Studies*, to which Drey refers. In the background lay, too, Schleiermacher's plan from 1810 for a theological faculty. With a ready program for Roman Catholic theology in the new age of philosophy and Romanticism, Drey could set to work on his own systems: the unpublished *Praelectiones Dogmaticae* (1815–1834) and the *Apologetics* (1838–1843).

Drey's career came between the earlier Catholic Schellingians and the creator of a mature Romantic theology. His contacts with Sailer had been mediated through the Landshut professor's disciples, men such as Zimmer and the Swiss Alois Gügler, both of whom were followers of Schelling. In Ellwangen, Drey used Zimmer's *Introduction to Dogmatic Theology* as a text—he considered it something of a model in openness to the times joined to fidelity to the church.[3] It may have been that Thanner's writings of 1809, based upon Schelling's philosophy of identity, served as a link from Schelling to Drey. Thanner had even introduced faintly Schelling's notion of organic development into theology.

Drey was also familiar with his countrymen, the Swabian pietists Bengel and Oetinger. As with Schelling, those Protestant mystics were part of his heritage. Their personal theology drew from mystical experience and led to a history unfolding upon a better future. In Schleiermacher, Drey found a support for some of his methodology, especially for the joining of emotion to faith.[4] Jacobi, always popular with Roman Catholics, strengthened the Romantic dynamic of intuition by interpreting it as faith. Drey then was a point of intersection where prophets and giants from the early nineteenth century met, and through him their thought reached Roman Catholic theology. Mediating between Sailer, Zimmer and Thanner, and Drey's own pupils, Staudenmaier, Möhler and Kuhn, Drey's genius lay not in the formulation of a new christology or ecclesiology but in his employment within Roman Catholic fundamental theology—that is, apologetics and the philosophy of religion—of seminal themes, some of which came from Schelling.

Schelling's philosophy from 1800 to 1814—the years that attracted Drey's attention—was like a plant. At the center was idealism; from that core unfolded not only a philosophy of nature—nature mirrored in the life of the spirit—but a philosophy of art. The form of this ontology was process. A further, tentative suggestion lay with history viewed as God's self-realization in religion. The mind's intuition could look into all of this life of the spirit and see archetypal ideas, their structure and their expression in system. Schelling was not hostile to religion or to Christianity, seeing them as part of the life of the spirit, which found its best expression in his own idealism. Religion and Christianity were a work of art, a symbol of *Geist*. But Schelling wrote philosophy not theology; when he turned to Christianity and its beliefs, he did so within his philosophy. So the task before Drey and his students was the employment of idealism in a theology of Christian revelation.

Religion and Revelation

Because the young Roman Catholic theological students were coming to ministry without any system, Drey in 1819 presented the entire field of theological studies in his *Short Introduction*. Schelling's influence is

clear in the areas of the book that touch upon subjectivity within religion
and revelation. The opening of the work strikes the reader as a pool upon
whose surface play the colors of Romanticism, as an assembly of various
writers and movements. Through the knowing subject, he wrote, we
descend to the ground and so to religion:

> All faith and all knowing rest in the darkly felt or clearly recognized
> presupposition that everything finite that exists not only has pro-
> ceeded from an eternal and absolute ground but, in its temporal
> being and life, is rooted and is still being born by this primal
> ground.[5]

For Drey, the activity of nature and the immediacy of spirit give a general
revelation of God in the universe. A counterpoising of dark feelings and
clear recognition suggests the movement (after Schleiermacher and in
Schelling) from the early Romanticism of spirit to the dark Romanticism
of the abyss. In the style of Schelling's early systems from 1800 to 1804,
Drey observed the tracing of all forms and natures through a cohesive
universe of relations back to the primal ground. Religion proceeds from
the exploration of spiritual subjectivity:

> In that nature which owns consciousness, the annunciation of those
> connections and intertwinings cannot be separated from conscious-
> ness . . . but is one with original consciousness, is that very reality.
> This annunciation and its feeling is religion. Religion then is the first
> appearance in the human spirit, the original revelation of God in the
> human person as it becomes conscious of God just as it is becoming
> conscious of self.[6]

Feeling, experience, the full range of consciousness, intellect and
will—all flow through religion. The fall of the human race has impaired
or distorted religion. So revelation is a restoration of religion, and Christ
is the central point in history. Drey saw a continuity between the primal
revelation, which comes to explicit expression in human consciousness,
and the second revelation in Christ, which both transcends the order of
being and history but also articulates and expands the older broader
revelation in religion:

> The revelation of God is the presentation of his essence in another
> which is not God, and which in this way exists outside of him.
> Outside of God is the universe, and only this. All revelation of God,

therefore, can only take place in the universe, and the universe itself, nothing else, is this revelation. Like religion, revelation is from the beginning; it continues on and can never end.[7]

Drey struggled to express the intimate relationship of history to revelation that was so radically stated by Schelling and others. Religion looked to a more explicit revelation; the Christian word was the harmony and the fulfillment of the event of consciousness.

Drey had to distinguish the form of a subjectively oriented philosophy of religion from the content of a theology that in the last analysis was either full of pantheism or empty of true revelation. His careful use of Schelling is, of course, a microcosm of the entire problematic of Romantic idealism and its relationship to Christian revelation. Both agree that *Vernunft* is the place of revelation, inasmuch as both reason and revelation proceed from the same God who is absolute knowing:

> Revelation is something conceived by the eternal, absolute reason in God. It proceeds from this reason, and so is not fully alien to human reason in which it reveals the godly. . . . The meaning and significance of that true and effective revelation is lost for science when its [revelation's] facts and teachings are not brought into reference with the unchanging ideas of reason.[8]

Although it is true that religion exists with consciousness, neither the religious history of the human race nor true revelation are fully and immediately a by-product of intellectual life. Revelation is, for Drey, an analogous term designating a process that moves from intuitive reason to historical revelation through religion. For Schelling, the history of revelation is not a separate action of the absolute but a symbolic realization of the absolute's presence in reason and particularly history. History is not salvation-history but theodrama, the representation of the life of God.[9] And metaphysics is always broader than revelation and history. The way from the religiously tuned powers of the intellect to revelation passes through religion.

Like Görres, Schlegel and the later Schelling in their systems of the world religions, Drey devoted considerable energy to an analysis of religion. He too saw in the universal history of religion a power that was something more than human social drives. Drey seemed to hold for a special, revelatory action and word in all religions, in the religious activity or dimension of mind. Religion is a developing consciousness of what in Christ is clearly revelation. Time had to be spent on the topic of religion because in its concept modern thought watched the meeting of two basic forces: divine revelation and the analysis of consciousness.

It is clear, however, that Drey struggled to affirm a special, distinct revelation within an idealist, subject-centered approach. Within history God acted over and beyond psychic life. Revelation is more than religion: something new brings a specific, effected presence of God to history. Revelation is not, for Drey, purely past (a primal revelation) or intellectually educative (Lessing) but is a positive, historical, direct intervention of God. Reason without this special revelation is by its psychic nature a kind of participation in the divine reason and mind, and so is revelation. Reason, however, does not enter easily or naturally into immediate contact with the being of God, nor will reason—even in its mysterious, intuitive dimension—absorb revelation.[10]

The new philosophy is not a replacement of religion and revelation but a metaphysical form for explaining religion. The structure of reason is, in its essence and depth, open toward a special realm. Drey summed it up:

> Religion is the bond of man to God. Religion is certainly objective, although it is first encountered subjectively in the entire human spirit. . . . Religion differentiates itself from pure subjectivism when it portrays this bond to God as an external fact. This fact is revelation, and as such lives on in a lasting, present and fresh insight by being transformed into an organism—the church.[11]

The gospel, the church, the Spirit—these are the objective side of religious consciousness. Drey struggled to think dialectically, to affirm the objectivity of revelation in religion and to point out that in the last analysis it was the structure of human subjectivity where religion and revelation were unfolded.[12]

Drey's goal was for revelation to become in theology a *Wissenschaftslehre*. There should be a construction of dogmatic truths (the word "construction" is Schelling's) and Drey defined theology as "a construction of the faith of the Christian religion through a knowledge based upon the teachings of the Catholic Church."[13] Idea and history, science and organism meet in a construction. Higher knowledge flows from and leads back to basic and formative ideas, and then ends in an arrangement that is both the fullness of the idea and the scientific system. Not only is revelation a historical expression of the life of the spirit, it is an ongoing dialogue with the Holy Spirit.[14] The result of the human spirit's meeting God need not appear as random fragments blown from the essence of the absolute, for spirit is the origin and place of religion and revelation; because spirit is mind, it will guide revelation to become system.

The Subject's Idea

In the early 1800s, Schelling had broken with Fichte; Hegel was as yet unknown; German intellectuals were impressed by the systems Schelling was publishing, the philosophy of identity. In 1802 the *Presentation of My System of Philosophy* employed, alongside the previously favored "absolute," the term "ground."[15] A philosophy of forms unfolded there from knowing subjectivity. This philosophy was neither a subjective monism (Fichte) nor an epistemology of categories (Kant), but an objective idealism. The act of knowing, the horizons of psychic life, Schelling wrote, encompass both subjectivity and objectivity. Subjectivity, objectivity and their dialectic are the fields in which the powers of spirit render the real ideal and the ideal real. The goal of this dual process is the point of identity of the real and ideal—absolute in God, developing in the world; there nature is maximum spirit and spirit is fully concrete.

Then, in the *Further Elaboration*, a paraphrase of the system of identity published the next year, more elements and terms of the philosophy appear; reality is organic; the absolute is the ground of thinking and being; system is a construction of the absolute; construction is a living system of ideas.[16] Mediating between the infinite and the universe of beings are eternal but active forms: the ideas. The All images itself in the ideas and through them pours out being into particularity. "The ideas are the sole possibility," Schelling explained, "of grasping the absolute fullness in the absolute oneness, of grasping the particular in the absolute . . . and of grasping the absolute in the individual."[17]

An idea for Schelling is a reality that is abstract but capable of effecting particularity; moreover, it is the entire intellectual atmosphere or system surrounding that reality and its apprehension. The idea is the union of the real and the ideal, the universal and the historical:

> These external ideas, as such, can become objective only to the extent that they, in their individuality as special forms, become symbolic. That which shines through them is the absolute unity, the

idea in and for itself; form is the body with which they clothe themselves and in which they become objective.[18]

Schelling applied this to Christianity. "Idea . . . is an expression of the absolute—that is, of God himself revealed as the idea. This is why the concept of revelation is absolutely necessary in Christianity." Christianity, Schelling concluded, is religion-in-history; its idea is the divine being intent upon a historical realization of religion:

> Christianity's leading idea is God become incarnate. . . . He stands as the boundary between two worlds, decreed from all eternity yet a transitory phenomenon in time. He himself returns to the invisible realm and promises the coming of the Spirit: not a principle which becomes finite to stay finite but the ideal principle which leads the finite back to the infinite and, as such, is the light of the modern world.[19]

The ideas are living, they are capable of more than one realization, they are developmental. What Drey and Schelling both called "the inner history" of Christianity is the appearance of archetypal figures and teachings. Drey's work required finesse, for although idealism came to discuss revelation it ended by absorbing it. Drey applied the philosophy of ideas to Christianity, searching for the primal ideas in the New Testament and then interpreting theology as a history of their interpretation. He laid the foundations for a theology that was open to transcendental method and historical process.

> Both Christianity in general and its nature can be perceived and investigated either as pure concept—a system of concepts—or as a living power which forms its own world. According to a definite distinction between Christianity as a religious system *in abstracto* and a religious system in living form, one can ask: which is the essence of the system of the Christian religion and which is the essence of the church?[20]

If the ideas of Christianity are treated only as scriptural words, then all theology is merely exegesis. But if "idea" is the continued incarnation in objective appearance of the primal revelation, the historical life of Christianity is made tangible and visible again and again throughout history in the life of tradition and church. Drey has ingeniously turned Roman Catholic theology into an objective-idealist theology, in somewhat the same way Schelling seriously modified Fichte into an objective idealism. The new philosophy of intellectual subjectivity has as its polar opposite the real of historical revelation. Just as nature pursues its spiritualization, so history will not rest content with a record of empirical facts. The issue is not what happened in the chronicles of history, but what is the idea that history discloses.

Although Drey was quite conversant with Schelling's philosophy of identity, the clearest influence upon Drey was Schelling's *Lectures on University Studies*, particularly the two sections "The Historical Construction of Christianity" and "Theology." This book by Schelling continued to have an extraordinary influence upon Roman Catholics years after its publication. Seminal for many German intellectuals after its publication in 1802, its importance for Drey and other Catholics only increased after 1815. Staudenmaier wrote as late as 1834: "This writing of Schelling now begins to have the influence that it always deserved to exercise. It contains for historical Christianity so much and such great thoughts that we cannot understand why its influence has been delayed."[21]

Drey's *Short Introduction* referred to the book's "stimulating remarks" about both a more scientific view of Christianity and a scientific format for theology.[22] Schelling argued there that what distinguishes Christianity from earlier religions is history. History is a flow in which the various polar pairs can exist, meet and be synthesized. The ideal becomes real, the esoteric becomes exoteric, the infinite is present in the finite, the necessity of the natural is loosened by the freedom of history:

> The real sciences can be distinguished from the absolute or ideal science only because they contain a historical element. Theology, however, apart from this element, stands in a special relation to history. It is primarily in theology, which does deal with speculative ideas, that philosophy becomes objective. . . . Christianity is in the highest sense and in its innermost spirit historical.[23]

For Schelling, the process of revelation is coextensive, is one, with history: "On account of the universality of its idea, the historical construction of Christianity presupposes the religious construction of history as a whole."[24] Christianity is the fulfillment of Greek and Indian religions at a definitely higher stage where the mystery of nature yields to lucid history as the place of the disclosure and very being of God. Schelling stated that incarnation is the basic idea of the higher religion, Christianity: God's birth in the finite world. In a few lines he summed up his philosophy of religion-becoming-revelation in history:

> The ideas of a religion directed toward an intuition of the infinite in the finite should preferably be expressed in reality; the ideas of the opposite kind of religion, in which every symbolism belongs only to the subject, can only become object through activity. The primal symbol of every perception of God within religion is history—but history is endless, immeasurable. History must be represented through an appearance which is both infinite and still limited: not the state (which is real), nor the unity of all things in spirit (which is ideal). This symbolic intuition is the church as a living work of art.[25]

Yet another religious idea expressed the dialectic of ideal and real that Schelling saw admirably presented in incarnation. That was the kingdom of God: "The divine unveils itself in the ideal world—above all, in history; here the mystery of the divine kingdom is disclosed."[26] Kingdom, rather than incarnation, was the choice of the theologians for the idea that was the seminal ground of Christianity.

Idea and construction go together in the arrangement of religion and revelation as a manifestation of spirit in history, and in the insertion of Christian beliefs into a framework of related, dialectical ideas. The theologian, Drey said, has the task of selecting primal ideas that will be fruitful in unfolding their intellectual depth and potency and yet will be an accurate elaboration of the gospel:

> It belongs to the logic of my system of theology to pursue this approach. After I present in the Introduction the necessity and reality of a revelation, and after I have presented the idea of Christianity in general, I explain in dogmatic theology the basic idea in its full expanse and in all its aspects. . . . Then I show how those dogmas are present in the first preaching of the gospel.[27]

Breakthrough: Polar Tension and Development

Arthur Lovejoy pointed out that Schelling's philosophy of history was something new: an evolutionary theology that broke with the static or devolutionist metaphysics of Western Hellenism.[28] The fire for the fusion of the ideal and the real construction came from Schelling's (and then Drey's) elevation of organic life into a basic principle. By 1798, in his book *On the World-Soul*, Schelling had proclaimed nature to be organic; like consciousness, it lived out an evolutionary history. First nature, then history and art, and finally religion could all best be portrayed as an organism whose development was the matter of the spirit:

> Philosophy is nothing other than a physics of our spirit. From now on all dogmatism is reversed. We treat the system of our ideas not in their being, but in their becoming. Philosophy is becoming genetic. . . . The system of nature is at the same time the system of our spirit.[29]

Schelling quickly moved from Kant's static cosmos to Romanticism's fluid nature:

> The insight into this inner necessity of all natural phenomena certainly becomes even more complete as soon as we reflect that there is no true system which is not at the same time an organic totality. . . . This organization as a totality must preexist its parts . . . , and this dynamic organization of the universe in all its aspects is what we want to present.[30]

Consciousness was historical just as nature was organic. Applied to religion this means that God's subjectivity was also a revelatory life. Schelling wrote:

> No matter how one pictures to oneself the procession of creatures from God, it can never be as a mechanical production. God is not a system but a life. . . . The absolute unity-in-form of the ideal and the real . . . comes from organism. That is the highest expression of nature whether in God and of God, or of nature in the finite.[31]

Drey decided to describe the development of faith and theology as the flowering of an idea. Not only does the idea lead to a universal science of all particulars but the ideas possess the facets of development, organic growth. He wrote in a sketch for a private journal that all that we now assemble under the term "church" was educed from a simple idea in the early preaching of Christians: the kingdom of God. To be at the service of history and culture, that idea expanded into various external forms, which we see as the constitution of the church. Nevertheless, even if he advocated the seminal idea and its history as basic to his theology, Drey knew how to criticize theologies current in his day where the church had become no more than an idea, where the church owned no visible forms, no concrete self-realization.[32]

Whereas the idea of the organic had been suggested by Romantic idealism, the kingdom of God had been a popular choice of theologians for the central topic of Christianity. It was easy to use Schelling's philosophy of the development of an idea to explain the kingdom of God as the primal idea of revelation. The kingdom of God is an organic idea, an evolutionary principle, a theological history; Drey chose it as theology's central idea:

> Through the absolute necessity and truth that this idea of the kingdom of God has for reason, the same characteristics of necessity and truth come about by the appearance of this kingdom in the history of the human race, and by all the teachings of Christianity that uncover and explain the mysteries in history—namely, the plan and the organization of the kingdom. Just as Christ clearly transformed the entire (religious) history of the past into ideas (and his Apostles did the same), so no scientific theology transforms the history of Christ into pure ideas, and so binds together history before and after Christ into a whole.[33]

Drey was not Schelling. His emphasis upon revelation, upon the objectivity of Christianity in the organic life of the church, gave his work a very different emphasis. Drey rejected the theological monopoly of idealism, that "pure philosophical contemplation that treats everything positive and historical as an allegory or a symbol of ideas."[34] Catholicism should present a saner approach, one lying between rationalism and orthodoxy. Drey learned from Schelling, however, that the new philosophy or theology need not fear objectivity, for spirit develops through nature and nature makes spirit concrete. The horizons of faith and theology can include history as well as revelation.

Theology, however, has to own a Christian identity (which Protestant liberalism seemed in danger of losing) and a historical development (which Roman theology seemed to lack). The consciousness of a constant identity is evident in the first disciples' preaching, something prior to the church. Yet, in Catholicism primal Christianity continues to live as something tangible. Drey wrote:

> In this basic view that Catholicism has of itself as the unbroken continuation . . . of primal Christianity, there is an easy mediation

of inner, subjective faith through an objectivity based on history. . . . In the real intuition into Christ and his history, in the perfect agreement of the phenomenon of this history with the ideas of religion, the faith of the first Christians found its realization, which convinced them of the truth, and which became strong and living.[35]

Drey's approach was to retrieve the essence of early Christianity and to find in the past and present the vitality of the church of the first century. The first generation of Catholic theologians drawn to Romanticism and idealism barely reached the philosophy of the organic. If it had stopped with them, the religious philosophy of identity might have dissolved into a ghostly epistemology or mathematics. Drey went ahead of his disciples such as Möhler and Kuhn, and liberated a living community and its developing but ancient tradition from the dangers of popular contempt or rational empiricism.[36] Drey, by employing the philosophy of a developmental construction of religious ideas in history, and by locating this in a dialectical and not merely historical framework, shifted the emphasis, for Catholics, from an idealist philosophy of religious consciousness to church and tradition. Tradition no longer merely forms from antiquity but preserves and sets off faith-realities, surviving bright and triumphant.

Church Father at Tübingen

The Tübingen theologian's conversation with the new philosophy took place at three levels: first, his study of the theoretician of the times, Schelling; secondly, his creative theological application of motifs from the modern way of thinking already weakly exemplified in Zimmer and Thanner, and more vigorously in Schleiermacher; thirdly, Drey's efforts (often left incomplete) to formulate a systematic theology constructed along some of the lines of a post-Fichtean philosophy, a theology more truly theological than Schelling's thought but more traditional than Schleiermacher's.

Drey's journals show a study of Schelling's publications after 1806—for instance, the essay on freedom and the dispute with Jacobi. Drey taught at Tübingen for over twenty years after Schelling returned to academic prominence in 1827. Unfortunately Drey was not able to examine closely the new philosophy of revelation emerging in lectures not far to the east, in Munich. Some of its characteristics—such as the history of religions and revelation as developmental—he understood.

Schelling's final system was not published during these years and, when it appeared in Paulus's edition in 1843, Drey did not review it. Nevertheless, perhaps in lectures whose notes in manuscript we lack, Drey lectured on Schelling's positive philosophy of Christianity—and in a negative tone From Berlin in 1844, Schelling wrote to one of his sons studying at Tübingen, asking about "a Dr. Drey, an adversary of the *Philosophy of Revelation*. . . . Where can one find his ramblings? How did he get a copy of my lectures (as grounds for his remarks)?"[37]

For a decade after 1822, Drey was distracted by political and ecclesiastical intrigues. His theology was criticized, his person not accepted for a bishopric. Poor health limited his theological labors. Although he lived to 1853, he took little part in the controversy around the new movements, neoscholasticism and historicism. Like an organic idea, he lived on in his students and school.

PART THREE

Freedom for Systems
1826 to 1841

6
The System-Builders

IN THE TEN YEARS from 1826 to 1836, we have the last decade of a period of cultural history. Those years record a final self-confident assertion of the Romanticism born in Jena or Heidelberg and chart the fading voyages of the mystical and heroic self through nature and history. They mark also a further striving for a comprehensive system that begins with the subject—whether that be a finite self or a god—and concludes with the world and the god complete. To the north in Berlin, Hegel struggled to finish this type of worldview; to the south in Munich, the professors at the new university drew from the remaining powers of idealism and Romanticism a last time of designs and dreams. By 1836 Hegel had been dead for five years, Schelling was tiring, the young J. A. Möhler was dead, and the forces that would determine the rest of the century were gathering strength.

The years leading up to 1826 continued the crescendo in German cultural life that had been begun almost fifty years before. Musicians and writers as well as philosophers found new powers and sought new vistas. The aged Goethe labored on completing *Faust II*; Hegel expounded his philosophy of all art and all religion. Composers struggled toward broader forms. Perhaps all sensed that this was the last decade that held out hope that the earlier dream of encompassing infinite emotion was attainable. This is the time of Beethoven's last string quartets and piano sonatas, of his ninth symphony and *Missa Solemnis*. Schubert wrote his grand, unhurried compositions for chamber ensemble, piano and orchestra. For the philosophers and theologians, there was still the vision into a better future of intellect and freedom, still the pursuit of a total system, still the confidence that only easy insight into the infinite can bring. Schelling was able to express his mission optimistically:

> This eternal freedom is enclosed at first in one form, in one particular freedom. It penetrates through all but remains in nothing; finally, it

breaks through into eternal freedom. But that form in which it was enclosed always consumes itself again and again. So freedom, like the phoenix, arises transformed through fiery death—this is the content of the highest science.[1]

Roman Catholic thought in the nineteenth century had its system-builders. Schelling remained its mentor, its counterpart to Hegel. Joining him in Munich in 1827 were two men who, as we have seen, were formidable constructors of vast religious edifices; Joseph Görres and Franz von Baader. Not far way in Vienna was Friedrich Schlegel. This group made up a part of the third period of Roman Catholicism's dialogue with German idealism as Catholic philosophy and theology confidently worked from within the thought-forms of the modern world. Two other groups defined the relationship of Schelling's thought to Catholicism. There were the students and intellectuals who were part of the exciting Munich restoration of Ludwig I at whose center is Schelling. Other professors and students in Tübingen or on the Rhine heard with interest reports of Schelling's new and final philosophy, a Christian philosophy. The philosopher had never been more dynamic in the lecture hall, never more certain in the claims he made for his philosophy. The man and the philosophy stimulated Catholics to develop parallel expressions of their own work in encyclopedias and courses in philosophy, in theological systems.

So, in this third and final part of our history, we will look first at the great system-builders—men whom we have already met in the earlier time when Romanticism and idealism began and who now return in the maturity of their gifts; next, at the dialogue between Schelling and the theologians who were a highpoint of the Catholic Tübingen school; and finally, returning to Munich, we will describe a younger generation, even as idealism and Romanticism, along with Schelling, fade away.

1. Friedrich Schelling

Schelling and the New University

Ludwig I became king in 1825 at the age of thirty-nine. Growing up in a time of unprecedented change had not made him fearful but had filled him with ideas about being a king and building a capital city. The king was as interested in his city's being the showplace for the arts as he was in its reputation for scientific and religious renewal. Architects representing Graeco-Roman classicism and others whose approach was Gothic (both were highly derivative) worked next to each other on the Ludwigstrasse designing the governmental buildings, the new museums, the academies. Munich returned to its musical heritage as church choirs again performed the motets of Palestrina and Orlando di Lasso, the composer from an earlier Bavarian court.

On a trip to Florence the idea came to Ludwig to make Munich a new Florence: classical in art, Catholic in faith and life. Amid the splendors of northern Italy, J. N. Ringseis, disciple of Sailer at Landshut and Ludwig's physician, mentioned the idea of moving the university from Landshut to Munich. Only there could it compete with Vienna and with the Protestant north: with Göttingen and with the new school in Berlin. In January 1826, Eduard Schenk, also a member of the Landshut-Sailer group,[2] received the commission to prepare a brief presenting the reasons for moving the university. The following November, the school was opened in Munich and Ringseis was named the first rector. The establishment of the university allowed the Catholic restoration to flow into more areas of culture in Bavaria. Hellenic colonnades sheltered the professors of Romanticism and idealism. Romanesque frescoes looked down on historians and political theorists entranced by the texts of medieval mystics or of Persian myths. Ludwig drew Protestant scholars to the faculties as freely as he worked to restore Benedictine monasticism.

While working with the king and Schenk on possible members of the first faculty, Ringseis exclaimed: "Schelling must come—to give the university brilliance, movement!" The king agreed and later said he valued the recruitment of Schelling "as much as a victory in battle."[3] Ringseis recalled in his memoirs that professors were chosen so that the university might have a Christian tone.[4] Würzburg and Erlangen would remain distinctively confessional but men such as Baader, Schelling and Görres were supraconfessional: genial, provocative, yet Christian in a global, general style. Schenk contacted Schelling in July of 1826 and the king himself, visiting his domains, met Schelling in Nuremberg and expressed his hopes that the philosopher would come. Among the king's advisors only one argued against the choice: Sailer, now bishop of Regensburg. The more Schelling had left metaphysics and the philosophy of nature for religion, the more Sailer had become disturbed. "A call to Schelling," he wrote, "seems to me upon reflection problematical. Schelling's philosophy—as much as its creator may have intended it to do so—can't keep itself free of pantheism."[5]

Schelling wrote from Erlangen asking that he might come to Munich not in November of 1826 but a year later so that he could see into print "a work on whose content I have been working much of my life." In fact, the *Ages of the World* was, again, not published. Schelling arrived in Munich in time to begin lecturing as the semester started on November 15, 1827; he promised he would present a new religious philosophy, a cosmic and transcendental yet Christian system. He would be the response to Hegel in Berlin. Goethe wrote congratulations to Schelling on his professorship and to the king on such academic perspicacity. The Munich newspapers were filled with descriptions of Schelling's first lectures. The sometimes malicious Salat, witnessing such a sad finale to his treasured Catholic Enlightenment in the new marble halls of the university, described how not only students but military and court officials, artists and physicians, came to the *Aula Maxima* as to a theater:

> At 6:00 P.M., on a winter evening, the crowd assembles in the chosen hall. . . . A carriage comes, and Schelling accompanied by two of his best students enters. Ahead of him is a servant, wih two lamps in his hands. He withdraws as soon as the sublime teacher has mounted the *Katheder*. The doors are closed and the lecture begins.[6]

A year after Schelling's arrival, Schenk said publicly: "Schelling is the crown of our university."[7]

The Final System

His positive philosophy, Schelling announced, would include "plants and animals, societies and states, world history and art—all as members of a great organism growing out of the abyss of nature and rising up into the world of spirits."[8] Schelling saw himself launching the last, crucial attempt to hold back the forces of darkness and nothingness threatening freedom and objectivity, the same mission that three decades earlier had excited the Tübingen comrades, Hegel, Hölderlin, Schelling. Now Hölderlin is insane, Hegel is approaching his death, and Schelling wise through suffering feels himself alone. In these inaugural lectures Schelling proclaimed that "the decisive and proper name" for his philosophy is *Christian*. This adjective, however, he soon came to avoid. Ringseis was an eyewitness and described the Schelling presence:

Schelling's reputation in Munich was great, proven by the number of his hearers. He praised the youth of Bavaria as "highly impressionable, gratefully receptive of a word which would strengthen and raise them." Naturally, there were hearers who were not able to understand his lectures, but that would have been true anyway. Perhaps at that time no German capital was more capable or more open to offering Schelling so favorable a situation as Munich was. A kind of philosophical excitement went through the student body because of the considerable interest in art and science, and this was linked to a new interest in religion.[9]

In Munich from 1827 to 1841, Schelling lectured only on his positive philosophy of existence. It had three parts: the first treated God in an idealist manner, as primal being and origin of the universe of being (this first part included a history and critique of modern philosophy); the second part was a grandiose philosophy of mythology; the third continued this into a phenomenology of revelation. None of this material beyond the first three lectures was published in his lifetime, although, as Schelling complained vigorously, it was widely circulated in student notes, and one version was to be published without permission in Berlin in 1843 by Schelling's enemy from Würzburg, Paulus.[10]

We want to have an overall view of Schelling's philosophy of religion in order to understand its role as a climax of that philosophy that had its roots both in idealism and Romanticism, and because by this philosophy Roman Catholics will finally evaluate Schelling and the limitations of this era.

The object of philosophy, he began, is the life of the absolute realized in the divine life, in the human spirit and in world history. The absolute becomes fully itself through tension and process. The empirical record of that process is a history that prior to Christ we call "myth" and after him we name "revelation." The structure and history of the human spirit is such that it unfolds the life of God. Spirit's history is theogony, a realization of a God becoming itself.

Schelling's positive philosophy is always and simultaneously describing three things: (1) the life of God as God, through his divine potencies, exoterically becoming himself fully; (2) the vital, historical line of finite beings that has its own development but also bears inwardly the realization of God; (3) the history of human consciousness, both collective and individual, which is bringing nature and spirit to unity in art, religion and in their finest expression, philosophy. History, religion and theogony are one.

Spirit still dwells within the framework of transcendental idealism but spirit's self-realization lies in religion. Mythical forms are the place, the process where the archetypes in human consciousness depict and realize the external development of God, theogony. Religion is the theogonic process as played out during the epochs of human history. It belongs to philosophy to find the right form and the essential content of religion and revelation. "My task is the philosophical explanation of systems of religion and myth."[11]

Schelling's analysis of the mythical systems of Egypt, India, China and Greece was an interpretation of the totality of myth, a search for the presence of divine powers in each particular system. "The process that begins with the tension posited amid the potencies is a theogonic process, for the potencies effect it and they are in thmelves theogonic. But at the same time it is an extradivine process, not only a process of nature but one that we at first call mythology."[12] In the epochs of mythology the three potencies play out their roles as gods. Every mythological system includes a story of concrete gods and this narrative is a telling of the race's social experience. So it is myth that forms peoples; nations emerge not from political pressures but from spiritual movements. "Mythology does not determine but *is* that people's fate (just as a man's character is his fate), its destiny allotted to it from the beginning."[13] Myths, like language, are a disclosure of the becoming God who meets with the human race.

Not only does myth mirror theogenesis, the history of myth records psychogenesis. The human spirit finding its way ahead to full freedom is a reflection of God's own development for freedom. The world of gods arises in the human mind spontaneously, for God's way to himself and the path of human history are one. "Mythology comes into being through a process that is necessary; its origin is lost in a realm before history. Consciousness may resist the process in certain particulars but it cannot impede, much less reverse, the whole." In this theogony, myth has taken over the role that art and nature played in Schelling's earlier writings. The lives of the gods and goddesses are creations that pictorialize forces active in our (and in God's) minds and wills. "Seen objectively, mythology is in fact what it claims to be: true theogony, a history of the gods. The ultimate history of the gods is the creation, the real genesis in consciousness, of God."[14]

The Second Potency's Realm: Christianity

The history of our planet is the realm of the second divine potency, who is the objective, existing counterpart to absolute subject. Like the other two *Potenzen*, the Son was present in every religious system, but Christianity is the final, explicit stage of his life. Schelling's lectures on trinitarian theogony led quickly to the generation of the Son and his relation to world and history. The Son is potency and lord of our world. To beget the Son is to begin creation and history. The Son is the realization of God's freedom for being, the breaking of the necessity of not telling. "Before all willing, through the mere necessity of his being God, God, to the extent that he is being-for-itself, places himself in a second form. . . ." The Son is the object of the divine knowledge and will. The epoch of the Son is a period of exist and return, of risk and realization. Emerging out of freedom this *Potenz* finds that glory comes after solitude and obedience. "The *actus* of this self-realization lasts until the time of the complete birth [of the Son]; only at the end is the Son the real Son. Because this end is the end of creation, the Son is begotten at the beginning of creation, but is only realized as such at its term."[15]

Although every religion qualifies as revelation, Christianity marks a higher stage of the process that mythogenesis began. Neither Schelling's knowledge of theology nor his theological acumen equaled his competence in the field of mythology, Theology was yet another field for him to master, and in the late 1820s, when the need for such research made itself felt, Schelling was fifty. His treatment of Christianity is quite limited. Nevertheless, we know that he was acquainted with some of the theological literature of the time: with D.F. Strauss, with Schleiermacher, whom he considered to be the most intelligent of dogmatic theologians, and with F. Schlegel and a few publications of his Catholic disciples.

Schelling treated only two Christian doctrines, the Trinity and the Son as Christ, but he spent considerable time on the topic of Christianity. Christian revelation begins at that transitional moment when out of mythic history the objectification of God begins. The second power, objectivity, is beginning its return to God, a god it will find complete and free. Creation and history are the place of activity where lordship is won by the second power. When the Son becomes a power in history, human religion is elevated from the "natural activity" of the potency to its clearer revelation. What in *nature* is necessary and obscure becomes in *history* intuitively clear. In the depth of Christianity one can intuit theogony, the becoming of God. Tilliette describes the *Philosophy of Revelation*:

> It is a speculative theology, an interpretation of dogmatic state-ments. But above all it is a philosophy of Christian religion. Within this vast philosophy of religion it appears as the second panel of a diptych: mythology-Christianity. The relationship of Christianity to paganism is the joint that allows the exposition to expand.[16]

The epochs of the worldwide history of religion prior to Christ are individually touched by error, and yet "the process as a whole is truth." Each stage has prepared for the next, but the entire process is found in each moment:

> The content of all true religion is eternal and hence cannot be abso-lutely excluded from any epoch. A religion that is not as old as the world cannot be the true one. Christianity must, therefore, have been in paganism, and paganism had the same substantial content.[17]

The theophanies of the Old Testament do not seem to be much superior to Asian religions or to paganism. Every rite, all doctrinal teach-ing, point to something more profound, and so it is not possible to locate revelation or freedom within only one religion:

> If we take paganism, Judaism and Christianity as the three great forms of all religion, the revelation of the Old Testament is merely the revelation that runs through mythology; Christianity is the reve-lation that has broken through this husk (paganism), and thereby transcended both paganism and Judaism.[18]

Paganism and Judaism are both prototypes of Christianity. "Chris-tianity was the future of paganism."[19] The acceptance, however, of this revelation is not submission to dogmas destined to be explained away by reason (as the Enlightenment claimed to have done) but insight into the work of God. The shift is one from the essential to the existential order. Theogony is not only consciousness but, more, relationship to God. Revelation, Schelling says, is the movement from the rational order of nature and myth to the real existence of God active in us.

We may be surprised to see Schelling's philosophy of revelation climax with christology. Christ is the content of Christianity just as for Christianity history is the content of the universe. As theogony unfolds in the history of human religion, the potency of the Son is present in all religions, but Christianity brings a clearer view of the turbulent fullness of the godhead as well as the furthest removal and incipient return of the divine powers. Creation and history are tragic. Over against the lordship of the subject, the solid assertion of objectivity appears not only as distinction but as alienation. So, the second potency's process is lonely and ends not only in incarnation but in the cross.

Only two christological themes interest Schelling: the birth of the Son in eternity and time; and the term of that begetting, the *kenosis* of the incarnation. Schelling's christology is a historical and ontological elaboration of Philippians 2:6–8. The Son's preexistent divinity was not full godliness but a "form" of such. Caught up in the epochal movement of the godhead through the universe, the second potency cannot rest with its first form and in a free self-emptying seeks the fully divine. Paul's *kenosis* suggests an idealist origin moving to existential incarnation and crucifixion. The crucifixion, born by the Son's obedience, is a psychological condition of furthest alienation from the Father. Freedom before, through and after the cross: only he who has the form of God independent of God can renounce it and through death arrive at glory with God.

Resolution

The three *Potenzen* are the three lords of time. The third potency is spirit. For the idealist, *Geist* is the source of being, the creative force, the ultimate identity. Spirit underlies every stage of the developing universe and is the ground of mind and will. Though active from the beginning it must wait for the incarnation of the second power, for only after the climactic moment of the Son can the coming of the Spirit occur. Only if God separated at the beginning would he find freedom and possess the infinitude of created forms at the end.

History has undergone two important transformations: one from being to mythogenesis; a second from myth to revelation. We glimpse at the end of the Munich system a third and final epochal shift. Christianity was the future of mythology; idealism is the future of Christianity. The pattern of the idealist system, of the fall and its return, remains operative here; the ideal and the real in the human person are to be resolved in spirit. Schelling's eschatology is protology; it looks backward for ideas. In bringing the Spirit, Christ has brought the possibility of the final era of full freedom. Freedom is the keynote of the time of resolution. The threat of chaos and evil is being subjected to science, to knowing and to fashioning freedom. All other religions must fade except that revelation which is also *Wissenschaft*. This science interprets idealistically the Pauline *gnosis* and *charismata* of the Spirit as a knowledge that now knows no limits and no superstition. No protected corners of darkness escape its light. Schelling did not describe at length the final stage of theogony, the activity of the third potency bringing resolution to the cosmos. "The development after Christ will be subject to the same disturbances, restrictions and counter-forces as would affect any natural evolution."[20]

Although Schelling failed to bring his system to a conclusion worthy of the fulfillment of spirit and the resolution of divine life, he did offer an interesting, final theory. Surprisingly, he turned to the church and de-scribed an ecclesiological dialectic that calls for completion. There has been a Petrine church, which is Roman Catholicism, and a Pauline church, which is Protestantism. These should find their fulfilling resolu-tion in the Johannine church, a church of love. Sometimes we gain the impression that the Johannine church has roots in Eastern Orthodoxy; sometimes it appears to be only the church of freedom and idealism. The origins and influence of this theory are many and complicated; one source was Franz von Baader's efforts in Eastern ecumenism. It is remarkable that Schelling ended his philosophical career in ecclesiology.

This final system of Schelling, the one from his long life of philoso-phy that is the most concerned with religion and revelation—what influ-ence did it have upon Roman Catholics? There was no reaction like the impetuous enthusiasm of a Zimmer proclaiming in 1804 that Roman Catholics had found in Schelling "the right philosophy"; there was no inspired appropriation by a Drey or a young Görres. But for the next decade Schelling was still important to Catholic students and intellectuals who wanted to hear his lectures or who wanted to imitate his ambition in their dogmatic and moral theologies, in their philosophies of life and history.

2. Friedrich Schlegel

In this era of great projects and in the Vienna of the composers Schubert and Beethoven, Friedrich Schlegel worked on a philosophy that was, as he said, both an all-encompassing search and an organic unity; almost infinite systems were constructed with care from particular ele-ments. In Schlegel as in Schelling, we find a thinker who fashioned what might be called the universal Romantic system of Christian mystical idealism. Schlegel's wrestling with a religious psychology and a historical phenomenology of religion encouraged others at work upon similar systems for the times. F.A. Staudenmaier at Tübingen wrote of him: "He was among the spirits whom destiny determines for the destruction of an old era and the introduction of a new one. . . . He provided no single, special system, but prepared in advance [that effort]."[21]

In the 1820s, the Vienna-Munich-Tübingen axis created a distinct type of late idealist system: inconceivable without Romanticism, and assisted by Roman Catholicism. Speculative Christianity was developed by Schelling, Schlegel, Görres, Baader, Drey, Staudenmaier—all in different ways. This intellectual approach could appropriate other religions to Christianity and could conceive of all aspects of religion as facets of art. What was sought and partially produced was a framework for understanding Christian revelation in an evolutionary world. Psyche and history—early themes of Schelling and Schlegel—are still fixed points among the system-makers. As the struggle to comprehend history intensified, so did the interest in mysticism. What emerged was a new emphasis upon traditional, Christian themes. Christianity was located in an evolutionary stream of religions, mysticisms and cults. Even Schelling (losing none of his distance from organized religion, Protestant or Catholic) affirmed that his system begins with a trinity of divine powers and ends in christology. It would be interesting to have a comparative study of the great systems written in these years, for we know their common sources, forms and goals. This metaphysics of experience probing the godhead and attentive to history and religion seemed to some Christian thinkers—for instance, Schleiermacher—a strange partner for Roman Catholics. The Protestants failed to see the affinity between the inquiring Catholic mind and an evolutionary system where grace flowed into nature. Basing themselves on Kant and Fichte, either enamored of or opposed to Hegel, the northern Protestants had little idea of the Bavarian and Viennese systems.

Schlegel and Schelling: Pantheism

The markings on Friedrich Schlegel's road to conversion to Catholicism in 1808 had been philosophies, sciences, paintings and cathedrals. Then too, his Sanskrit studies enabled him to link the mystical writings of India with the mysticism he had read in Jacob Boehme: this also may have suggested Catholicism. Public reaction to his conversion was mixed. Goethe, who, like Hegel, criticized Roman Catholicism as primitive and repressive, wrote: "This is a sign of the times . . . , a strange case that in the highest light of reason and understanding, of world-comprehension, an extraordinary and highly educated talent is misled to bury itself."[22] As Friedrich and Dorothea became Catholics, his book on Indian thought was finished. With a new religious worldview and a new mission, with Romantic idealism expanded by the thought of the East, Schlegel moved to Vienna and to a new circle of Romantics. He had decided that his future thinking would not pursue the mysterious absolute manifest in the structure of the real and the ideal; it would explore a living God revealing himself in the life of the soul. "Reason in and for itself gets no further than a lifeless self or an eternally repetitive ego, which is the self. No real thou ever emerges. . . . Let us presume something more than reason: love."[23]

Before the two explorers into the light and darkness of the absolute could recognize the similarity in their thought after 1827, they had to pass through a period of criticism. Schelling was not mentioned by name in Schlegel's *On the Language and Wisdom of the Indians*, but a clear challenge was presented. Not Eastern metempsychosis or Manichaean metaphysics but pantheism represented for Schlegel the low point in Eastern thinking; the formless night of pantheism where total unity turned out to be only emptiness.[24] Whereas Schlegel arrived at more objections about the absolute of idealism, Schelling in the middle period of his philosophy strove, as we have seen, to produce a new system on those very issues; its fragment was the *Essay on Human Freedom*. To take seriously freedom and necessity in history, to perceive good and evil in cosmos and self, is to expect in God not only fullness but plurality and change. Otherwise we cannot account for freedom and evil. Beyond the surface of "God" is the infinite sea of the godhead with structures of both good and evil.

Schelling had to reply to Schlegel's charge of pantheism:

> For it cannot be denied that if pantheism meant nothing but the doctrine of the immanence of all things in God, every rational view would have to adhere to this teaching in some sense or other. That the fatalistic point of view can be combined with pantheism is undeniable; but that it is not essentially tied to it is made clear by the fact that many are driven to this pantheistic outlook precisely because of the liveliest sense of freedom.

Schelling radicalized idealism by leading pantheism to deeper realms of speculation:

Inasmuch as freedom is unthinkable in contradistinction to omnipotence, is there any other escape from this argument except by placing man and his freedom in the divine being, by saying that man exists not outside God but in God and that man's activity itself belongs to God's life?[25]

After the publication of Schelling's book on freedom, both thinkers began to notice a similarity in their thought. Jena lay in the years before; Schlegel too had expounded the idea of a universal and primal revelation that was the product neither of reason nor of a special contact by God. God stands outside, he maintained, but reveals himself "everywhere in the old traditions and theologies."[26] After his conversion and after the comparative study of mythologies, Schlegel, rejecting an unmediated access to the divine through intellectual activity, probed the idealism and aesthetics of mythical stories and symbolic rituals. Religion had true flesh and blood, and its long history was developmental. Schlegel presumed that Schelling had been influenced by his ideas, and Schelling mused about how "Schlegel on his path has come to certain ideas that strikingly confirm mine."[27]

By 1820 Schelling held the opinion that an abstract, transcendental description of God and godhead, of the three divine powers active in history, should be fleshed out by the history of myth and religion. All gods everywhere were humankind's mental and historical realization of the life and revelation of God's life. He wrote Schlegel, "In this idea, I consider you to be the main predecessor and I recognize an ever greater agreement with you in individual aspects."[28] The Academy of Fine Arts honored Schlegel with membership and he traveled to Munich to meet Ludwig I and Schelling.

Schelling, Schlegel thought, had gone beyond the dead abstractions of his earlier idealism and now proclaimed God to be personal, philosophy to be empirical, and system to include life and revelation. "The ghost of the absolute seems to have disappeared from his system."[29] The insertion of Eastern mythologies into Schelling's process-system, which made up a third of the system, certainly owed something to Schlegel and when he learned of Schelling's positive philosophy where the world's mythologies and Christian doctrines such as the Trinity and Christ made the idealist dialectic tangible, he wrote: "In a special way my attention has been directed to him and to the turn he is taking. He stands very high in my esteem.''[30] Schlegel defended Schelling against the followers of Jacobi and argued with Bishop Sailer for a university chair for the philosopher. "Schelling . . . is at a decisive turning point in his philosophy, even in his entire process of thought. . . . A Protestant? He has certainly not been one for a long time."[31]

After 1826 Schlegel constructed system after system. A new burst of creativity drove him to search out a system of systems: to integrate history, mythology and psychology with Christianity and social theory. "Really, I believe I am right," he wrote, "in feeling that a new epoch has begun for me. . . . I feel again like holding lectures on philosophy. . . . Often the stream of my thoughts interrupts my sleep."[32] Schlegel's *Philosophy of Life* presented what was to be the basic pattern for the several constructions of life and history that followed upon each other. This work began with the subjectivity of life: from life all flows, and in experiencing life we meet what modern philosophy calls transcendental forms and object-creating powers. Schlegel did not hesitate to introduce elements from what he viewed as Christian political theory or from Roman Catholic theology. God is the master, the fulfillment, the initiator of all; human consciousness is a place for a richer life given by God; and history is the stage upon which human and divine life intermingle. Unlike Schelling, Schlegel emphasized a distinct, objective revelation of God in the evolving world.

Another system, *The Philosophy of History*, corresponded somewhat to Schelling's *Philosophy of Mythology*. Schelling wrote of Schlegel's work in progress in 1828: "This work touches the one decisive question, and he is at present working out its solution."[33] That question seems to have been temporality's colors and organisms, the body of history. Attention has shifted from psyche to history. Schlegel included myth in his philosophy of history, but his focus stayed with the intellectual history of civilizations and nations. Primal history, Chinese and Indian views of religion, politics and morality, Grecian and Roman culture and art escort him through the centuries until Christianity, the German nation and medieval polarities lead into the "ruinous" late Middle Ages and then to Protestantism and its powerful influence in the modern world. This series of lectures just barely arrives at "the dominant spirit of the present age,"[34] and ends.

In his three last and maturest works . . . Schlegel pursued the thought of the philosophical presence of God in history, nature and language as well as in self-experience. The correspondence of this varied manifestation of God to the fifth revelation, Scripture, seemed to him a sign of a new harmony for faith and knowledge.[35]

As 1828 began, Schlegel held a third series of lectures on the *Philosophy of Language and Word*. All these systems were to have been delivered, in some form, in 1829 in Berlin and Munich, but Schlegel's sudden death intervened. If that lecture tour had taken place, we would have had together in Munich four great system-builders of the age—Baader, Görres, Schelling and Schlegel—listening to each other. And imagination can project a meeting in Berlin between Schlegel and Hegel. The Viennese philosopher planned further lectures on God, creation, the spirit of the modern age, all coming together in an eschatological finale. All of these structures and fragments were to be assembled in a *System of the Totality of Christian Philosophy*. If Schelling continually revised one linear pattern, reworking its three epochs, Schlegel was writing the same system over again but changing the subject matter. Philosophy was not logic or history, but the articulation of his thinking about life.

Schlegel's writings and lectures had been sustained by his strong personality; his life spanned the time from Goethe to Metternich.

With the philosophical works of his later years, Schlegel, along with Schelling, became one of the leading representatives of Christian thought in Germany at that time. His striving for a personal foundation of philosophical reflection found its parallels in the movement of *"réalisme spiritualiste."* One result of this was Bergson's philosophy of life; for Schlegel's thought on memory, language and revelation placed him in close contact with the movement of French traditionalism whose foundation lay with Bonald.[36]

As a Roman Catholic, as an advisor to Metternich, Schlegel became increasingly conservative. Yet he remained liberal in his understanding of the world religions, of the primacy of the subject's psychological life, of the hiddenness of God. The ecclesiastical and political conservatism that entered during the 1830s was not to be experienced by Schlegel, whom death allowed to be fully a Romantic. His powers of imagination lessened as he grew older; if the hopes and plans for the systems were generous, his mind no longer produced the flood of ideas and insights that his early journals record. He lacked the theological interest necessary to complete his Catholicism with a theology. His philosophy was really an analysis, a compartmentalization, of history.

Vienna was not so open to new systems after 1840. Anton Günther tried, without success and without as great genius as Schlegel or Baader, to compose an anti-Hegelian but late idealist system for Roman Catholicism. The tragedy of the Viennese Günther was that for all practical purposes he overlooked the achievements of Schlegel or of Schelling. He stood, like the Kantian Hermes, outside the course history was taking. He thought in the past and so pleased neither German thinkers of the next generation nor Rome. He lacked the perception to see that the time for systems of Catholic idealism had passed. The advent of Gregory XVI, the death of Hegel, the pressured move of Schelling to Berlin, the polemics of Döllinger—these were the signs of the advent of another *Zeitgeist*.

3. Joseph Görres

This third section of the history of Roman Catholic theology in dialogue with idealism focuses upon older men who remained with the interests of their youth. Our narrative looks not at exegesis or theology but at systems of the philosophy of history and religion floating like icebergs in the stream of the first third of the nineteenth century, and we are led back to Munich to take up again the story of two of the creative and intriguing figures of German intellectual life, Joseph Görres and Franz von Baader. They became Schelling's colleagues at the opening of the university, but they were not his disciples. They pursued their own quest, working to express once and for all the power and the breadth of an era just beginning to slip away.

Mercury from the Rhine

Görres by 1818 had turned from Asian mythology to Prussian politics, from the philosophy of nature to journalism. He founded the *Rheinischer Merkur* to mix Roman Catholicism with liberal politics. Its condemnation by the Prussian government, along with the notoriety achieved by Görres's *Germany and the Revolution*, led to a warrant for the political journalist's arrest. Fleeing to Strassburg with his family, he became an increasingly visible figure in politics and religion. Then Görres came to the conclusion that there were only two social systems still viable: there was the unconditional negativity of a state supremacy, and in

Catholicism there was the tradition of the great thinkers and mystics. Roman Catholicism should be a bridge to the world religions and a power to confront autocratic principalities. Görres decided in 1824 to affirm publicly the return of his person and his thinking to the Church of Rome.[37]

J.N. von Ringseis, Sailer's disciple and chancellor of the university, was responsible for bringing Görres to Munich in 1826. He had been an enthusiastic disciple ever since, as a Landshut student, he read Görres's *Glauben und Wissen*. Ringseis had visited him when Görres stood under the threat of Prussian arrest, a threat that could only enhance Görres's stature in the eyes of a Bavarian. It was not hard to win Ludwig to create a professorship for this leading journalist of German and Catholic interests in Europe, and the king ignored the objections of the Prussian court.[38] Görres's lectureship was in an academic area the king considered important: general and literary history. The Munich court hoped that Görres would bring with him his periodical *Der Katholik*, and so make Bavaria a center of public thought. "His call was viewed by contemporaries as a victory for Sailer, Ringseis, Schenk, Brentano and Diepenbrock; a return of science from the north of Protestantism and the Enlightenment, a gain of the spokesman for Catholic Germany and a thinker who could be given the assignment of leading the religious and scientific restoration."[39] Sailer, who had been skeptical of Baader and hostile toward Schelling, wrote that Görres would be "the concertmaster" to lead in harmony the varied voices of the Catholic renaissance that the king and his advisors were assembling.

Out of that "orchestra" of philosophers, historians and artists came the periodical *Eos*. Baader and Görres worked as coeditors; the latter wrote an opening article on church-state relations and the former wrote on religion as a healing for Europe's woes. In its four years, *Eos* ("Dawn") received articles from a wide range of contributors including Schlegel, de Lamennais, Bonald. Bishop Sailer wrote encouragement from Regensburg. The young Döllinger's commentary on Dante's *Paradiso* was illustrated by Cornelius. Baader, however, soon found Görres "too papist," and *Eos* ended its brief life.[40]

Not only was he in contact with European circles of Romanticism, but Görres had an eye for all that was happening in France and Great Britain. He viewed his causes for Bavaria and the Rhineland as part of the larger struggle by Roman Catholics during the nineteenth century to achieve freedom from Protestant oppression or sterile neglect. Daniel

O'Connell in Ireland, the influence of de Lamennais upon de Mérode in
Belgium were, in his mind, connected with the riots in Cologne over the
imprisonment of the Catholic archbishop Droste-Vischering. *Eos*'s policy had been to show that ideas are important, and that the cultural
changes occurring since the Enlightenment are not to be feared even if
Christ and religion are ultimately accepted as the only sane foundation.
Higher, political authority such as monarchy and papacy was treated
conservatively but social issues such as economic and religious freedom
were discussed in a tone of reform.

Görres the System-Builder

Görres wrote to his daughter shortly after arriving in Munich, "I am
beginning my sixth or seventh life." He mentioned that he was getting
along well with Schelling and that all the distinguished professors had
arrived:

> Schelling and I were both at fault for postponing our first meeeeting.
> We are mutually compatible. There is something strange in him, the
> *natura naturata* in him is not so agreeable; there is something of the
> animal, impetuosity . . . but he is intelligent. He understands
> quickly, he retains and is judicious. There is an honest look in his
> eyes, which particularly pleases me. Lacking anyone better, the
> Protestant party has taken him over, although they had some reserva-
> tions about such a step. . . .[41]

Görres soon became the center for the Catholic intellectuals filling
the halls of the new university on the Ludwigstrasse. Görres's home was a
center for friends, colleagues and visitors. One met interesting foreigners,
the higher clergy, educated women, artists as well as scholars. Döllinger,
Ringseis, Clemens Brentano were often there; less frequently, Baader.
Schelling was absent. Görres, almost fifty when he began to lecture at
Munich, would arrange history into a format of politics and mysticism for
two more decades.

While Schelling presented his system of idealism rooted in existence
and religious history, Görres summed up the goal of his lectures on
"World History" with the phrase "making life visible in history."[42] The
semesters saw him follow a general philosophy of history with a presentation in some detail of human temporality from Genesis to the French
Revolution:

Görres was one of the last surviving generalists, living through and beyond, like Goethe, the expansion of knowledge which followed the year 1800. He enjoyed working at Sanskrit, medicine, Carolingian history, Persian, geography, occult or mystical texts—and all at the same time! As a historian—as we know the profession today, and as his younger colleague, Döllinger, pursued it—the aging Romantic sounded (so one of his hearers described it) like Merlin speaking out of a subterranean cave.[43]

For Görres, system was no longer (as it had been once) physics or idealism, but universal history. History is religion—not only Christianity but Catholicism. Its underlying principle is the divine word forming and penetrating the history of spirit and world. And history and religion are politics. Like Schlegel, Görres was impatient to get to the special development of nations where he could explain the direction of historical events and the role of the church. Finally, Görres's vision was one of evolution. In a remarkable way, he adapted Schelling's dialectic of divine powers active in material forces, anticipating Darwin and Marx:

The eternal substance has been searching for eons for the missing form belonging to itself, and it has evolved into today's world order. The suns have given birth to the planets; out of the inorganic, the organic slowly freed itself. Crystals became planets and in further development the animals emerged. In the world of animals the higher came from the lower, the ape; and eventually the tree of the newly formed human race emerged. . . . Then came families, tribes, state.[44]

In the spirit of the times, he struggled to bring together God and history. There is no plan outside history itself, and in history chaos is a real principle. "History recognizes no god over it, but only a God in it. He first becomes himself through history and he has created progressing humanity in his own likeness."[45]

In the last analysis, Görres's goal was apologetic rather than philosophical. He looked ahead and saw in the future a secularization rushing into all areas of culture. He did not hide his conviction that the theory of upward evolution was true, but he glimpsed on the horizon a withdrawal of its reference to God. Anticipating Feuerbach, Görres discovered something new and terribly important about the systems of idealism. They could be divested of any divine origin or goal. The future of the idealist system resembled its Fichtean beginnings. It could end up as a process of personality and organism from which the God who was there to become himself had disappeared. Just as Schelling in his youth saw idealism as the better expression and right fulfillment of Christianity, so the successors of Hegel would easily omit religion and revelation from their philosophies and politics. "All science," Görres observed sadly, "is secularizing itself . . . , becoming profane, servile, fickle."[46]

Schelling and Görres: Later Contact

Görres was an independent thinker. His approach and goals were those of this time of system-builders, but the relationships of Schelling and Görres are not so easy to outline. Schelling did not mention Görres in those works where their thought is similar, and we cannot be certain of how Görres influenced Schelling. One area does draw our attention: mythology. Horst Fuhrmans is of the opinion that Görres and Schelling resemble each other at deep levels in their thinking because they are two monumental examples of late Romanticism. "Any reader of Schelling's writings after 1809 knows how close the pages lie to the vision and tone of Görres."[47] The case for the Rhinelander's influence is strengthened by the appearance at a relatively early time, 1810, of systems whose substance is a phenomenology of mythologies. *Glauben und Wissen* resembles not Schelling's systems contemporary with it (1805), but his *Philosophy of Mythology* composed twenty years later. In 1834 Schelling mentioned in a letter to Victor Cousin in Paris that the school of Görres and Baader held his sympathy.[48] Schelling's sympathy, however, had its limits.

Around Görres and Baader swirled the rumors that their circle was excessively conservative and Roman Catholic; they were called "the congregation." Schelling had, moreover, no interest in the turbulent dialectic of church and state, or in Görres's demands for economic or ecclesiastical reform. Görres had set aside his pioneering interest in mythology, but Schelling was mastering more and more works on that subject and achieving a picture of world religion more coherent and more extensive than that of Görres or Schlegel. Still, there is no doubt that Görres's books in that field, along with those of his teacher F. Creuzer, had been a major source for the second part of the Munich system:

> Schelling is one of those persons of rare inspiration who knew how to speak the dead language of myths as his native tongue, who produced music from the voices of silence. . . . He had before his

eyes a hundred studies on myth, above all, the works of Creuzer and Görres classifying mythologies by history and geography. What attracted him most was their schemas. Despite his eulogy of Creuzer for a grand vision (with regard to Görres he kept a silence which was heavy with meaning), Schelling was capable of criticizing haste, lack of discipline and a tendency to pile up material (in these works).[49]

Schelling's *Philosophy of Mythology* was original and coherent. It explained with style and vision the similarities of the world's religious poetry and structure to each other. Schelling's arrangement came not from texts or dogmas but from a transcendental format worked out over three decades of philosophizing. The content was Görres's but the form owed much to Schelling.

Did Schelling influence Görres? Görres stood apart: once a son of early Romanticism, he was accustomed to being at the center. Alois Dempf is of the opinion that Schelling's lectures at Munich did touch Görres: "Metaphysics and myth and their tensions—here is certainly the main influence of Schelling on Görres; not so much a particular teaching of Schelling's philosophy of nature but rather the significance of metaphysics as the total framework for an economics of the spirit."[50] This may be true, but there is little evidence in Görres's later writings of such an influence between the two Munich professors. "The fact is that Görres, like almost all the philosophers around Schelling, essentially modified Schelling's philosophy and in this reconstruction of individual parts often lost sight of it altogether."[51] Schlegel and Görres were attracted to the Orient but Schelling remained Hellene. He remained the sovereign idealist; paradoxically, his speculative genius gave to myth a more significant meaning and a relationship to Christianity that the work of Creuzer certainly lacked and that even Görres's and Schlegel's efforts only thinly implied.

Subjectivity/Revelation: A Finale in Mysticism

As the 1840s began, Görres was suspect in Rome: too much freedom in his political thinking, too much curiosity in his exploration of the mystical. The personal intervention of King Ludwig kept his works off the Index.[52] Görres's final years were a struggle to produce one last philosophy of reality, human and divine. This vast canvas, however, was not a philosophy of science and nature or a philosophy of history but a

Mystik, a three-thousand-page epic of supernatural psychology and history. *Christian Mysticism* encompassed a system that was to combine the new natural sciences with traditional mysticism. The most varied topics were treated: the effects of the stars, the sacramental and magical activities of metals and plants and rituals; vampirism and spiritism; the idea of a demonic antichurch, magnetic aura. Görres accepted clairvoyance and mesmerism as scientific and religious. Christian mysticism, he believed, should be illumined by the powers that science uncovered in magnetism, chemical exchange, electric fields. All of this Görres incorporated into a system that was to appeal to the intelligentsia of the age and support the Catholic faithful. "We can still speak of the influence of Schelling in this work, to the extent that Görres is unthinkable without the natural philosopher Schelling. Yet the *Mystik* is worked out in an independent way and proceeds from a new perspective."[53]

If we assemble a school of spirituality out of those Protestant and Catholic, baroque and medieval, mystics—Eckhart, Boehme, Tauler, Suso, Silesius—who attracted German thinkers' attention in this period, then Görres like Baader, Schelling and even Hegel attended the same mystical school. Görres had gone back, upon his return to Munich, to the study of the natural sciences, and at the same time he was composing an introduction to a collection of the works of the Dominican mystic and disciple of Meister Eckhart, Henry Suso. As the years passed, Görres was also drawn by patristic and medieval thought and grew to appreciate traditional orthodoxy. The task of the *Christliche Mystik* was to take account of these spiritualities without neglecting either Asian religion or mysticism's shadow side—the dark Romanticism of demonology and parapsychology. Christian mystical theology would be both a view of revelation in history and a fulfillment of natural philosophy in the psychology of religious experience.

It was as if in the third and fourth decades of the nineteenth century the intellectual situation of decades earlier was reversed. Then philosophy of nature had led the Romantics to religion. Now mysticism, the replacement of pantheism—for mysticism after 1806 did in many quarters replace pantheism—would bring natural philosophy to graced fulfillment and be supported by science. All should see that mysticism rather than being a bizarre and isolated mental state was the fulfillment of the "insight" of idealism and of the "power" of physics. This final system was a unique attempt to produce a natural philosophy of mysticism, a psychology of religious phenomena in the idealist manner.

The mystical system was a distraction for Görres from the political arena as the years approached his death in 1848. He had become as suspicious of secular democracy as of imperial bureaucracy. He felt importuned not only by Protestant Prussia but by the conservative papacy. Görres was an interpreter, a pointer, a prophet, a weathervane. As hard as it is to believe, Görres planned yet another great system: it would be called *Genesis* and, he wrote, would cost him ten times as much effort as the prior *Mystik*.[54]

When Schelling left the University of Munich for Berlin in 1841, Görres wrote a lengthy article bemoaning his departure; it was, he said, a sign of a new Protestant hegemony over speculative thought.[55] Hegel he now viewed as the unhappy realization of the essence of Protestantism, and he rejoiced that Schelling's departure for Berlin meant the arrival there of a happier philosophy. He criticized Schelling's absorption of Christian dogma into idealist categories but he praised, as other Catholic critics after 1840 did not, a philosophy of religion constructed not only on nature and metaphysics but upon history, myth and the mystical. Görres and Schelling never lost a cool, mutual appreciation, for they were similar in their hope for that one system, subject-centered, that would present in process the one and the all.

Shortly before his death, Görres wrote that Europe was on the edge of a new society and a new church. New doctors of the church would appear, he said; masters of new times, helmsmen of the modern, capable of bold steering as the earliest fathers had led the church through Greek wisdom. Clearly he did not see Schelling or Hegel among these church fathers, or Pius IX. New teachers did emerge, and they sat in Schelling's lecture hall—for a while. They were Feuerbach and Marx, Engels and Kierkegaard.

4. Franz von Baader

In his trip to Russia, Baader had failed to secure even a gesture, much less a pact, of ecumenical cooperation between Orthodox Russia and Protestant and Catholic Europe. His goal had been not only political arrangements insuring peace and exchange, but moves of an ecumenical nature toward a union (if not unity) of churches. In 1824 Baader returned to his projects in Munich: to projected editions of Suso and Tauler, to surveys of European politics, to counterattacks against claims of an increasingly conservative papacy. Bishop Sailer argued for Baader to be given an important professorship, but he was assigned only an extraordinary lectureship in history.

In 1827, at the University of Munich, Baader was an old man and a tired lecturer, but he remained hard at work on what had always been his grand design: a synthesis between the Catholic tradition and modern philosophy, a reconciliation of his church's essence with ecumenical change. F.A. Staudenmaier described Baader as "a living system." "When we follow him we find the totality of the idea . . . , the living and creating spirit active in its development."[56]

Baader saw the approaching illnesses of the modern world in both church and state. Neither Rome nor Moscow nor Berlin understood how to bring together the new drives for freedom in the individual and society. As had been his way with the natural sciences and with transcendental philosophy, the modality and the instrument of Baader's own system remained mystical subjectivity and organic development. Like Görres, Baader was convinced that a synthesizing renewal, capable of resolving the age-old problems of science and faith, would come through the mystics. Görres, however, completed one last system of this coloring, *Christian Mysticism*, and Baader did not.

Schelling avoided Baader. He rejected efforts to restore their friendship and he annoyed Baader by mocking the mystic, Saint-Martin, in his lectures. What had earlier brought Baader and Schelling together was the marriage of metaphysics and mysticism, a search for God amid the processes of nature and history. What separated them was a disagreement over how traditional a philosophical theology of creation and revelation should be. Baader saw that Schelling's positive philosophy, for all its confession of being Christian, never became a philosophy of revelation, or a theology. Schelling always considered his thought to be a honed fulfillment of religion, whether Christian or Indian. Some truths of Christianity were symbols of what dynamic insight could perceive in the transcendental structures of consciousness and history. Schelling's first system of 1800 and the brief writings on Christianity and theology of 1802 had held that lofty view and it lived on in the final system.

From Baader we have a rather autobiographical critique of Schelling's great Munich system of idealism, mythology and revelation.[57] Baader attended the cycle of lectures with enthusiastic Catholic students, some of whom argued with Baader when he attacked Schelling. He found Schelling's major points deficient. Schelling gave too much and too little to the world's religions; without such, an independent, tribal mythology could not evolve toward Christ. On the other hand, Schelling offered too little empirical evidence that the mythologies really fit into his dialectical system, and that they can be harmonized with the gospel: "The light of Christ did not come from the swamp of mythology." Baader shrewdly observed that, for Schelling, it is not the Old Testament but the world mythologies that are the source of Christianity. But this confuses the bearers of a historical revelation with mythopoetic forms of consciousness.

As we observed, Schelling ended his positive philosophy of world religion haltingly, with a vision of the dialectic of church division and unity resolved in a Johannine church. Such an idea probably came from Baader; as early as 1818, Baader was interpreting his ecumenical efforts with Orthodoxy and especially with Russia in those terms. Eastern Christianity, he said, was a unique and ancient form of church. Although it was intellectually isolated, it had a divine role to play in the West. In "Asian and European Catholicism," which has been called "the most significant ecumenical writing of the nineteenth century,"[58] these ideas are set forth clearly and challengingly. Where Baader disagreed with Schelling was that the philosopher was expounding an idea of salvific potential, whereas Baader was its agent in the field of ecclesial polity.

Baader made no secret of the fact that he was disappointed in the final works of Schelling and Hegel. His own writings, either directly or obliquely, always kept the philosophy of the times in mind. He wrote:

> We see the error of both Schelling and Hegel as they treat the relationship of nature to spirit. For Schelling spirit is never free of nature or emancipated from nature. (He thinks that freedom would mean being without a nature or being incorporeal.) While, on the other hand, Hegel pictures a natureless spirit that is only a ghost moving over fallen nature.[59]

In a melancholy tone, Baader summed up the entire enterprise of his era: "We have a confused reconciliation of naturalism and theism, of nature and Scripture, of believing and knowing."[60]

His critique of Schelling's *Philosophy of Revelation*, however, did not keep Baader from lecturing on and publishing between 1828 and 1838, his own final system *Lectures on Speculative Dogmatics*. "The only true mysticism," he wrote, "is speculative or doctrinal mysticism."[61] Couched in structural wanderings and opaque language, this six-hundred-page mix of progressive social theory, Catholic orthodoxy, transcendental philosophy and chiliastic mysticism proffers only the beginning of a system. We must have a system, Baader began, whose foundation comes from above. A Christian philosophy displays its true nature in the form of a constantly rotating circle of concepts, which, in the style of Neoplatonism, we contemplate; and yet, we must begin with the conviction that all speculation is subject to the conditions of its own historical setting.[62] Baader chose as his leitmotif the kingdom of God. The system will have four parts; the ground of the kingdom, its destruction and return, its continuation in history, its fulfillment in eternal life.[63]

Baader began with many lectures on the nature of science and religion, on faith and philosophy. The spiritual nature of the human personality is an image of God. After a lengthy survey of modern philosophy occasioned by this transcendental analysis, he moved to the idealist problematic of God and creation. The system reached only as far as Baader's favorite topic, the Trinity. How he would have treated Christ and the church is left to our imagination, for declining health and preoccupations with philosophy as well as the papacy kept him from continuing what was to be the fulfillment of the philosophies of science he had composed fifty years before.

Baader was in his middle sixties; his once fabled energy was spent. He could not follow the younger, liberal Catholics such as Möhler into the landscape of history; he remained entranced by the mystics, still hoping from their intuition to find a unity of tradition and freedom. He helped to guide the *Eos* circle and its journal; he dominated the conversations at dinners given by Görres or by Sailer, now the bishop of Regensburg. Church authority, however, was for Baader not a topic to be set aside by piety: it belonged to politics, not revelation.

For over a decade, Baader had been questioning the self-descriptions of the papacy. The primacy of the pope, he wrote, should not be numbered among the deepest truths of revelation.[64] Papacy is not the same as the church, nor is the origin of the church principally the origins of hierarchy. The papacy does not own in isolation the highest principle of church life. Baader will admit an "autocratic" authority for the papacy, but he warns against autocracy's becoming despotism. The pope should not behave like a heaven-inspired monarch. What is challenging the papacy, he insightfully pointed out, is the current evolution of society's sense of itself. More and more the papacy does not correspond to that social change. At the opening of the University of Munich, Baader took as his theme "Freedom of Intelligence" and he made reference to one of his recent articles, which suggested that the laity be restored to roles of minister and theologian in the Roman Catholic Church. The Vatican of Gregory XVI implied in important circles that Baader might be subject to ecclesiastical censure; certainly his writings did not please the conservative party of the Bavarian clergy. Baader, however, distanced himself from those who appeared radical, such as de Lamennais, because he saw no hope for his work if he were cut off from the Catholic community. He knew that as a prophet moving mercurially from panentheistic systems to ecumenism, from Russian politics to lay power, he appeared antipapal, dangerous and perhaps anachronistic. Nevertheless, he kept on developing new ideas.

Baader spoke before the Royal Academy of Science in 1835 on "The Proletariat" and wrote a memorandum the next year to Ludwig I on the necessity of taking "social evolution" seriously.[65] In protesting against both the theology of the Roman papacy and the politics of the Prussian court, Baader typified the confusing interplay in Munich of liberal and conservative policies and, of course, he never ceased to support limited monarchy for the state and papacy for the church. The last years of his life were lonely: cut off from his beloved Russia, alienated from the older generation of philosophers and from the younger clergy, disillusioned with the pope and Ludwig I, he died in poverty in 1841, the year Schelling moved to Berlin.

Baader's influence came back to life in movements that began after his death. He was a precursor of ecumenism, a pioneer of liturgical and ministerial reform through the laity, a rediscoverer of Western mystics. Kierkegaard spoke of his importance, and Adolf von Kolping, the German founder of Catholic social action, learned his theory in Munich from Baader's lectures. Some have seen his ideas in the social teaching of the popes after Leo XIII, and others have described Teilhard de Chardin as his intellectual descendant. The final system never found its incarnation; language and form failed Baader, but his universal spirit lived on.[66]

7
Between Schelling and Hegel:
The Catholic Tübingen School

JOHANN SEBASTIAN DREY's theological faculty at Tübingen flourished and his offspring in the various areas of theological science were numerous. Johann Adam Möhler, Franz Anton Staudenmaier and Johann Evengelist Kuhn were the highpoint of the Catholic Tübingen school, the result of their mentor, Drey's, work in theology. The Catholic *Tübinger* were self-confident in their use of modern philosophy, firm in their independent but loyal commitment to tradition and faith. They lacked, obviously, the limitations of Zimmer, Sailer, even of Baader, for they were heirs to decades of German Christian intellectual life of depth and power. In their youthful vigor they spoke only of further goals and horizons; encyclopedias, systematic theologies, complete theological courses. And yet a certain, scarcely seen mist of doubt has entered. Could modern thought amid Christian faith avoid pantheism and agnosticism? Still, these doubts lay below the surface of the world of Tübingen, and the professors and students there were not ready to give up the enterprise of a Catholic, modern theology despite the dangers and the discouragement.

These Tübingen professors and disciples of Drey are both the peak and the denouement of the dialogue between Romantic idealism and Catholicism. Möhler, Kuhn and Staudenmaier were all excited by Schelling when they were young. Moreover, Kuhn and Staudenmaier felt the need in the 1840s to write an evaluation of the final system of Schelling's philosophy of revelation. We will look at these three thinkers for examples of the Catholic German theology in the nineteenth century most deeply engaged with modern thought. They also show the origin of Catholic interest—over and beyond the idealism of Schelling—in Hegel. Kuhn was a systematic theologian; Staudenmaier's interest remained philosophy of religion and fundamental theology, while Möhler, theoretician and historian, directed his generation toward that future path that will replace subject-centered philosophy in Catholic thought: history and ecclesiology. Together, and with others, they form the third generation of Catholic theologians who worked within the modern problematic. Their careers spanned a large part of the past century: through the entire first half, from Sailer and Drey to the Hegelians and the neoscholastics.

> What drove the Tübingen theologians was love for the church of Christ; what determined their search was a veneration for Catholicism, which was to be vitalized anew. Their writings, however, are inconceivable without those of Jacobi, Fichte, Schelling, Schleiermacher and Hegel. It would be rather inept to present the influence of German idealism on the *Tübinger* as the effect of practical or political considerations. The substance of their Catholicity depends upon no particular philosophy. . . . What makes them great is the liberated self-possession by which they have placed the great philosophies of their time at the service of theology.[1]

Franz Anton Staudenmaier

"Schelling! The name recalls one of the greatest and deepest, one of the most notable and most powerful figures who ever lived or ever will live."[2] So Franz Anton Staudenmaier, at the beginning of his academic career in 1832, summed up someone who had been for him more of an inspiration than a teacher. Staudenmaier's theological career was to be a trek around and over various philosophical peaks. He labored at producing a synthesis of Roman Catholic theology with the giants of German philosophy. Schelling was studied, Hegel was employed, and then both were critiqued. Hegel had often proclaimed that a philosophy was the spirit of a time expressed in thinking, and Staudenmaier, echoing Sailer, exclaimed: "It is vain to withstand the spirit of the times. . . . We must recognize it, penetrate it, but not in every way adopt it."[3] We have in Staudenmaier a theologian at the crossroads: he represents the third generation of Roman Catholic interest in idealism and in Schelling, and he represents the Tübingen school at its best:

> The life and work of Staudenmaier displays, as does hardly any other of his colleagues in Freiburg and Tübingen, the greatness of Catholic theology in the nineteenth century. The dimensions of this huge torso—almost all Staudenmaier's large works were left

uncompleted—are drawn from a review and reconstruction of life in that century: the establishment of new political forms, the formulation of modern science, the introduction of technical civilization. All of this entered the stage of history with trumpet blasts in the 1830s and 1840s.[4]

Like Schelling and Hegel, Staudenmaier was a speculative Swabian. And like them, he produced system after system, each left incomplete like fragments of classical statuary. At the *Gymnasium* in Ellwangen from 1818 to 1822, he read the Romantics, filling his exercise books with excerpts from Novalis and the Schlegels, from Goethe and Schiller. He studied Baader's and Schelling's philosophies of nature and transcendental philosophy. At the age of twenty-two he wrote *On History*, a booklet fleshing out his own theories with the fragments he found exciting. That same year, a Roman Catholic theological faculty was established at Tübingen with Drey its head. Staudenmaier's studies in Tübingen began that first year, and before they were completed Möhler's *The Unity of the Church* appeared, a book applying a high Romantic idealism to new areas of theology. Not only the idealist philosophers were enthusiastically read at Tübingen, but Protestant theologians such as Schleiermacher, Marheineke and Rosenkranz were studied with respect.

After ordination in 1826 and a year's pastoral experience, the young priest returned to Tübingen as tutor in the Catholic seminary. He won a theological prize for his historical study on the popular selection of bishops. After publishing a first book on the problem of the human person as the image of God, Staudenmaier received in 1830 a professorship in Giessen; from there, too, came a doctorate. He brought to the small school, with its tendencies toward Josephism and Kantianism, a third direction, something new—history. Patristic and systematic theology were cultivated in the Catholic Tübingen faculty through the medium of historical research. He and his colleagues founded at Giessen in 1834 the periodical *Jahrbücher für Theologie und christliche Philosophie*. In its pages and in Drey's Tübingen *Quartalschrift*, Staudenmaier surveyed the theological riches of the times, criticizing amicably Anton Günther, praising Friedrich Schlegel. As he reviewed Schleiermacher, he pondered whether the Protestant theologian's interpretation of Christ might have fallen short of the absolute, incarnate Word of God as accepted by the Christian traditions of the East and West. Nevertheless, Staudenmaier wrote, Schleiermacher was the greatest Protestant theologian since Calvin.[5]

Schelling's Genius

Staudenmaier's theology, like his personality, was open, approachable, and receptive:

At the beginning of his thirties, for a moment he was the very incarnation of a new theology, a theology which would come into existence through dialogue with theologians of other confessions and with the Romantics and their beloved Plato; a theology which would be at home with Hamann, Jean Paul, Lessing, Goethe and Novalis. It would overcome the sterile alternatives between theological rationalism and supernatural positivism.[6]

Staudenmaier's thinking, like Schelling's, evolved through several periods; in its gathering of disparate sources it was an endless search for the final system. What interests us is not the heavy material of these systems but their form where Staudenmaier encountered and accepted idealism. Particularly in his first writings Staudenmaier critiqued, praised and used Schelling's thought between 1802 and 1809. The decade after 1834 was a time of reflection by the Catholic systematician upon the giants of modern philosophy. There is no question that the young professor in Giessen saw Roman Catholicism as capable of producing a systematic of dogma in idealist format. A study on the Carolingian Neoplatonist, Scotus Erigena, served well as a historical apologia for this enterprise. As Staudenmaier pursued Schelling's and Hegel's writings, he could see that Erigena's history of the divine archetypes active in space and history and flowing out from the divine freedom and mind was in the same vein as the new philosophy.

Two early articles went directly to the heart of the problem of how idealism could relate to revelation. The first examined pantheism; the second insisted that history was the locus for the activity of God in the world. The first essay pointed out that pantheism has a long history in Western religious thought. For Staudenmaier, Hegel was typical of modern thought; Schelling was a variant as he went beyond the world of the transcendental *a priori* and recognized that the forms of the mind were the form but not the content of a revelation of a personal God and his kingdom:

Schelling continued to develop free and historical movement as a fundamental truth of the personality of God. God's movement brings with it act, life and creation. Hegel, however, stayed with logical necessity (also present in Schelling's philosophy) and moved backward not only to Spinoza but to Greek pantheism.[7]

What is rather startling in this article is Staudenmaier's description of the divine personality as will, an insight drawn from the *Essay on Freedom*. The solution to the problem of pantheism, the theologian concluded, was not to derive theology from orthodox statements or causal effects. If the ambiguity of history and the sublime aseity of God were preserved, the freedom of the divine mind and will to both be and not be in time and cosmos would be sustained.

The theme of the second article was history, and Staudenmaier did not hesitate to draw on earlier works of Schelling. The rationalism, he wrote, fashionable around the end of the eighteenth century is without content or activity. Schelling has gone beyond his philosophy of mental identity to one of history and existence, to a system of freedom as guarantee for the freedom of God's activity. The only true principle for history is "the personal, powerful, holy and wise will of the godhead, God himself."[8] This essay was filled with ideas from Schelling: the dialectic of freedom and necessity; history as the drama of the godhead, the systole and diastole of the heart of God in history. Staudenmaier concluded: "Christianity is the system of divine freedom."[9]

As these essays, and a first encyclopedia, were being published, Staudenmaier was finishing the first volume of his *Philosophy of Christianity*. Vast in its plan, this unfinished work (dedicated to Anton Günther) began with questions and topics fundamental to a theological system in the nineteenth century. The time of the post-Kantians, of Jacobi and his Catholic disciples such as Köppen is past, and a time of synthesis has come. A bold philosophy of Christian revelation meant the systematic unfolding of the divine ideas about nature, spirit and self precisely as all of this is disclosed in scriptural revelation.

There was no doubt that Staudenmaier saw a specific metaphysics latent in the Christian message, and that this metaphysics began with the subject and proceeded through development. A treatment of the divine ideas began the work; in God, the objective and the subjective, the concept and the reality, are one. God is neither the prototype of the world, nor the world itself; rather, in and from the ideas of God the world came forth. An idea, Staudenmaier explained, is a bridge between concept and reality. Such an approach permits to theology subjectivity without pantheism. Schelling was the genius who brought together thinking and being; he stood daringly on the pinnacle of subjective idealism.

While laying a historical backdrop for his philosophy of Christianity, Staudenmaier surveyed the evolution of Schelling's thought from its beginning. First came the philosophy, where nature and spirit own parallel histories; there the absolute becomes fruitful idea and organic vitality. Next, Staudenmaier praised Schelling's acceptance after 1802 of the divine archetypes and of a fall. Finally, there is the philosophy of the will of the godhead, and the (mainly unknown) positive philosophy of revelation. "And so," Staudenmaier concluded, "Schelling's system is essentially metamorphosed as it moves ever nearer to the Christian reality."[10] Schellingian motifs such as life, idea, personality when applied to God must lead ultimately to historical revelation . . . , even to incarnation.

Subjectivity and Revelation

Although in philosophical form the early Staudenmaier warmed to Schelling, a parallel intellectual enterprise was at the same time drawing him away. In 1837 a first study on revelation appeared, dedicated to Drey. Idealism, he wrote, oversteps its limits when it concludes that "religion is the self-consciousness of God in man."[11] If that were true, revelation would not be the free gift of God but the necessary emotion of the human being.

Revelation takes place in varying levels of immediacy, and Staudenmaier began not with the special, biblical revelation but with the mediation of God in nature, spirit and history. Although he criticized the idea that God is not God without the world, the Catholic theologian observed parenthetically that such an idea is "of a fearful depth and terrible height."[12] Christian revelation, however, is more than the invisible presence of God's intimacy in history and self, those "organs and symbols of the intuition of God."[13]

Staudenmaier chose more and more not metaphysics but life as his theme. The vitality of God and the plurality of the divine archetypes lead to a free incarnation in history. All of the Old and New Testaments flows from a revelation in the historical life of Jesus. He is the identity of the finite and infinite. But even as it labors to defend a special revelation not deduced from mental life, the small volume on revelation assumed the stance of idealism and devoted most of its time to arranging idealist insights into a legitimate Catholic theology.

The Critique of Schelling

Staudenmaier matured, his academic responsibilities increased, the theologian turned to Hegel where he found some new insights but no fully satisfying structure. Usually Staudenmaier wrote of Schelling's philosophical career as still unfolding, for the Munich lectures were inaccessable outside of Bavaria:

> In a truly reconciling fashion, the genius of Schelling, rich in knowledge, entered philosophy. The objective world receives its old rights back and is reconciled with spirit. His teaching is that of the essential identity of subject and object in which alone truth dwells. But we can give no sure and complete judgment on this system for it is not complete. There have been many unjust attacks on Schelling—that he was a Spinozist, a pantheist. We do not agree. His earlier systems might suffer from all of this, but he then decided for a personal God. . . .
>
> In recent times we have learned from his own students that he has come fully to Christianity, opting for a free creation, and the personality of God and man. In his early periods Schelling could have gone two ways, for both were contained in his thought: the logical and necessary, and the free-historical (Christian). The second, Schelling followed; the first, Hegel.[14]

But by 1842 Staudenmaier had seen summaries of Schelling's positive philosophy and he published a long essay on this philosophy of Christianity. As with other Roman Catholic summaries of Schelling, the philosopher's final departure from Bavaria for Berlin seems to have been the occasion. Evidently Schelling remained for the Catholic theologians a great figure who was attempting an enormous task, but who was increasingly a man from a philosophical world that was passing.[15]

A succinct summary of Schelling's philosophy of revelation began the long article. The new, positive philosophy of existence and its relationship to consciousness was greeted as an honest attempt to avoid pantheism in the development of God's life. Staudenmaier's concluding section on Christ was almost longer than Schelling's own presentation of the Johannine *logos* and the Pauline *kenosis*; for the great idealist's powers weakened as he approached (Staudenmaier observed) the second and third potencies. The christology is brief, the pneumatology is bare.

Schelling remains *the* philosopher because, unlike Hegel, he has allowed the Lord of Being to be free and multiple, not static but filled with potentiality for all. The affirmation of a prior fullness in God separates Schelling from Hegel. The relationship of God's life to its own history of development, moreover, has lost its pantheistic character. But Schelling is still unable to answer the question—the very question that guided him to theological issues in 1804—of how the finite emerges from the infinite. One cannot deduce from the nature of God what is contrary to God.

Schelling has confused finitude with sin, and freedom with every being-in-process. Here we have a particularly insightful objection from Staudenmaier, one valid for the entire range of Schelling's philosophy. For sin and redemption are impossible without human and divine freedom, whereas religion and myth depend upon a distinction between God and the world. There is no real polarity in Schelling's idealist monism; metaphysics and grace are one. Schelling has written so much about freedom but ultimately the metaphysics of a necessary cosmic process reduces every freedom to "only a game."[16]

The great philosopher has not succeeded in transposing a metaphysical cosmogenesis—all of reality conceived as process—into Christian theology. To critique this theogenetic cosmogenesis, Staudenmaier, in an interesting turnabout, employed anthropology. If the absolute was not the Fichtean self but the life of the spirit, this meant that the life of God is involved with finite life. Paradoxically Staudenmaier maintained that Schelling neglected humanity for deity. A metaphysics of finitude is not the same as human sin, and participation in divine process is not the same as human freedom. Even his ultimate promise to ground philosophy in existence is not kept. Schelling's thought remained a description of God or of the totality of spiritual consciousness. The human person seems to be no more than the vase where the divine chemicals mix. Redemption is not personal salvation but God's revelatory presence in finite consciousness. This consciousness, moreover, as the concrete expression of the human return to the divine, never gets beyond being a myth. Anthropology empty of sin and present as myth is feeble, hollow.

Is this Christianity? No, but it stands closer to Christianity than did early idealism. Schelling is now taking history and historical Christianity more seriously. Crucial aspects of the Judaeo-Christian tradition, however, are not so easily fitted into his vast system. God cannot become God, for a divine power cannot *become* fully divine. Religion proceeds from the dialectic of sin and freedom, not from that of necessity and process. It comes as no surprise that Schelling has failed to make Christ a central religious figure. The monist ontology of grace and being obscures the teaching and redemptive role of Christ. Staudenmaier knew Schelling's proclivity for describing history as a Greek epic or play; Christ, the theologian objected, should be more than a figure acting out a solitary role in a Greek drama.

Staudenmaier did not know this at the time but his pages of succinct evaluation, in this article on Schelling and in his volume on Hegel, are the mature summing up by Roman Catholic theologians of this period in Western thought. As we shall see, Kuhn, Döllinger and others will also feel the need to evaluate Schelling's place in their history. But in Staudenmaier, heir to Drey and colleague of Möhler, we have the best critique from systematic theology.

At the end of his life, the Tübingen theologian turned his efforts to political thinking: he struggled for a new ecumenical and well as political consciousness. The earlier decades, ones of excitement over *Wissenschaft* and *Idee*, lay behind. Like the students of Hegel in Berlin, he sensed the future lay with politics. Staudenmaier's metaphysical framework remained idealist but his theology of revelation more and more moved to a christocentric position. Through all of his systems he struggled to reconcile (a word he often applied to Schelling) the idealist stance with fidelity to Catholic Christianity. He concluded (as the young Schelling had in 1796) that truth was to be found between orthodox supernaturalism and rationalism, and that ultimately the expression of thought is a system that is always in development.[17]

2. Johann Adam Möhler

From our vantage point after Vatican II, we know that it was not to be J.S. Drey or I. Döllinger but the lesser known Johann Adam Möhler who was to have the most far-reaching impact upon the Roman Catholic Church. Vatican II was an event of ecclesial renewal, and the thinking of Möhler stood behind many of the German and French theologians who fashioned the council's change of direction. Möhler had been quickly forgotten after his early death in 1838. But Geiselmann, Fries, Ratzinger, Kasper, Küng would all admit some debt to him; Yves Congar rehabilitated him for the French- and English-speaking worlds. What made Möhler original was his way of viewing church and tradition not as dogmas or canons, as explicit as they were eternal, but as an evolving collective consciousness, unpredictable but Spirit-guided.

We know that Drey viewed the church and the consciousness of the Christian as a vital process of insight into the Christ-event; this owed much to Romanticism and idealism. Writers on Möhler inevitably mention his indebtedness to Drey but often fail to trace the influence further to philosophical sources such as Schelling and Hegel. Schelling's philosophy of consciousness and being, shot through with history, was first stated in 1799; his view that no being was immune from polar dialectic served as a remote stimulus for Tübingen fundamental theology and ecclesiology:

> Drey, Möhler and after them Staudenmaier and Kuhn were, from the beginning, convinced that their substantially Catholic thinking can be identified (with some qualifications) with the absolute philosophizing of the Romantics. . . . They believed that their Catholic faith in the incarnate *logos* would eventually present the true and absolute philosophy.[18]

Son of Tübingen

When Möhler was born in 1796 on the Tauber, northeast of Stuttgart, Napoleon was triumphant in Italy and the pope was soon to be his prisoner. Goethe was finding the tranquility of Weimar nourishing, Kant was disturbed by Fichte's *Doctrine of Science*, and the young Schelling was leaving Tübingen for the first time for Leipzig. Möhler was at the seminary in Ellwangen when it moved in 1817 to Tübingen to form the university's Catholic faculty. One of his teachers was J. N. Bestlin, an intense if forgotten disciple of Sailer, and Möhler met the aged Sailer himself in 1818. The Catholic theologians in Tübingen were excited about their opportunities to engage the new philosophies in their writings and to study the views and origins of their Protestant colleagues, and so Möhler decided to begin serious study of Luther.

After ordination and two years of pastoral experience, he returned in 1821 to Tübingen to act as tutor and to pursue doctoral studies in classical philology. The next year he began to lecture on church history; it was to be the field he would choose as his dominant area of interest. Möhler's obligatory trip for theological refinement passed through Jena, Göttingen, Berlin, Vienna, Landshut. He would not have found Schelling in Munich: the new university had not yet opened its doors and Schelling was teaching—for the first time in decades—at Lutheran Erlangen. In Berlin, Möhler met some imposing minds: Schleiermacher, Neander and Marheineke. Marheineke had published in 1810 his *Christian Symbolics*, which arranged its material around some thought-forms of Schelling, but since then he had turned to the philosophy of his colleague Hegel. J. G. Plank at Göttingen and Neander at Berlin urged Möhler to study the first and second centuries. Plank had begun to write a comparative historical symbolics; Neander in his studies on Julian the Apostate and John Chrysostom served as a forerunner for all who were to research not only the brute data of history but to locate them in their social and psychological context. In Schleiermacher, Möhler found not the early Romantic of the *Reden* but a theologian lecturing upon the social dimensions of the history of Christian dogmas. By the end of the trip the motifs that determined Möhler's work for the rest of his life were seminally present: spirit, church, faith, love, freedom and history.

In the 1820s, German Romanticism was still vibrant, it still held out hope for a future of freedom and synthesis and religious power. Möhler—like Novalis, Schlegel and Görres—viewed the previous cultural epochs, the Reformation and the Enlightenment, as understandable but linked together in their aloofness to religion. Romanticism had brought those times as well as late medieval and baroque Catholicism to a new time of vigor. Möhler commented:

> The emptiness, the vagueness and indifference of the recent times had become intolerable. The religious spirit dares again to assert its own rights. Science, art, life—everything has assumed a more serious, a more defined form. Catholics and Protestants have, with one and the same effort although in different ways, collected their strength and moved to a higher position, one above the depths to which they had fallen.[19]

But, to secure this new and higher position, one had to go back—to the history of the early church.

Romanticism and Ecclesiology

At the age of twenty-nine Möhler published his first great work; it was a description of a church that moved through century after century, retaining—in the face of newness and schism, heresy and reflection—its unity and its identity. *The Unity of the Church* brought to its author the attention of German theologians. Möhler discovered "the theology of Drey in the writings of the fathers of the church."[20] A theology of change and unity is drawn from the Christian thinkers of the first three centuries; theory, then, flows from history.

The church, Möhler wrote, has always lived not out of an eternal and legal constitution given to the Apostles nor from a divine logic, but out of a life that pulses with growth and dialectic:

> The church is the eternal, visible form of a holy, living power of love, which the Holy Spirit imparts. The church is the body belonging to the spirit of believers, a spirit that forms itself from inward out. . . . . Tradition runs through all the periods of the church and is alive at every moment. The incarnational expression of the Holy Spirit gives life to the collectivity of the faithful.[21]

It would be a century and a half before Roman Catholicism understood and adopted as its own the theology held in these words.

Patristic research suggested to Möhler patterns of thought not unlike those of modern philosophy. He knew how to use Schelling when he described ecclesiology as the science not only of a life but of a living subject. What marks the originality of *Unity* is that it took as the subject for its developmental system neither the human mind nor God but the church. *Wissenschaftslehre* has become ecclesiology. Möhler will influence Roman Catholic theology in 1965 as well as in 1835 because he has replaced the ecclesiologies of medieval metaphysics and canonical nominalism with the modern developmental philosophy of consciousness.

It is certainly not coincidental that at this time Hegel's thought concluded with the state, and Schelling's ended first with the myth-making nations and then with Christianity and the Christian churches. Möhler as a Catholic theologian carried the direction of objective idealism toward a climax in society further when he wrote, "The Christian life (the life of the church) is true and divine philosophy."[22] If we want the essence of Christianity and the church, Möhler asserted, we will find it not in words or in formulas but in life. The Holy Spirit is the spirit or life principle of a community that develops organically and historically. For the leitmotif of his theology Möhler selected not the heroic, solitary individual self of early Romanticism (Schleiermacher), nor the world-creating ego of Fichte (from the time of the French Revolution), nor the process of the world or of God (the later Schelling), nor the logic and concepts of the world-mind (Hegel), but life: historical life and community life:

Unity in the Church is a mirror of Möhler's inner life, the expression
of his inner vitality; it is a confession and a praise of God. The
Romantic idea of life replaces the concept. This is the key that
explains the puzzling changes in his thought. . . . The worldview
that had determined Möhler's understanding until then was deism, a
separation between God and world, and its stepchild, mechanism. In
contrast to this worldview, the enthusiasm of Romanticism enters to
serve as the background for the new image of the church. That view
of the world is colored by the mutual presence of world and humanity in God.[23]

The times were right: Catholics were irenically inquiring into the
causes of the Reformation and the historical meaning of Protestantism,
and they no longer felt inferior in the modern world. It was time to apply
the modern philosophy of self, nature and religion, even of art, to particular theological areas, such as the church.

Möhler's book expressed in a refreshing way the elements by which
the church both retains its identity and responds to the changes of history.
When the church is viewed as a living collectivity, there can be growth
without division and mature reflection without heresy. In all that grows
we find polar tension; drawing on the philosophy of nature made famous
by Schelling almost three decades earlier, Möhler described church life.[24]
In a community enlivened by the holy yet epochal Spirit, individuals can
flourish in their individuality as the community grows in depth and
breadth. Brightness and power can shine through particular members and
through the individual truths of faith and theology.[25] The community of
believers is like a living organism where love and insight grow and where
guarantees of truth come to the individual. Möhler may have had in mind
Fichte and the early Schelling when he located the source of heresy in
"egoistic assertions cut off from the community's life and love."[26] Regardless, now the freedom of the Fichtean self or of the Romantic hero, a
freedom without constraint but also without objectification, has yielded to
life within the organic society.

The church is not an archive or a museum, but an organism that is not
afraid of history and culture but lives from the Spirit and from the times.
The gifts of the Spirit contribute to the integral life of this organism—the
community. The controversial issue of correct thinking in the church is
part of the life process. The consciousness of the church belongs not to
one or two members, but is, or should be, really a collective conscious-

ness; it unfolds in fidelity and in newness God's revelation in Christ, but this unfolding happens in history. The articulated, historical side of church life is what we call tradition. Tradition is not a collection of writings but the community's consciousness bearing and reflecting upon revelation under the silent direction of the Spirit.

Toward the end of the theoretical part of this book, Möhler introduced one final, Romantic motif. He resolved his evolutionary theology of the church in aesthetics. The "inner essence," the "spiritual unity" of church is mirrored in nature, and in art. As we saw, after 1800 Schelling drew into his own idealist philosophy the strong impulses of Romantic art by concluding his first systems in art. The work of art was a place where one could see and intuit the union of the real and the ideal, matter under spirit. "Liturgy is," Möhler wrote, "the presentation of religious ideas, movements and facts through forms in space, through bodily symbols and symbolic actions."[27] In Christianity the idealizing power of the Spirit finds expression not only in word but in the reality of sacrament—religion's art.

Both Sailer and Schleiermacher had confronted their churches with the principle that, in faith and theology, Christians could proceed from that which is within to the external, from the subject to the object. Romanticism painted subjectivity with the colors of the interior, the intuitive, the productive, the mystical. Roman Catholic theologians, following Baader and Schlegel, looked not for a rejection of the mystical but for its objectification. Schelling had guided his students from intuition (idealism) to mystery (nature) and then to religion (mysticism). Möhler's ecclesiology is essentially mystical, for the principle of church life is not canon law but an unpredictable development.

Möhler's genius was to apply evolution through dialectic and historical consciousness to the community, to bring together in time the historical reality and the revealed ideal of the church. Although it is true that Möhler turned to history, the framework of his thought, however, is not yet the historical research of von Ranke or Döllinger; it is still a philosophy of history. There was evidently no compulsion in modern philosophy for theologians to sacrifice the objectivity of revelation concretized in the life of the church. It was important, Möhler wrote in 1827, for the community to reflect upon its life, but it was also important to think about what Christ had done for it. This turn toward the historical, Christ-bestowed reality of revelation, as an *an sich* with its absolute truth, indicates a move away from the subjectivism of early Romanticism and from a faith that was either individual mysticism or the climax of transcendental reason's creative powers. Möhler was searching for the objectivity of tradition, the flesh and blood of revelation in history . . . and he hoped to find help in Hegel.[28]

From Schelling to Hegel

Möhler was not influenced by Schelling as explicitly as had been Drey. The younger historian and ecclesiologist absorbed the cultural milieu of his times. In terms of his philosophical position Möhler soon moved beyond Drey and Schelling to the sharper lines of the Hegelian dialectic. It is often forgotten that Schelling's idealism was objective idealism. Spirit becomes fully absolute through objectification in nature, art, history, religion. For Möhler, however, Schelling's philosophy seemed to have too little objectivity. Hegel attracted Möhler because he had ended his system in concrete society. It may have been Schelling's persistence in developing the transcendental analysis of the knower or in concluding his thought in intellectual systems—for example, those of mythological systems—that impressed Möhler as a thought too faintly objective.[29] The Tübingen theologian decided that it was not the undetermined godhead that was unfolding its life in the cosmos, but the Spirit-directed Christian community. Despite Hegel's cry that Roman Catholicism was a religion of unfreedom, younger Catholic theologians such as Möhler came to prefer the Berlin philosopher. As Möhler labored, the *Einheit* of Drey and Schelling became the *Symbolik* of Hegel.

Influenced by the writings of Marheineke and Schleiermacher, Möhler wanted to write a symbolics that would go beyond dogmatic propositions to their historical context, and then to the spirit and idea that lay behind the different positions of separated Christians.[30] The *Symbolics* described the intellectual life of Catholicism but the churches of the Reformation were part of that development. Möhler struggled with Hegel's writings to find a kind of dialectic that might relate and even reconcile positions that previously had only been parallel. The theologian found himself stretched between two untamed forces: the objective meaning of revelation in church tradition, and the varied, sometimes opposing, Protestant and Catholic articulations of deeper revelatory ideas. In the wake of Hegel, Möhler set out for his next intellectual world—not the aesthetic expression of a Romantic ecclesiology, but the synthesis of a dialectical history of theology.

As the spokesman for the Catholic point of view (which, in the last analysis, directed the *Symbolics*), Möhler became embroiled in controversy in Tübingen, especially with F. C. Baur. This, and the uncertainty of the next stage in his theology, left him exhausted. He turned down a professorship in Bonn offered by the Prussian government, for the archbishop of Cologne—on the advice of Hermes—judged Möhler's books too novel. He was happy to accept a position in Munich in 1834, a chair arranged by his friend Döllinger. Möhler did not live to become the speculative theological genius of the Tübingen school or a young Catholic counterpart to the later Schelling. Unfortunately, the move from Tübingen to Munich, the strain of lecturing in exegesis as well as history, did not permit Möhler to improve his failing health. Unable to withstand a cholera attack, he died in Munich, Holy Week, 1838.

We have in Möhler the thinker of the times who is most gifted in theology and also least influenced by idealism. Quickly forgotten after 1848, his ideas were to spring Roman Catholicism open after the long, narrowing reigns of Pius IX and Pius XII. His fresh approach to the theology of church and tradition will have a profound impact at the Second Vatican Council.

3. Johann Evangelist Kuhn

J. E. Kuhn was born just about the time Schelling was moving from Würzburg to Munich, in 1806. Kuhn pursued the typical educational pattern for the priesthood: the prescribed internship of pastoral ministry followed five years at the Wilhelmstift, the Catholic seminary at Tübingen. There, from 1825 to 1830, his professors were Drey for dogmatic theology, Möhler for church history and J. B. Hirscher for moral theology. He studied philosophy with K. A. Eschenmayer, a scholar long engaged in appreciative employment of Schelling's thought.[31]

On Jacobi and Schelling

It was Eschenmayer who in 1812 had tried to reconcile an angry Schelling with his less gifted critic Jacobi. Hirscher's theology, too, had absorbed philosophy through the filter of Jacobi: his ethics strove to find a basic, transcendental form, and, not unlike Sailer, he located that organizing point for morality in the ideas of the love of God and faith. These were the primal forms of conscious life. Kuhn's theology changed as the times changed, but its spirit reached back to Jacobi. The Tübingen theologian looked upon the Enlightenment as something that both Jacobi and Romanticism had overcome. During his career he moved through the great philosophers up to Hegel, and then, later in life, he drew back from idealism to the history of dogma.

Kuhn won a prize in 1830 for an essay comparing Jacobi's thought to other systems of German philosophy, especially to Schelling's. After gaining his doctorate, Kuhn's writings and personal study stayed with the problems of fundamental theology and the philosophy of religion. The ground and nature of knowledge and a legitimate objectivity surrounded any presentation of faith and revelation. In a first essay on speculative Christian philosophy, Kuhn looked further into revelation and philosophy. Granted the intricacies of the idealists' analyses of the highest spheres of knowing, and granted that philosophy encompasses the depths and limits of human knowledge (even knowledge about the absolute), theology is knowledge about something else: Christianity. What is marginal for nature and reason is central for theology: history. The philosophy of religion, the philosophy of revelation, are history-grasped-as-science. "The philosophy of Christian revelation," he concluded, "is the presence of Christ revealed historically not dialectically."[32] The necessary analysis of other religions and of primal revelation must not obscure either the uniqueness of Christ or Christ's inclusion of all worldviews in himself as the *logos* of God made concrete and active in history. Romanticism, Tübingen theology and an awareness of some sterility in idealism had already pushed the younger theologians such as Möhler and then Kuhn ahead to history and to its two theological forms favored at Tübingen: revelation and church.

As we saw with Möhler, nineteenth-century academia had the custom of qualifying a university professor by funding him for "a scientific journey," a trip to excellent centers and renowned professors of his choosing. This gave him a view into the contemporary milieu and problems of his own field. Significantly, Kuhn's first stop was Munich. In 1831 Schelling was lecturing there on the concluding sections of the philosophy of mythology and beginning the philosophy of revelation. We do not know how long Kuhn stayed in Munich but we are surprised to learn that in a public discussion he rather challenged Schelling.[33] At the end of his trip Kuhn suddenly found himself professor for New Testament studies at Giessen; at twenty-six, he was Staudenmaier's colleague. First publications told the academic world that the young scholar's interest, however, lay not with exegesis but with philosophy in theology.

Subjectivity, Revelation and Myth

Kuhn's first book surveyed modern philosophy from Kant to Hegel. What is striking about his treatment of Schelling is that he focuses on the early and middle Schelling:

> From that spectacular period that began for philosophy in 1780 with Kant and Jacobi, and was heightened by Fichte at the turn of the century, one man stands out. The rich magnificence of his spirit filled his perceptive contemporaries with wonder and respect: F. W. J. Schelling. The influence that this hero among philosophers, through his writings and lectures, exercised upon his age is a matter of history and cannot lose anything of its value even if we view his opinions on solving the problems of philosophy as far from successful.[34]

Kuhn assumed as fundamental to theology Schelling's philosophy of a dialectic between the real and the ideal rooted in the identity given by the absolute spirit. The absolute's parallel being in *Natur* and *Geist* still held the imagination of thinkers. Schelling is not a pantheist, Kuhn concluded, because he philosophized about the form of consciousness and not about objects made into God. The philosopher's early theory of insight is significant because it is a faithlike principle. Kuhn applauded the move of the center of thought from world to God, but doubted that this shift had been carried off successfully. One has the impression that Kuhn was sympathetic to Schelling's philosophy of identity as a background to religion, but mistrusted it as a theology of revelation where access to God should come from historical revelation and not from the consciousness of being. When Kuhn asked whether Schelling had been attentive to experience, the question was addressed to the early Schelling, and not to the philosopher of positive existence. "Idealism will remain perpetually the weapon for science and the support of realism," Kuhn concluded as he himself set out to find a course between pantheism and theism.[35]

All of Germany was involved in debate with D. F. Strauss over his life of Jesus, and Kuhn wanted to deepen his knowledge of scripture as a preparation for confronting that sensational work. The New Testament, he concluded, was not best viewed as a Palestinian mythology nor was it

well exegeted through concepts such as consciousness and life. The
gospels were a historical record of a unique revelation. Kuhn's controversy with Strauss has some bearing upon Catholic theologians' stance
toward Schelling. As early as 1802, Schelling had analyzed myth as the
expression in idealism of religion, and his final system was one of God's
becoming himself extrinsically in the processes of the world. This
exoteric evolution was first recorded in myth. Some Roman Catholics
viewed sympathetically the idealist's exaltation of myth as a medium, a
bridge between historical revelation and ontology. Strauss's psychological reduction of Jesus' miracles to myths projected by consciousness was,
however, a further but different understanding of myth in the religious
thought of the nineteenth century.

We cannot decide here how Strauss and the generations of demythologizers who followed him were influenced by Romantic idealism,
by pioneers of myth such as Schlegel and Görres. What is clear is that
Strauss and his disciples understood myth, and its presence in Christianity, quite differently from Schelling, Görres and their mentor Creuzer.
Schelling affirmed an idealist sublimation, universalization and realization of a religious event in the developing life of God; in the development
of history, the mythical core yielded to the religious truth and then to the
idealist insight. Myth was an earlier, not later, form of religious truth—
and it was not a psychological insight set free from its religious trappings.
The Roman Catholic theologians did not agree with Schelling's philosophy of mythology, as we have seen, but they seem to have appreciated the
style of the philosophical enterprise, something that was lacking in their
reviews of Tübingen Protestant demythologizers.

Kuhn's Critique of Schelling

Kuhn succeeded Drey as professor for dogmatic theology in the
Catholic Tübingen faculty. During the years following 1839, he read
deeply in philosophy, studying anew Hegel, Schleiermacher and Schelling as well as Hermes and Bautain. The times seemed to call for a
summing up of Schelling, and so in Drey's Tübingen journal he published
a critique. It is 1844; in Berlin, Schelling will soon cease lecturing because his audiences have grown small; Kierkegaard and Bakunin have
absented themselves from the lectures; Paulus, his colleague turned
enemy, has surreptitiously published a student's record of the final system.

Kuhn's article began by comparing Schelling's earlier, negative philosophy of concepts with the new, positive philosophy of being; it ended with an interpretation of Christ in the *Philosophy of Revelation*. Kuhn showed a lack of interest in the era of Fichte, as he dismissed the early periods in Schelling's thought as "only a game with concepts, not a science."[36] The philosophical affirmation that God can be real only if he exists in history and discloses himself in nature and history was typical of its time and must be judged as too close to pantheism, too subject-centered. The entire approach of the early Schelling was mistaken, because it forgot that philosophy is not an exclusively *a priori*, lordly theory but a gift of experience.

Next Kuhn claims that the positive philosophy has not admitted experience. Schelling differs from Hegel by treating the godhead as origin, as the beginning of all, even of God. The philosopher cannot escape a basic difficulty even by a strong move toward Christianity; biblical religion is monotheistic but Schelling, since the *Essay on Freedom* (1809), is always exploring a God whose being is process and duality or trinity. The Schelling system only works if, in its origins, God and the triune powers of God are distinct from each other and separate from the ground of the godhead. "The personal being of God," Kuhn wrote, "cannot be—potentially or really—mediated through nondivine or extradivine beings."[37]

The longest section of Kuhn's essay argues that Christian revelation really ends not in a transcendental ontology of divine self-realization but in a revealed teaching based upon history. Schelling erred: Christianity is not philosophy or idealism, but godly revelation in history. The person of Christ brings not ontological harmony but a teaching, a life and a grace. Schelling indiscriminately mixed concepts and events, and so he never reached the stratum of history, the marrow of life. Kuhn himself was moving from ontology to history and his criticism showed that shift. Schelling cannot in fact do justice to history's colors, and revelation is ultimately history. Because of the philosopher's preoccupation with a God who is becoming, the theology of freedom is weak, and salvation seeks out freedom. For Schelling, history is only material, philosophy only hermeneutic; for Kuhn, revelation is God's word in history, and there are hermeneutics in faith and community as well as in science.

At the end of his essay, Kuhn pondered his own era, the epoch of the great system-makers, a time coming to an end. The imbalance of that age had been caused by the drive to build the definitive system, and to build it alone. Life is too diverse to be imprisoned in one system. Schelling struggled over and over to fashion a union of all that fell under "science" and "revelation." He wanted that symphony to be fully his own, unrelated to the past giants in theology and philosophy, all of whom were judged by their success or failure in anticipating Schelling. This compulsion for the one, eternal system was a gnostic illusion, Kuhn declared: "It was only a dream of science, a dream of power that turned out inevitably to be powerless."[38]

In a strange paradox, Kuhn turned to Hegel for guidance into the realm of the objective. Hegel seemed to present better the dialectical resolution of the varied powers of history than Schelling did. Hegel's God might be incomplete in the midst of history, but Schelling's philosophy of history was a mosaic, many of whose fragments were floating in the air of abstraction. Even though he had founded objective idealism and despite his assertion that his was a philosophy of existence, his thought seemed too cerebral:

> In Kuhn we find a definite turn from the Romantic philosophy of Schelling as the bearer of helpful categories for theology to Hegel's philosophy of spirit. This move had already been pointed out by Möhler. Kuhn shifts the center of interest away from knowing, from the living and the organic, to a transcendental objectivity of spirit and its structure, and thence to the community of the faithful. Now dogmatic teachings and ecclesiastical statements are not forms of a living consciousness, even of the community, but the conceptual formulation of the objective, Christian spirit.[39]

In his early forties, as the revolutionary year 1848 approached, Kuhn's life underwent some changes. He reduced his theological work and entered politics as a member of the Stuttgart parliament. When he returned to the life of a theologian, he set aside his conversation with speculative minds and turned to patristic and medieval thought. His essays on the history of dogma centered not on the post-Kantian philosophers but upon Augustine:

> There are three reasons for this change in approach. First, idealist philosophy had lost its power, and the philosophy of history had become historicism—the desire to know with von Ranke "how it really was." At the same time, Kuhn was deeply involved in controversy with F.C. Baur's school at Tübingen. Finally, Möhler's

move to the first centuries of Christianity affected him (as it did Newman and Döllinger). This move to early Christian sources is connected to the first reason: the fading of idealist philosophy.[40]

Kuhn stood at an intersection where transcendental philosophy met the objectivity of Scripture and historical revelation. He found Hermes and Günther excessive in their rationalism, and Schelling and Hegel too fixed in a philosophy of process. The old giants such as Jacobi and Baader were dead, figures from a time past. But the rising neoscholastics seemed to be only another rationalism with fresh propaganda, a theology with its own language and mental categories but not the lucid expression of faith that was needed.

The young Kuhn had never really known the era of Fichte, of the mature Goethe or of the young Schelling, and in his later years at Tübingen he was attacked or forgotten by the neoscholastics. He died at eighty-one, missing by only a dozen years the beginning of the twentieth century.

Catholics and Idealism: The Third Generation

Schelling, Baader and Görres were, by the late 1830s, men of an older generation. Hegel was dead, and the left-wing Hegelians in Berlin and Tübingen were attracting attention in theology as well as politics. The times were changing, slowly transforming world and thought. With the passing of decades, the freshness of idealism and Romanticism faded and became part of a world that was past. As often happens, a time of conservative retrospection—penetrating even into Tübingen—followed one of freedom and enthusiasm. What could not be denied was that Catholic theologians had gained for some years a strong sense of identity. Catholic theology was not ashamed of itself; it could confront D.F. Strauss and the memory of Hegel. By the time Schelling left Munich for Berlin, younger Catholic theologians no longer considered him a factor in their own development. They were independent, and were moving away from idealism. Neither Hegel nor Schelling had produced the final system to resolve the dialectic of finite and infinite, of understanding and faith.

Schelling had taught Landshut to think out of subjectivity, and he had taught Tübingen to think developmentally. What has remained from the work of these theologians is not their relationship with the great idealist philosophers but their own theological imagination. Even if changes within the nineteenth century chilled the summer of the Tübingen school, some of their approaches to Christianity had a permanent effect. The Tübingen professors struggled to integrate their discovery of the role of history in church and doctrine with philosophy, and complete success eluded their own systems.

This autumnal period, however, of the history of Roman Catholic theology and Romantic idealism portrays not failure or exhaustion but only an inevitable decline, a fading away of a once powerful era. The final word (and Möhler and Kuhn saw this) will belong to history and to process: not to Schelling's philosophy of history—the unfolding in cosmos and humanity of a God becoming—but to an ecumenical and social history of Western Christianity.

8

The Decline of the Munich Circle

MARTIN DEUTINGER AND Ignaz von Döllinger are the last figures in our history. Both were associated with Munich; neither was a theologian of the Tübingen school, and both were at the University of Munich, as professor or student, where they encountered Schelling. They differ, however, in the fields they mastered. Deutinger stood in the tradition of philosophers of religion and systematic theologians, whereas Döllinger was a church historian.

Against the repeated calls for a rejection of modern ways of apprehending self and world—sounds that grew in intensity after 1841— these thinkers took seriously the culture of the modern world and worked within the horizons of subjectivity and history. For different reasons each felt the need to write a final evaluation of Schelling and they both were actively present at the event that solemnly concluded an era of Catholic theology: the Assembly of German Scholars of 1864. Deutinger and Döllinger—their lives saw an end to this period in Germany of independent and modern Roman Catholic theology.

1. Martin Deutinger

Martin Deutinger was born in Upper Bavaria on Good Friday, 1815. At that time, Schelling, to the south, in Munich, was working seriously on the first draft of his *Ages of the World*. Deutinger began his career as a teacher in 1841, the year after his mentor Franz von Baader died and the year when Schelling moved to Berlin. Six years later Görres was dead and Ludwig I, under whose aegis the Munich Catholic restoration had unfolded, abdicated. The union of Catholic Romanticism and German transcendental philosophy as developed by Bavarian and Rhenish thinkers had come to an end.

Deutinger is the last Catholic intellectual of stature to accept Schelling's thought seriously and enthusiastically. Deutinger died at the age of forty-nine, in 1864. The meeting of scholars called together in Munich by Döllinger had just shown the deep fissure between the modern-German and the scholastic-Roman camps. Vatican I was only five years away.

In Schelling's Train

Martin Deutinger's father was a miller and his son delighted in the solitude of the mill and the flow of the stream. An uncle after whom Martin was named held all the important positions in the Munich archdiocese except that of bishop. This older ecclesiastic, who had been formed by Sailer, encouraged Martin not only to enter the priesthood but to pursue an academic career.

While attending *Gymnasium* at Munich and Freising, the young student of natural science and philosophy was captivated by Schelling's thought, "becoming so excited he ripped the buttons off his coat."[1] In 1832 Deutinger moved to the seminary of Dillingen (where, thirty years before, Zimmer and Weber, those very first disciples of Schelling, had pored over his early writings). There a convinced Schellingian, Hubert Beckers,[2] lectured on philosophy by expounding the works of Schelling's middle period—for example, the *Essay on Freedom*—and by drawing somewhat on the philosophy of myth and revelation then being presented in Munich. Deutinger longed for the *aula maxima* at Munich where he could hear the great man himself. But he feared the rumors might be true, and Schelling, irritated at the rigid methods of the new regime, would suddenly leave Munich.

Deutinger was soon fortunate enough to be able to pursue his theological and philosophical studies in Munich. Schelling was still there presenting in those semesters his tripartite philosophy of religion. The positive philosophy of existence and Christianity began with an ontology of idealism. A history of modern philosophy was inserted into this "grand introduction," all of which only prepared for the vast history of mythology. Finally came the fulfillment, the concretization of the philosophy of myth in the revelation of the Second Power of the Godhead, Christ. This was still a time of a fluid melding of philosophy and theology, and Deutinger's occupation for most of his life was philosophy: the philosophical questions basic to all science and life, the philosophy of psychology and morality, the philosophy of art and religion. In the young, meditative but excitable priest, we find the Romantic triad: nature, art and religion.

Between 1833 and 1835, Deutinger heard Schelling on God, myth and revelation; Baader on speculative dogmatics and natural philosophy; Görres on universal history and theosophy. During those years the intellectual climate of Bavarian Catholicism was such that preparation for the priesthood could be undertaken in classrooms where professors like Baader, Görres, Döllinger and Schelling lectured. To look through Deutinger's notes of lectures attended is to see that he was strongly influenced by Baader and Görres in the area of Christian philosophy.[3] Deutinger was from his first student years a zealous hearer of Schelling and reader of his writings. His marginal comments in copies of Schelling's works show clearly that the early philosophy of nature and the conceptualization of freedom influenced him in a search for his own principles.

The *Essay on Freedom*, however, left his mind stimulated but dissatisfied. Schelling had not solved the issue of the relationship of the absolute to the world, of human to divine freedom. The library at the Georgianum, the ducal seminary next to the University of Munich, contains Deutinger's own careful recension of Schelling's lectures on the philosophy of revelation. Franz von Baader's influence was stronger. Baader was not so much a source for particular ideas as the mentor of a general approach. He sustained young Deutinger's fundamentally subject-centered analysis of thinking and belief, showing that the great Christian mystics approach the relationship of self to God and God to world rather as Schelling, Görres and Baader did. Although the orthodox mystics never bothered to question, deny or replace the objectivity of their Christianity (for instance, the sacraments, the life of Christ), they did quietly move those elements to the side. Their objectivity stood in the shadow of the subjectivity of the godhead. Deutinger agreed with Baader that the mystics showed a profound subjectivity, which was met by an equally forceful objective revelation of divine life.

From the older philosopher, Deutinger drew also a commitment to the Trinity as a cornerstone of all thought, for Baader never tired of repeating that the Trinity was the highest principle of all being, life and knowing. Despite his sometimes bizarre systematizing with numbers, Baader developed trinitarian theology in a far more traditional manner than did Hegel or Schelling. Trinity was a *factum* for him; the triune God before creation was the absolute mystery and not the product of an idealist view of God in self-development.[4]

Deutinger, at first inclined toward botany or art history, was drawn to philosophy and theology when he read Möhler's *Symbolik*. He wrote:

"[Möhler's] *Symbolik* is being discussed everywhere and I want to gain my own view of it."[5] In 1837 the young man who dreamt of a chair at Munich was ordained. After four years in pastoral work and with essays published in Görres's *Historisch-politische Blätter*, he became professor of philosophy at the clerical lyceum in Freising near Munich. Time was available for him to read deeply in the theologians and philosophers whom this period favored—Augustine, Erigena, Pseudo-Denys, Tauer—and to study more thoroughly the professors he had just heard in Munich, and Anton Günther. Deutinger's first lectures and courses covered almost all the areas of philosophy. At twenty-seven he worked to arrange them into a possible encyclopedia of philosophy, which he began to publish in 1843. These volumes interest us because they show a young, gifted seminary professor developing what he esteemed to be the right philosophical approach for Roman Catholicism. We will look first at Deutinger's usage of an idealist format for this system, and then look more closely at his relationship to Schelling by presenting his critique of Schelling's last system.

Man is knowing subjectivity. Deutinger began his system with the customary analysis of the powers of knowing and willing. Objects not only focus and limit but realize human subjectivity. Our being finds itself not in dialogue with abstract being but with being made concrete. Deutinger's approach is that of objective and developmental idealism tempered with a Roman Catholic affirmation of the objectivity of creation and the history of revelation.[6] A first volume of preliminary methodological questions about the nature of knowing moves through an extensive psychology to a metaphysics of thought. Concept, idea, dialectic and system are all pillars of this moderately idealist structure.

What is striking is the presence in Deutinger of psychology. Instead of idealist epistemology drawn out at length, a "phenomenology" explores the characteristics of being a person. The pages at the end of the third volume execute a move—very much in the style of the philosophical systematicians of the nineteenth century—from knowing to the highest knower and known, that which in itself presents an identity of knowing and being. The psychological interest of Deutinger is present in his discussion of the limits, the temporality, the freedom for self-determination in each individual.[7] But they do not exist in a vacuum. Existence, nature, freedom—all presume a ground, for in us they are neither self-grounding nor self-explanatory. This primal ground we call God, who is beyond both knowing and being.[8] Repeating a phrase popular with Schelling, Deutinger wrote: "God is not a being or Being, but the Lord of Being."[9] The philosopher then deftly drew the conclusion that the absolute personality cannot be a solitary being but must be triune.

It is not clear whether Deutinger was unfolding the congruence of Christian revelation with philosophy, or whether he held that idealist metaphysics does ground and explain what revelation affirms: the trinitarian, inner life of God. The system at this point makes no distinction between philosophy, theology and revelation as it moves swiftly from epistemology and ontology to Trinity. A comment that was a final warning concluded this philosophy of self and God amid thinking and being: God's freedom is not a freedom to become something other than he is but a freedom to create. So, unlike Schelling, Deutinger saw process and personhood not as forming the inner life of a God becoming but as enabling the freedom of a perfect God to create.[10]

This first philosophical system was a subjective psychology; it was also an objective idealism whose absolute ground is a God with traditional attributes bestowed upon him by Christianity. Not only in the title of positive philosophy, but in the approach of objective idealism and the problematic of creation, the world of Schelling is still present.

The Decline of Munich

With a doctorate from Würzburg and a many-volumed system in print, Deutinger still had to wait until 1846 for a position at the University of Munich. Döllinger was there, the aged Görres still lectured, but Baader was dead and Schelling had moved to Berlin. The young professor had a success in philosophy that, some said, had not been seen since Schelling's departure. The lecture hall was too small for the number of hearers, and the courses in thought and aesthetics again attracted government officials and artists as well as students. It seemed possible that Deutinger would introduce a new generation of brilliance.

Deutinger began:

Every person in the revelation of that life and thought which is within only proceeds from there outward. . . . This search and delineation of the highest ground of knowing we call philosophy. Philosophy, then, is an essential task of human life. Before we come to a termination for philosophy, time itself will have ended.[11]

This professorship lasted less than a year. Deutinger was caught up in the private and political scandals that surrounded Ludwig I in 1847. These events should not have concerned a scholar at work in Ludwig's Bavarian Florence. Nevertheless, through their wasting influence upon the king and their real destruction of his reign, they became a major factor in the decline of this bright time in Roman Catholic intellectual history in the past century. The smoldering violence in the years approaching 1848 discernible throughout the German principalities was not absent from Bavaria. Ludwig's amorous obsession and political malaise were about to ruin or leave incomplete the bright promises of the 1820s. With the rigid minister Abel anxious for the power of a Montgelas but without the openness and talent of that prince of the Enlightenment, steps were taken to control all who lectured on religion at the university. As we shall see, Schelling felt these measures; insulted, he was happy to leave for Berlin. Deutinger's tongue was sharp and he spoke too strongly about the behavior of the court and the vagaries of the king. He lost his position in 1847, as did Döllinger and others.

Döllinger quickly regained his position, but Deutinger did not. Exiled to Dillingen, he was saluted as a hero. The philosopher, however, hated Dillingen, his "Patmos," and he suffered until he could return to Munich. That was not to be until 1858. The years in exile allowed him to pursue new studies, and he puzzled over the relationship of modern philosophy to earlier thinkers—for instance, Cusanus. He gave himself to the needs of the clergy, founding conferences, publishing editions of Christian classics, founding a short-lived periodical (a cousin to Görres's *Eos*) named *Siloah*. This "journal for religious progress within the church" reviewed theology and politics, science and art.

Deutinger undertook trips to enjoy a world he deeply loved: art. Florence, Rome, Prague, Dresden, Paris found him admiring the displays of their museums. What is particularly interesting is that this philosopher came to art and life not simply as a viewer, but as a photographer. He took thousands of pictures with this new invention after 1850 and collected twenty thousand photos, sketches and reproductions to prepare for something novel: an illustrated history of Western art. But no publisher saw its merit.

Deutinger and Romantic Idealism

Deutinger composed a lengthy philosophy of art that showed some resemblance to Schelling's history of myth in the *Philosophy of Mythol-*

ogy. For Deutinger, poetry and religion are both revealed expressions of the same absolute. They are the externalization in appearance of its identity of knowing, willing and being. Mythology and art, whether Egyptian or Greek, display in history modes of the way we look at God. Polytheism, monotheism, pantheism are cultural results inseparable from their parallels in art and poetry.[12] What Deutinger scarcely alluded to was, of course, at the heart of Schelling's theory: the cultural process where poetry and religion are one in realizing diverse ways of the pleroma of God's life. For Schelling, in the world's religions and arts God is displaying his process of self-becoming; for Deutinger, God is above cultural evolution. Art leads to religion, to Christianity. "There is that awe before being like to God, before the heavenly descent and calling which has become active and firm in the human person." As Schelling had once proclaimed that art was the fulfillment of philosophy and then later that Christianity was the fulfillment of myth, so Deutinger wrote, "Christianity is the true fulfillment of art."[13]

It is interesting to read Deutinger's evaluation of Romanticism. The issues this movement faced, some decades past, were, he wrote, those of full freedom, of the overcoming of dualism, of imagination, intuition and mysticism. "The Romantic school developed itself maturely out of a kind of active analogy with Schelling's thought; between both emerged the new, real-ideal poetry of *Weltschmerz*, which in its deepest structures finds fulfillment in Hegelianism."[14]

Martin Deutinger's writings show that he, too, belonged to the age of the great system-builders such as Schelling, Hegel, Görres, Baader. He was primarily a philosopher and secondly a theoretician of art, and in these interests he resembled Friedrich Schlegel. When he turned to theology, as a capstone to his philosophical tomes, or, at the end of his life, as exegesis, he chose themes that were popular with the Protestant and Catholic faculties at Tübingen. He shared a memory, increasingly faint, of the rejection of the Enlightenment with its superb contempt for the emotional and the mysterious. He had been educated in Catholic circles that viewed Hegel negatively and no longer expected a profound resolution to the problem of faith and thought to come from Schelling.

Deutinger's philosophical approach, however, proceeded from subjectivity as the place where knowing and being met; his language was that of transcendental analysis. "The first foundation for the spirit that reaches thought is the unchanging being of the human person; from that being outward, a movement to knowable objects is possible."[15] Yet he criticized the modern systems of mind and process even as he employed them. He lived at the edge of an era, and at the end of his life he found himself isolated intellectually. His theological career from 1836 to 1861 passed from systems of Greek and idealist philosophy through an aestheticism of sculpture and painting to a final apologetic drawn from the Johannine writings.

As storm clouds covered the sky of German culture between 1848 and 1864, Deutinger fought for an open theology: "To exclude," he wrote, "is not Catholic. For Catholicism feels at home with the general and the universal, and brings into itself all the treasures of nature and life. Excluding nothing but sin, the Catholic ethos ennobles, spiritualizes and divinizes all natural powers. This universality is not indifference to opposition and error when faced with the knowledge of divine truth, but the highest truth, which assumes all contradictions into its solution."[16] Here is Deutinger's *Aufhebung* and it is Catholicism, not idealism, that provides the higher principle, even if metaphysics and history must be contemplated without fear. Every era must be taken on its own terms; the Middle Ages are an exemplary epoch where a synthesis once occurred, but they are past. Deutinger invoked the venerable spirit of Sailer to support the tradition of an open philosophy and theology, which had been active for over half a century in Landshut and Munich.

A Critique of Schelling

In his youth, Deutinger, and some of his lesser known contemporaries, were still translating motifs from Schelling and Hegel into Catholic thought. Some hold that Deutinger was, among Roman Catholics, even at this late date, a particularly perceptive reader of Hegel and Schelling.[17] But by 1845 Deutinger concluded that what Schelling had aimed for was an impossibility: the philosopher had been trapped by human subjectivity and by divine necessity. True, Schelling had improved upon his earlier metaphysics and had labored over a positive, Christian philosophy, but it had not done justice to revelation. The consciousness of time is at fault; the tension in the relationship of God to the world is imperfectly resolved. In 1855, a year after Schelling's death, Deutinger, not university professor but university preacher, was composing for his last philosophical work, *The Principle of Recent Philosophy and Christian Knowledge*, a chapter on "Schelling's Final System of Philosophy."

What Schelling was about was the renewal of philosophy through the principles of both authority and freedom. Of the great philosophers after Kant, he came closest to the correct method of a positive philosophy. "Schelling stood for a Christian and positive philosophy in contrast to the logical absolutism of Hegelian thought, which misrepresented every particle of individuality and freedom."[18] But, Deutinger asked, did he succeed? "Schelling's new, later, positive philosophy is a speculative-historical system, which contains . . . individual sections that are truly great." The later system is still not published, Deutinger observed, but notes offer enough information to evaluate it, which Deutinger subsequently did in detail.

Schelling impressed favorably many of his hearers in his lectures in Munich in the 1830s, but the changes he had made were not radical enough. He had taken from Baader rather than from Hegel an affirmation of freedom for God and for history, but he did not go far enough in relating correctly God's freedom and nature to creation: "The result is that we have now only a historical pantheism in the place of Hegel's logical system."[19] Sadly, Schelling had not passed beyond the "old leaven" of the immanence of things in the divine being.

Schelling wanted to go beyond the *Vernunft* of Kant and the *Logik* of Hegel to being. This philosophy, however, should not imply that God is a being like us, but that being is godly. Schelling developed "the idea of an absolute self-conscious *Geist* in which all the lines of world and history develop and run rogether as will and beginning."[20] But, Deutinger argued, Schelling did not fully succeed, because he ignored the distinction between logic and theory, and the reality of world and God. Although it intended to be a positive philosophy of existence, Schelling's final system had no real content: for him, God enters history not to act as God but to become God. Moreover, the "history" into which God enters in Schelling's thought is not real history. Schelling wanted a philosophy of God-in-history, but what he produced was not God in history but God in the soul: in the individual and collective consciousness of peoples. If God is bound to this process of revelation in spiritual personality, he is not free.

The history of mythology can be convincingly proposed as a process of God-consciousness in the human race. It is something else to see the same process as that of God becoming himself. Mythology does not in fact bear witness to an essential revelatory moment of God, of a God passing from the natural to the free. Schelling had not made philosophy Christian, Deutinger concluded, but he had christianized philosophy. God's free activity in history has been transformed backward into an unfree cosmogony. Neither a real God nor a real world history can come from an "eternal but blind Being." Schelling's trinity, the "Potencies," are cold and impersonal. These three powers, an ill-conceived leitmotif for divine development, undermine the incarnation and creation, the Trinity whether as Creator or Savior. For Schelling, Jesus Christ would seem to be not an incarnation, a God becoming man but, rather, a becoming of God. The human personality stands between nature and will, before free creation and free revelation of a God beyond. This ambiguity of the human condition is absent in Schelling's philosophy.

There are great sections and ideas in Schelling, Deutinger sums up, but:

> This is not a philosophy for the future but one that rests on its past reputation. Nothing more can be done with it—as we have known for some time. What consoles us is a feeling that, nevertheless, this philosophy goes beyond every positive sublimation of the Spirit in philosophy to date. What we also sense is sorrow, the sorrow of a paganism sensing that its redemption is most near precisely when that paganism is conscious of its own untenability and abandonment.[21]

Deutinger had returned to Munich as university preacher in 1858. Aesthetical pursuits continued but philosophical work was set aside in favor of biblical research. His second period in Munich was a time of sermons, lectures in Scripture, writing in art. Although he was only in his forties, his eyes and nerves were failing. No professorship was available. He was psychically shaken by his own failure to unite the various fields of academia. Schelling had failed him, as had Günther. Those geniuses, Baader and Görres, had produced no system that held.

Deutinger's last public appearance was in connection with the extraordinary assembly of German Catholic intellectuals held in Munich in 1863. The goal of Döllinger's congress was the reconciliation of the division between the older idealist thinkers and the younger neoscholastics. Döllinger hoped to save something of the vitality of the first half of the century. Deutinger gave a major address, which was ignored. He seemed in his presentation of a vague metaphysics of freedom like a voice from the past. Broken by further discouragement and fatigue, he was dead within a year. Deutinger was a figure who lived between the times. His interests in Schelling, art, in a system of knowing and subjectivity, were of another time. Moreover, he had been born too early to comprehend the next period of the nineteenth century, after 1848. Younger than Döllinger but distracted from theology by aesthetics and idealism, he thought out of that earlier time of synthesis.

Deutinger as a student heard Schelling lecture on revelation and myth. Surprisingly, he also found riches in the earlier philosophies of identity and nature. In fact, he tended to employ the early Schelling's philosophy of identity in his philosophy and to critique, from the perspective of a believer and a theologian, the final philosophy of Christianity. Nevertheless, in both his distance from and his devotion to the great idealist, he—and his words at Schelling's death—sum up the era as it draws to a close:

> For all who ever heard his lectures or read his rich writings, the memory of Schelling will always remain in the highest honor. There is no one who has the least real acquaintance with the profound intellectual production of this man, regardless of how his views are linked to the thought of Schelling, who is not filled with extraordinary respect toward him. His spiritual greatness called forth the astonishment of our century.[22]

2. Ignaz von Döllinger

Ignaz Döllinger absorbed through family and education the atmosphere that fashioned the Catholic renaissance in southern Germany. Nevertheless, he is a figure from a later period in the nineteenth century. He experienced intensely the transition that took place after 1848 from the systematic theology of Romantic idealism to neoscholasticism and historicism. He fought for the right for Roman Catholic theology to speak out of and to a particular time.

As the presses poured out his essays and tomes, the decades passed; Döllinger tried to dissuade Rome from self-serving power, and he pleaded with German intellectuals not to surrender their creative freedom. After many controversies, from the vantage point of the year 1871, the great historian looked back at a time forty years earlier as the Munich University life began, and among many things recalled "Schelling's lectures, rich in their Platonic beauty, majesty, flowing."[23]

The Döllinger Tradition

J.J.I. von Döllinger not only lived in but through the nineteenth century. He was born in 1799 as the Romantics gathered in Jena were visiting Goethe and meeting Schelling; he died in 1890 as Sigmund Freud was exploring the phenomenon of hysteria. A career that began in 1826 with his first published book reached through many periods of German intellectual life. In his childhood the Enlightenment mixed with Franconian Catholic piety. Döllinger's father enriched his own life with a friendship with Sailer; later in Görres's circle the son learned about politics, papal and Prussian, and from Möhler he absorbed a new attitude toward Protestantism, at once more open and more critical.

We have already met the Döllinger family. Döllinger *père* was a medical colleague of Marcus, Schelling's propagandist among the physicians and professors at Bamberg. With Schelling's arrival in Bamberg in 1800, Ignaz Döllinger senior found the new, Romantic philosophy of nature to be the right format for the work he was doing in anatomy and embryology. He helped reform biology around the idea of organic polarities in tension, and he advocated for medical practice the guiding search for a dynamic balance of physical forces. Döllinger and Schelling joined the faculty of the University of Würzburg together in 1803, and their friendship grew over the next three years. Schelling worked with Döllinger, as well as with Röschlaub, Oken, Windischmann and other Catholic scientists, on the periodical *Jahrbücher der Medizin als Wissenschaft*, which he edited with Marcus during the Würzburg years.[24] The young Döllinger knew Schelling as his father's friend.

The father expected achievement from the son. He undertook his instruction in French, and the boy made such progress in Greek that he soon surpassed his teachers. By the end of his *Gymnasium*, he had learned Italian, Spanish and English. Würzburg was a crossroads of Napoleon's enterprises in Germany and Austria. As a boy in 1812, Döllinger followed one day the French emperor as he made his inspection: "in his green coat, the three-cornered hat on his head, with a sharply honed face with dark skin—like a bronze statue." Later, as with Görres, he would exchange admiration for dislike; both were angered by Napoleon's treatment of Pius VII. Johann Ignaz entered at seventeen the University of Würzburg and, after a few years of general and theological studies, he moved to the seminary at Bamberg. It was 1820, and his decision to commit himself to church and theology was firm.

It is significant that Döllinger did not attend the Catholic faculty at Tübingen. Unlike Möhler and Kuhn, unlike Staudenmaier (born the same year as Döllinger), he stood outside the Tübingen school. His contact with all that was modern was of the older sort. It came through the university world of his father, and recognized Schelling as a center of its aspirations. In Döllinger's first years at the university there was marked influence from the time of Romantic idealism, which in the 1820s was enjoying a final climax. At Bamberg, Döllinger pursued oriental languages and the study of the Greek fathers. Feeling the attraction of theology and particularly of the history of theological expression in the church, he set aside the natural sciences and philosophy for historical theology.

Ordination and pastoral activity were followed by a teaching position at a new lyceum in Aschaffenburg. Not far away was Mainz where he came into contact with the politico-religious life of the Rhine, meeting with priests who protested in theology and politics the Prussian oppression of the Rhineland. Their periodical *Der Katholik* was soon to be edited by Görres. Döllinger, intrigued by the writings of Friedrich Schlegel and Franz von Baader, drew up a plan for a theological encyclopedia to be written jointly with the Mainz theologians. That, however, would take considerable time.

A first book appeared in 1826, *The Eucharist in the First Three Centuries*. Praised by Möhler and others, it brought its author first fame. Ludwig I recognized a new talent and offered the young scholar the position of extraordinary professor of church history at Munich. From Landshut came a doctorate.

> The professorship for Döllinger at Munich, just at this time when his powers were beginning to burst forth, brought a decisive direction to his life. The Bavarian capital under Ludwig I was blooming into a European metropolis. To this city and to this university Döllinger remained true the rest of his life.[25]

Döllinger and Schelling: Idealism and History

Döllinger's long and productive life can be divided into three periods. The first concerns us because it coincides with Schelling's time in Munich after 1827. Döllinger was an active participant in the Munich restoration as it flourished in politics and religious science before meeting the conservative rebuffs and forces of the 1840s.

A second period ran from 1848 to the shock of Vatican I where the will of Pius IX brushed aside the views of the famous historian. For our history, this second period is important, too, for it is the epilogue to this history. At that time, in 1863, Döllinger called for an assembly of German intellectuals to face the split between historians, theologians and philosophers accustomed to work within the culture of their century, and a new generation that advocated scholasticism as the metaphysics of Christianity and as the judge of all theologies.

The third period of Döllinger's life, from his seventieth to his ninetieth year, was a time of disappointment and isolation. Uninvited to Vatican I, angered by the condescending neglect of his research by Roman scholars, he continued to reject the new papal dogma, which he evaluated as a product of an unfinished council and an immature ecclesiology.

When we turn back to the early years in Munich after 1827, we know that Döllinger's circle of colleagues and friends was not that of Schelling. The younger man was deeply Roman Catholic, and was impressed with Baader, who still labored over his image-filled mystical schemata. The circle around Görres was also important; the publication of *Eos* and the *Historisch-politische Blätter* drew the young historian into sorties amid the ebb and flow of battles over politics and religion. In Görres's house he met European intellectuals, experts in scientific research, students of mystical texts, and philosophers still struggling to bring all of this into one system. His gift for language, an asceticism channeled into immense work, an analytic mind in quest of the central form (the *Idee*), a genius for tracing problems to their social and historical roots—these were characteristics that made him a support for the aging professor of history, Görres. Döllinger was singularly free of competitiveness: he sought out friends and contacts; letters flowed to Bishop Dupanloup, to John Henry Newman, to Gladstone, to Kolping, the founder of German social action.

One interesting group of travelers to Munich illustrates the power of Munich Catholicism in which Schelling was a still active if aloof presence: Félicité de Lamennais and his companions visited the Isar capital in 1832. The French theologian of society and revolution had long conversations with the leading figures, not only with Görres and Döllinger but with Schelling. Hopes ran high for an intellectual alliance between France and Germany. Montalambert, Rio, Lacordaire were convinced that Schelling *au fond* was Roman Catholic, and that his philosophy (which they knew only by report) had reached a point where primal realities displayed themselves in ways congenial to the Catholic mind. Lacordaire, famous preacher and co-worker with de Lamennais, and soon to be famous as one of the restorers of religious life, planned to study with Schelling at length. De Lamennais wrote his impression of Schelling: "My admiration goes out to his marvelous genius as does my friendship for his person. He is someone in the world with whom my thought has much in common. If we had the time to penetrate each other's thought, we would find we are in accord on the essence of things."[26] At Christmas, 1833, Montalambert wrote to de Lamennais from Munich: "His sympathy for you surpasses that for all others."[27]

The Frenchmen went on to Rome, there to face papal severity and, of course, Schelling had no intention of abandoning his sovereign role as philosopher (which he had claimed since he was nineteen) for a renewal scheme of French Catholics. Sebastian Lösch nicely sums up the relationship: "The Tübingen *Stift*, from which Schelling came forth, and La Chenaie, where de Lamennais now lived apart from the world, were geographically too far apart to be able to come together on philosophical ultimates."[28]

As we saw, Döllinger knew the world of idealism and Romanticism. But, in 1827, when the most prominent Roman Catholics were constructing systems, Döllinger perceived the impotency of that endeavor. For him, threads from idealism and Romanticism led clearly to history: not to the history of consciousness and the historicity of existence, but to the facts of history. History, too, helped theology, for the great moments of the church's past explained how and why Christians believed as they did.

In a first church history, published in 1835, the language of Schelling is still present. The historian saw the organic elements in the church to be truths harmoniously fixed into a moving but total pattern. Schelling's explanation in 1802 of history as the privileged place of religion, of history yielding up to the scholar its construction of many facets, history as the unfolding of an idea, were not fully absent from the background of Döllinger's church history.[29] Nevertheless Döllinger had little sympathy for the superimposition of an epistemology and metaphysics upon the course of history. The ideas and themes of idealist philosophy may have been fruitful suggestions, useful background motifs, but they are no longer accepted as transcendental properties of the historian's consciousness; they are not the goal of history. History itself and not the system or the seminal idea comes first. "To curse the life-giving content of history," Döllinger wrote, "and to transform it into mere thought-products is to deface both science and reality. Rather, the interest in philosophy . . . has made room for history."[30] What the young Bavarian professor perceived clearly but stated with moderation was that Schelling's developmental idealism had prepared for history, and history had now replaced philosophy.

When Döllinger discussed scholarship and method, he moved away from the all-encompassing aura that had surrounded the knowing self since Kant. He agreed with Schelling that there is a unity to history that comes from its absolute source, God, and he gave a particular emphasis to the identity and limitations of the periods of history—each epoch is something unique and different. The revelation that Schelling casually announced to be present in history itself Döllinger found illusive. The meaning of the seemingly contradictory struggles and events of a time or a century do not give up their "revelation" so easily. Schelling and the other system-makers announced the revelatory meaning of history too facilely and they were not accustomed to tough research. For Schelling, idealism was the framework of history; for Döllinger history verified some of the thought-forms of philosophy after a struggle.[31]

Döllinger and Schelling both accepted history as developmental. Döllinger, whose specialty was Western Christian history, however, was not convinced that Schelling's vast system was truly developmental. The same few philosophical ideas appeared in each period: in the godhead, in Greek or Egyptian myths, in Christ. Schelling himself said that Christianity and paganism were not all that different.

Döllinger perceived dialectic, continuity and development in the church and in the history of theology; evolution bears dogma forward. Döllinger likened the evolution of the church's faith-consciousness to a seed from which a rare plant unfolds. Like Möhler, his friend, he held that the community's faith-consciousness analyzed in its historical periods holds the key for understanding change in theology. Theology is not an eternal system of beliefs but a history with life and birth, tension and distortion.[32]

A Final View of Schelling

Döllinger's historical sense both developed from and contrasted with the philosophy of history in Romantic idealism. In 1843, Döllinger assumed the role of theologian to write a lengthy article on Schelling's philosophy of revelation.[33] He left it unsigned. Schelling had gone to

Berlin; Döllinger was a prominent, independent thinker. Perhaps he wrote it as the summing up of an era coming to an end. That is certainly the tone of the piece. Regardless, the author of the article became known and caused Schelling pain to the north in Prussia. He was dismayed that the Catholic theologian was finding fault in his all too developmental system of world religion and Christianity.

A question began the essay: "Is Schelling's universal system truly a Christian theology, an explanation in thought of revelation and faith?" Schelling may believe so, but the fact is that there are insurmountable discrepancies between his views and the Christian understanding of Trinity, creation and incarnation. The idealist philosopher errs in thinking that myth and revelation come from the same source. They do not. Religion and myth may have a common source in the historical evolution of human consciousness; revelation, however, is not purely a product of *Geist* in history but is a divine act that is historical. The issue is the nature of God's contact with human life and God's elevation of history as message or church.

The correlate of revelation is faith. Does faith for Schelling involve power, commitment, trust and content, or is it only an educated reason speculating about its life? In Schelling's cosmogony, God appears to be blind and unfree, for he needs philosophers and believers to explain him; perhaps to explain him to himself. This worldview can only end up in dualism and pantheism. Schelling's philosophy of revelation chose Christ and the Trinity as the two important aspects of Christianity. For both Christianity and for Schelling's cosmogony, the greatest mystery is the Trinity. In Schelling, the three divine potencies externalize and realize the life of God. The source of all this, however, is the godhead behind God. This divine essence beyond its own powers is blind—blind because unspecified, unformed. God needs to be triune powers, and these need God, in order to be. Christ, the second power, is the objectivity of God; the incarnation and crucifixion are ultimate objectivity, ultimate in both the human and the divine spheres. Schelling praised Christ for accepting humiliation and alienation through his incarnation. In fact, Christ is not great because he is alien or obedient; Christ is not a player in a divine drama of self-realization. He is great because he is free. Jesus the Christ is a free messenger of God's gracious love for us. Only because God is complete can Christ be integral as God and man. Redemption is possible only to a finite person with real freedom. Human renewal is worth mentioning only as an action and event within God's freedom.

Döllinger turned, then, to an area in which he could claim some expertise: historical method. Schelling's method, he observed, is unsatisfactory. Why does this philosophy deserve the description "positive"? Where is the positive, scientific foundation for the exegesis of Scripture—for instance, the crucial *kenosis* passage in Paul? How accurate is Schelling's interpretation of mythologies? He seems to have little knowledge of the history of the Christian dogmas he treats. Döllinger's article differed from those authored by Kuhn and Staudenmaier. More simple in its Catholic orthodoxy, less philosophical, it lacked the reverence or the hope of a disciple. It is interesting to see the historian Döllinger raise the issue of method. Disciplined learning returns; Romanticism is questioned; before the roentgenizing lights of historical research, idealism seems to be only a skeleton.

Coda

Döllinger was a leader in Germany and in the German church. A delegate to the Frankfurt National Assembly in 1848, he was often theological advisor to the assemblies of German bishops and he served in the Bavarian state parliament. His research and publications, meanwhile, pursued topics of church history, and with increasing frequency, as the reign of Pius IX moved forward, he examined papal office and power. Döllinger rarely strayed from ecclesial interests: his three volumes (1848) on the Reformation were rather polemical; after 1854 and Pius IX's proclamation of the Immaculate Conception, he began to favor national political and ecclesiastical structures. The historian found himself (and Bavaria) caught between a powerful Rome and a state Protestantism— Prussia—which in his eyes had lost vigor and honesty. He was critical of Schelling's idea of a future synthesis of the three churches where the Petrine, Pauline and Johannine strands of Christianity came together. This was only an idea, not a political solution for divided Christendom.

After the appearance of Pius IX's *Syllabus Errorum* in 1864, the conflict in Döllinger between the man of the church and the historical researcher intensified. Papal infallibility was declared and Döllinger was unable to accept the Vatican Council's teaching. Rome forced the archbishop of Munich to excommunicate the aged scholar in 1871. Döllinger personally respected the excommunication and absented himself from priestly functions, but by order of Ludwig II, he remained *Probst* of the royal church of Bavaria, St. Cajetan's, until his death in 1890.[34]

Schelling married history with transcendental consciousness in 1800 and this become in 1827 the unfolding of all cosmic and world history. Developmental and objective idealism became in Döllinger history and historical research. Representing the younger Roman Catholics, Döllinger asserted that Schelling was not a Christian theologian, nor was philosophy history. Nevertheless, in his old age the dean of the royal canons looked back to Schelling and to an earlier time with pleasant memories:

> The older among us still enjoy that high pleasure that Schelling's majestic lectures once gave us. They were lectures rich in ideas, fashioned in the beauty of a style like Plato's. Today in Germany there is no longer a Schelling school . . . but this rich and powerful spirit will always have a place among the courageous and powerful and seminal thinkers of the human race.[35]

Conclusion

The Second Half of a Century

THE 1830s PASSED. Schelling modified his university lectures very little. Every third semester he began anew his three-part system, which commenced with the idea of being and ended in objectivity through Christ revealed in the crucifixion. He did not, however, release the lectures for publication. Schelling's positive philosophy was the last great attempt of the nineteenth century to create the total system—a system that was both subject-centered process and world structure, a system rooted in Christianity. Both the philosopher and his system, however, were forms left over from an age past. Goethe, Hegel, Schlegel, Baader and Schleiermacher were all dead.

Alexander Jung, a young intellectual devoted to Schelling's philosophy, recalled a visit to the philosopher in 1838: "A majestic staircase, rooms adorned with antique statues and mythological reliefs like a *glyptothèque* . . . and the master within, solemn and heavy with his oracles, suited to the decor of this museum."[1]

Schelling viewed the Munich of Ludwig's Catholic restoration with sympathy and detachment. He commented rarely on the theology of the Catholic church, but he knew how to enjoy his prominent position. He did not join the circles around Baader and Görres, remaining aloof from those zealous groups and their periodicals. Schelling must have been conscious that for years in Munich he had been training no small number of the Bavarian clergy who studied at the ducal seminary, the Georgianum. Deutinger was an example of those young men who had grown up in an atmosphere of open Roman Catholic life. Schelling was correct in his judgment that his contemporaries in southern Germany—Baader, Görres and Schlegel—were not his equal in the composition of a systematic presentation of God, history, religion and personality. Criticism still irritated him, and there had been public arguments with two younger Catholics, Kuhn and Möhler from

Tübingen. Schelling may have sensed that the younger Catholic scholars had distanced themselves from him. This attitude solidified after his departure for Berlin and found expression in the publication of those critiques by Catholic thinkers that we have discussed.

The End of the "Bavarian Florence"

In 1836 Ludwig I celebrated ten years of his reign. That time had been an expansion outward from university and court so that Munich and Bavaria might enjoy a rebirth in the arts, the sciences, and in Catholic thought and life. He had, not always with success, introduced measures for equality between the Catholic majority and Protestants and Jews. He had built museums to house his personal art collection (begun and expanded during numerous trips to Italy). A constitution had been approved, educational reform was encouraged, canals and railroads were built. On the one hand, the king had advocated intellectual freedom in his realm, and on the other hand he had viewed this entire renaissance as Christian and Catholic. "Religion must be the foundation of life," he proclaimed as he opened the new university in 1826.[2]

As the 1830s approached their end, the religious atmosphere in Munich altered. No longer were the times electric with revolution, Romanticism and restoration. That was fast becoming history. The problems of freedom and religious tranquility had not been resolved. In Rome, Gregory XVI, candidate of Metternich and foe of all liberal ideas, was elected in 1831 upon the death of Pius VIII. He was an advocate of maximum papal authority. Soon curial documents condemning the intellectual life north of the Alps appeared.

The king's powerful minister Abel was a harsh spirit jointed to a conservative nature. His rigidity made him anti-Protestant and quite uninterested in theology based upon modern philosophy. Abel's position in the government in 1837 led to a deterioration in cultural and intellectual life. Ludwig opposed this new conservatism, but his personality and power were not so strong as they had once been. More and more his counterparts in chancery, ministry and museum were not his friends but younger men with different interests. Things had gone so far by 1841 that he had to appeal to the bishops to avoid measures that insulted Protestants: "Act in the spirit of Sailer, a truly, authentically apostolic spirit," the king urged.[3]

Everything lofty and great in this period, all its activities and personages, were so weakened that they came to an end in political reaction. Perhaps this came about not merely because of the general impossibility of the task or from the inevitable decline from the pure idea (factors in the collapse of the Romantic restoration that were already visible by 1840) but particularly from the impulses given formerly by Schelling and his final philosophy, impulses left unfulfilled.[4]

Schelling ceased lecturing in 1840, because professors in philosophy were not permitted to be instructors in religious philosophy. This was now to be the prerogative of the Catholic theological faculty. Abel and the government withdrew the lectures in philosophy of religion from the category of obligatory courses. Both these measures seem aimed at Baader and Schelling. Certainly they facilitated Schelling's acceptance of a professorship in Berlin.

Schelling observed morosely the growing conservative spirit in Bavaria: "Everything going on around me would make it easier for me to leave Munich and the academic institutions of Bavaria."[5] Schelling and Ludwig I remained on good terms and the king only reluctantly gave permission for a move to Berlin in 1841, a move which came at the behest of the king of Prussia. Görres's *Historisch-politische Blätter* printed a few months after Schelling's departure a long article complaining that German intellectual life continued to center on Berlin: Leibniz, Hegel and now Schelling.[6] The author argued that Catholics have seen that, although Schelling's philosophy has little in common with church dogmatics, nonetheless it is concerned with God and with religion and is of high importance. Schelling had moved from the ethereal concepts and potencies of his earlier philosophy of identity to existence, and had attempted to work sympathetically if piecemeal within Christianity. At the end of the article the author wondered whether Schelling's kind of philosophy, very much the gift of the Reformation and yet recently appropriated by Catholicism, might be coming to its end.

It was King Ludwig's fate to couple a disastrous personal escapade to the years of political revolt surrounding 1848. He became not only personally embroiled with a dancer, Lola Montez, but he allowed her to assume some public role in combatting the increasingly powerful conservative party. Ludwig removed university professors who were critical of this entire situation, among whom were Martin Deutinger and

Ignaz von Döllinger. The two outspoken political theologians, Baader and Görres, were silent: Baader was dead and Görres was dying. Riots threatened a revolution. And so Ludwig's cultural renaissance came to its end as its institutions were diluted or closed. The king abdicated in favor of his son Maximilian in March 1848. The great student of Romanticism, Rudolf Haym, summed up the era:

> The end of "Munich Romanticism" cannot be treated as an isolated phenomenon; it has a close connection with the collapse of German idealism. The events of the year 1848 draw a clear, sharp line across the century, a line that separates the following decades from Hegel and Berlin, and from Schelling and Munich.[7]

Schelling in Berlin

Karl Jaspers described Schelling's appearance in the university and metropolis of the Hegelians as the last great event of university life in the nineteenth century.[8] The same mix of liberals and conservatives, of court ministers and churchmen, that had facilitated a departure from Catholic Munich awaited the philosopher in Berlin—only now it was Protestant. One observer of the situation in the Prussian capital wrote:

> While the entire German cultural world lay held in the chains of Hegelianism, more and more Schelling's name was whispered about. The Master, in a solitary life of thought, might have found a higher, newer solution for the problem of the world, for the reconciliation of Christianity with the sciences, physical and intellectual. . . . It was said that Schelling waited only for his Berlin appointment so that he would come forth as a prophet of a new philosophy.[9]

Because Schelling had not published his later system, Berlin was rather in the dark about his ideas. "They spoke of his mystical retirement, of how guests were led through shadowy gardens into a room to wait until doors opened upon an old man in a frock coat, solemn, like a magician."[10] Schelling would at least enter Berlin like a prophet and philosopher. The awaited reconciler of idealism and Christianity arrived in time to begin the winter semester of 1841. The year of Schelling's move saw the publication of books such as L. Feuerbach's *Das Wesen des Christentums*, Bruno Bauer's study on the synoptic gospels, and F. C. Baur's application of Hegel to the Trinity. An eyewitness described the scene:

> It was November 15th. About 5:00 PM a huge crowd of students pushed toward the largest auditorium of the university. . . . Professors could hardly find places. Schelling entered and slowly moved to the lecture area, a small, gray-haired man with an ordinary face and celestial eyes, the hero of philosophy. He stood for a while, the doors were closed, professors and students waited. Then he began: "Gentlemen, I am aware of the importance of this movement."[11]

The importance of that moment was bestowed as much by the students as by Schelling, for the crowd contained figures representative of the future of European culture. The Dane Kierkegaard, was there; the Prussian Engels; the Russian anarchist Bakunin; the Swiss art historian Burckhardt. Among the theological professors not content with Hegelianism, Neander and Vatke were in attendance. The historian who had been part of Schelling's influence in Heidelberg and in Munich, von Savigny, awaited the master, as did one of Schelling's most faithful disciples from the Jena years, the aged mineralogist Steffens. Von Ranke, *Ordinarius* in history since 1834, was present.

Schelling's presence in Berlin was new; his philosophy was not. His lectures more or less repeated the Munich cycle. An introduction dealt with God and creation from the perspective of an idealist science of the absolute in being and its potencies. Two major sections followed: the vast philosophy of mythology and of revelation, both of which had lengthy introductions relating their concrete content to transcendental idealism. The first lecture, however, was original, and Schelling permitted its publication (it was translated into English and published in the United States).

Schelling held his audience of several hundred for a few weeks, but men such as Engels and Kierkegaard were quickly disappointed. Engels represented a group for whom Schelling seemed too Christian.[12] Marx wrote that the philosopher should never have gotten mixed up in religion but should have remained with his Fichtean idealism and philosophy of nature. Kierkegaard represented another yearning for an end to speculation, for the liberation of existence and faith. At first the Dane thought Schelling would accomplish that by his tireless critique of Hegel and by his emphasis upon existence. He wrote in a letter:

Schelling is lecturing to an extraordinary audience. He shows forcefully that there are two philosophies: a negative and a positive. Hegel is neither, only a refined Spinoza. . . . I am happy I heard Schelling's second lecture. Indescribable! I have long desired for such, as have my thoughts within me. As he spoke the word "reality" relating philosophy to reality, the fruit of thought leapt within me for joy—as with Elizabeth.[13]

This enthusiasm was short-lived; by January, Kierkegaard, filled with angry disappointment, had given up on Schelling and was returning to Denmark: "I am returning because Schelling has not pleased me. I don't go to the lectures. . . . I can hardly stand him. There is nothing for me in Berlin. I am too old to hear such lectures, just as Schelling is too old to deliver them. His teaching about the potencies betrays the greatest impotency."[14]

Engels shared his disappointment in Schelling with Karl Marx as well as with the public; he wrote an anonymous pamphlet attacking the pseudo Christianity of the system. Marx wrote to Feuerbach that Schelling's mistake was to change the promise of the philosophy of nature into an egomaniacal system that tried to be everything: "Feuerbach is Schelling reversed. Schelling's fantastic dream of youth has become—with Feuerbach—truth; serious, virile reality. Schelling, in anticipation, became a deformed Feuerbach."[15]

Schelling had moved from reason to existence, and this lived on in Kierkegaard, Heidegger and Tillich. The idea of a positive philosophy continued in Feuerbach and Marx. The Christian content had no immediate heirs: a century would pass before Christian thinkers such as Teilhard de Chardin could fashion a system grandiose enough to include revelation, cosmogenesis, history and religious typology.

From the Philosophy of History to Research in History

Schelling had had considerable success in tutoring the crown prince of Bavaria. Maximilian enjoyed the philosopher's company, found his system intriguing and aesthetically pleasing. The young prince was irritated when his father gave permission for Schelling to move to Berlin. In his letters to Schelling in Munich and Berlin he expressed himself in the terms of Schelling's philosophy—"Christ exists in tension with the Spirit of possibilities." In a reply to questions about the future of the new king's realm and of Europe, Schelling gave a last view of the past and the future. Philosophy will end in politics, he wrote, for the movement of freedom begun by Kant and the French Revolution will find completion in the state, the state as guarantor not goal of individual life and freedom. The church has not yet reached its new essence, its proclamation of and ministry to historical revelation made universal. "The content of divine revelation will become more general, more conceptual. Divine truth must be transformed into general knowledge, a foundation for the first free and general church."[16]

In an earlier letter, from 1845, Schelling distinguished four theological directions: (a) the old rationalism, which had meant bankruptcy for both philosophy and theology; (b) a kind of half-orthodoxy proceeding from Schleiermacher, which avoided a full modern conceptualization and is a way for the half-committed to remain Christian; (c) a blind, rigid orthodoxy; (d) Schelling's own positive philosophy, which comprehends Christianity from its radical principle, a principle concretized in Christ but given with the foundation of the cosmos. When King Maximilian inquired in 1854 about the ideas that would govern the future direction of his age, Schelling replied that an adequate answer could come only from the depths of a true philosophy of history, from "a view into the law of the great periods of world history."[17]

Within a few months of this letter's composition, the historian Leopold von Ranke was invited to deliver a series of lectures to the Bavarian court on the epochs of history. While Schelling had been occupied with sketching an inner, necessary dynamic of history (primarily the history of religion and thought), Ranke's task was more modest. He wanted to see accurately the limits and characteristics of historical periods according to the data available. Ranke criticized mildly the idealist philosophers of cosmic and terrestrial history who could not distinguish cosmogenic and theosophical myths from historical events. Döllinger approved of Ranke's work. Interestingly, Ranke remarked that Schelling's perspective upon political history was "Catholic and monarchical."[18]

In 1800 Schelling—at that time the heir to Kant and the philosopher of Romanticism—had introduced "history" into consciousness, and thence into the absolute. Romantic, historical consciousness was a celebration of the vital processes of the world; a framework of organic evolution to explain the All and the absolute. History was the result of unconscious as well as conscious forces; in it, a prior idea or structure unfolded itself as higher forms spread out the life of God. Ranke rightly saw that the Hegelian schools, along with Schelling's retirement in Berlin, were signs that Romantic idealism had come to an end.[19]

While Schelling in Berlin wrote with warmth and respect to the Bavarian court, Catholic intellectuals at the University of Munich aroused his ire. Against Döllinger's critique of his final system he wrote: "Sooner or later, when these *messieurs* are no longer mentioned, one will recognize as the only documentation (of the age) a new and loftier theorem like the one I have attempted to prepare in my philosophy of revelation."[20] Schelling had heard that Drey, an old man, was "an enemy of his philosophy of revelation" and that a Dr. Kuhn "was on the same track."[21] Strange that Schelling had not already heard of Drey, who some time earlier had done so much to introduce his thought into Roman Catholic theology. This is explained best by a separation, not so much between ideological opponents but between intellectual worlds. Schelling was abreast of certain theologians and was knowledgeable in areas such as myth and religion but he spent little time on church history or upon specifically Catholic or Protestant systematic theology: perhaps some knowledge of the later Schleiermacher, a reading of Schlegel, but little more. At the end of his life Schelling thinks only of his *Philosophy of Revelation*, which he guards but will not publish.

Roman Catholic theology in the first half of the nineteenth century was to end in history. With Ranke and Döllinger, the Romantic characteristics of dialectic and development were fulfilled, or at least replaced, by historical research. During the 1830s, Catholic scholars turned more and more from philosophy to history. Möhler, Kuhn and Staudenmaier had absorbed Schelling's organic, developmental philosophy from the lectures of Drey. Möhler's *Einheit* and *Symbolik* were theological events; both books were grounded in church history. Möhler's thought ignored neither system nor research, but in his writings the subject's system had been metamorphosed into the community's history. The *Zeitgeist* pointed to historical research, especially to research in the early church, just as, decades before, the spirit of the era had led artists and intellectuals to epistemology and mythology. A third and last generation of German Catholics had studied Schelling but no one had found his final system satisfying. So they moved ahead, writing books on church history and patristic theology, constructing systematic theologies from history.

From Romantic Idealism to Neoscholasticism

The epoch we have been studying ended not only in history but in a form of ahistorical thought—neoscholasticism. The German neoscholastics labeled subject-oriented thought "Protestant," and the modern realm of the self was banished from Roman theology. But historicism and scholasticism were, more than perceived, rational frameworks, even if they convinced others that they were free of all subjectivism. To a world adrift amid storms of evolution and emotion, they did sometimes appear as detached viewers in the gallery of the real world.

As we have seen, Romanticism was a movement congenial to the Roman Catholic spirit. With the advocacy of a return to medieval thought, that connaturality was forgotten. The dimension of the holy in nature and being, mystical intuition, and organic development—these once exciting facets of Romantic life that had enhanced the Catholic mind were more or less rejected. Perhaps the Catholic thinkers, such as Baader and Görres, were partly at fault: over the years, the intuition into nature and consciousness that led easily to mysticism had ended up in parapyschology. The once great vision of organic nature was now only an excessively religious experimentation with the unusual or the bizarre.

We have observed one branch of the culture of Romantic idealism end in historians such as Ranke and Döllinger; now the second branch, which culminates in the medieval revival, deserves some attention. By 1841 a philosophical vacuum had been created. The transcendental format found less acceptance, thereby weakening the theoretical foundation for all the fields of theology. The era of great systems was passing; the historical handbook replaced the encyclopedia; the introduction sufficed for a philosophy of religion and revelation. History, however, is neither faith nor thought. Even in their choice of areas for research, Möhler and Döllinger sowed some seeds of uncertainty. They chose topics that disputed the claims of Rome; the early church's life might show some weaknesses in Protestant interpretations of Christianity but at the same time the Reformation was depicted as a historical inevitability. Clearly the time of *Aufhebung* was gone—the age when Schelling and Hegel offered a Christian philosophy resolving the differences of Protestant, Catholic and Orthodox churches. Schelling wrote in 1844 to a son studying in Tübingen "to view with humor the present (strained) relationships between Protestants and Catholics."[22]

We must look to social historians to relate to theology and church the conservative movements in economics and politics that were also emerging then in Germany and Europe, in Munich and Rome. The decades before and after 1848 show the momentum shifting to traditionalist groups in government and archdiocese. Earlier in Munich a strong allegiance to king and bishop (including the bishop of Rome) had been joined to a cosmopolitan openness in philosophy, theology, art and literature. This was no longer the case.

The papacy too had changed. Earlier the young revolutionary on the Rhine, Görres, had been inspired by the prophetic stance of Pius VII against the whims of Napoleon. The papacy under Gregory XVI, suave and power-conscious, became the establishment against which the Munich circle strove. The pope and his curia condemned Hermes and Bautain in 1835. The encyclical *Mirari Vos* expressed its fears of a universal rationalism and warned of a philosophy that relied upon its own strength and genius. Franz von Baader had soon made his views about the new form of Roman leadership known. The papacy, he wrote, should not be the leadership of a monarch, or the enterprise of a person "possessed" by the Holy Spirit.[23]

In Catholic centers such as Tübingen and Mainz, both the diocese and the theological school were increasingly dominated by ultramontane interests. The older, liberal figures were left undisturbed by neo-scholasticism, but the change in intellectual climate made them anxious. When Kuhn heard of the possibility of the immaculate conception of Mary becoming a dogma, he moaned: "The Romans had best try that out. For then we are finished. Those up there [the Protestants] will say: 'So that's how they make a dogma.' "[24]

Rome and circles of scholars throughout Europe came to favor a new philosophy, a replacement for Cartesianism and the Enlightenment but also for Romanticism and idealism. The "new philosophy" was, of course, an old philosophy: medieval, Christian, scholastic. No one was more important in this theological shift than Joseph Kleutgen. The person of Kleutgen linked Germany to Rome; the Jesuit from north of the Alps taught in Rome for thirty years, and he connected the two geographical areas first intent upon the restoration of scholasticism.

Kleutgen insisted that the philosophy and theology of the recent decades north of the Alps were an exception and an aberration: neither patristic, nor medieval, nor potentially Catholic. "Into this philosophy," he wrote, "as into one riverbed the two streams of the spirit of the times flow: pride and sensuality."[25] Kleutgen studied Hegel and Schelling not in the original works but in the writings of their Catholic students and critics—for instance, in the works of Staudenmaier, whom Kleutgen held up as an example of the wrong direction. In his own books Kleutgen displayed the lack of finesse necessary for seeing the nuanced variety in Catholic theologians' employment of idealism; he lacked the scholarship to read Schelling's (or Staudenmaier's) critiques of Hegel and of pantheism.[26]

Kleutgen repeated the opinion held by not a few that Schelling and Hegel had built upon the foundation of Protestantism.[27] Consequently, the discussion over the right cultural metaphysics for the modern world and the most useful philosophy for theology was carried on in the heated atmosphere of Protestant-Catholic competition. Every theology that had been subject-oriented and process-directed had to be recatholicized, not through Catholic creativity but through past thought-forms. The restoration of scholasticism was eventually accomplished by Leo XIII in 1879. Pope Leo himself was part of a group of seminary and university professors who deplored the state of philosophy and theology where dry textbooks presented a mixture of bland Descartes and ossified Scotus.[28] To what extent Italian scholars worked within post-Kantian thought lies outside our study. Turning to Aquinas, nevertheless, was more comfortable than turning to Hegel.

Kleutgen discerned scholasticism in the Greek and Latin fathers and he detected error in all that came after Duns Scotus. At Tübingen, Kuhn wrote furiously against this betrayal of a vital, intellectual Catholic Germany. The issue was the very freedom and contemporaneity of theology. Was a speculative exploration of Christianity to be the possession of a past, privileged time? Or was Catholicism to be philosophically alive, accepting thought-forms that emerged from the ongoing panorama of culture? The Tübingen faculty was the strongest proponent of the response that thought must be one with Rome in faith but not in theological expression. Approaching sixty, Kuhn was indomitable; some said too tough. During the uncertain years before Vatican I, Kuhn found himself hard pressed by episcopal and curial investigations. A number of sentences extracted from his flowing German prose had been given to the Holy Office. No condemnation was forthcoming but the elderly theologian put his pen aside and watched the confusion of these years. His opponent C. Schäzler was involved with true fanatics; some even attempted to get Sailer, the venerable father of Romantic Catholicism in Bavaria, condemned posthumously.

It was not merely fear or narrowness that formed and supported the return to neoscholasticism. The systems of the Roman Catholic idealist theologians were often left incomplete, and their mentors, Schelling and Hegel, had seemingly never reached the port of Christian orthodoxy. The more radical and more publicized Protestant liberal theologians were hardly an encouragement that post-Hegelian thought would prove to be a salvific road. Nor was the Catholic Church ready for history, or for the new and keen awareness of evolution and historicity that would pervade every horizon of culture in the coming century.

The return to scholasticism was led not only by the Italians and by Kleutgen in Rome. As often happens, the generation that followed those who broke through into the freedom and maturity of a contemporary theology took a step backward; their character was more careful and less spontaneous. The neoscholastics often possessed talent and scholarship. Nevertheless, most of their efforts, even as presentations of medieval thought, were mediocre. Intertwined with the advocacy of an eternal and Christian metaphysics was the polemic against all that was modern, because of its presumed origins in all that was Protestant.

The seminary began to fear the university, Rome wanted to control Germany. The seminary professors at Mainz (who now edited Görres's *Der Katholik*) joined this crusade. Their writings took patrology and exegesis seriously, but all fields were fitted into a scholastic format. In Bonn, the young layman Franz Jakob Clemens represented the new generation for whom Romantic idealism was past history. Clemens wrote in 1856 his *De sententia scholasticorum philosophiam esse theologiae ancillam* as a textbook and manifesto for the neoscholastic party. H. Denziger, professor at Würzburg, had completed his *Enchiridion Symbolorum*, the foundation of what came to be known as "Denziger-theology"—that is, an ahistorical assembly of proof-texts from papal and conciliar documents.

"Götterdämmerung." The Assembly of Scholars in Munich, 1863.

To every history there belongs not only its climax, when the powers of matter and spirit wrestle for success and mastery, but also its conclusion. The Roman Catholic theological renewal, the restoration of culture and Catholicism in southern Germany built upon Romantic idealism, climaxed as Görres, Baader and Schelling came to the University of Munich. There on the Isar they could influence Drey and his students in Tübingen, converse with de Lamennais in France, compare systems with Friedrich Schlegel in Vienna. Decline set in by 1835: the philosophers of religion and the theologian-historians looked at metaphysics with skepticism, while the bureaucrats of state and church evaluated modern thinking negatively.

If Munich in 1827 under Ludwig I was the climax of this age, its conclusion took place in the same city decades later. For in Munich, in 1863, an event occurred that solemnly concluded that history begun in the eighteenth century: this was the assembly of German scholars called by Döllinger. This unique gathering came together to face the divisions among Catholic intellectuals in the latter half of the nineteenth century. Young conservatives, old liberals, exegetes and historians assembled in the Benedictine Abbey of St. Boniface, itself built by Ludwig I to symbolize the restoration of monasticism.

Looking around at the seething polemics in Catholic Germany, Döllinger saw two movements. He called the two directions "Roman theology" and "German theology." The censure of persons and ideas by Gregory XVI; the condemnation of old Günther by Pius IX in 1857; the appointment of bishops and seminary rectors with ultramontane sympathies; the suspension of J. Frohschammer in Munich in 1862 contributed to the uneasiness. Certainly not without sharpening the conflict, Döllinger had turned his arsenal of historical data upon certain pious claims of the papacy concerning its venerable prerogatives. Not only history, however, but the philosophy of religion were battle-grounds. The older generation had watched with concern as neoscholasticism won victories in seminaries and universities. It was backed by the Roman theological and ecclesiastical community and augmented by a growing number of adherents in Germany. The age of Fichte, Schelling, Jacobi and Hegel was gone; no new Sailer, Drey or Möhler appeared. Döllinger, approaching seventy, presided over the assembly much as Wotan led the doomed gods into Valhalla in the *Ring* cycle of operas that Richard Wagner, living at that time in Munich, had begun to compose.

To the Abbey in September 1863, the scholars came "to discuss basic questions for the church and for its opposition to irreligious directions . . . with mutual understanding and support."[29] Led by Kuhn, the liberals of Tübingen, who wanted a narrower list of participants, let their pique best them and boycotted the meeting, so playing into the hands of their and Döllinger's foes.

Döllinger gave the major address: "On the Past and Present in Catholic Theology." The vision was broad and masterful, the approach historical and critical. Could there possibly be one, perennial thought-form?, he asked. Could a glowing time of the past really produce a way of thinking that transcended time and geography? What is the relationship between faith and culture? Is a modern theology possible for the Catholic tradition? The questions were the very ones that had opened the nineteenth century. Only then Catholic Munich was troubled not by the Middle Ages (which it had forgotten decades before) but by the Enlightenment.

Carefully, Döllinger led up to his first conclusion. Scholasticism is a building from the past and no amount of repairs can transform it into something contemporary. German theology, moreover, has the mission today to heal the wounds of the Reformation begun in Germany, and to develop the genius of modern thought in both its speculative and historical dimensions, for that philosophy, like the Reformation, is proper to the German spirit. Döllinger pleaded on behalf of theology for freedom and for critical judgment.

Days of discussion followed as the schools fenced with each other—often over political gestures rather than theological methods. The assembly ended peacefully enough but the inner chasm was obvious. Setting a precedent, the papal and curial attitude was one of warning and fear, not of encouragement. A further assembly planned for 1864 at Würzburg did not take place. Rome had other ideas. In 1864, the *Syllabus* catalogued—sketchily, anonymously and unscientifically—aspects of modern theology that were erroneous. Papal power was strengthened in the arena of theological discussion when infallibility was defined by the council in 1870. Was there a philosophical thought-form that could transcend history? Rome seemed to answer affirmatively in 1879 as Leo XIII restored the teaching of Thomas Aquinas as obligatory for Catholic higher education in philosophy and theology.

Modernism, we see, can mean many things. There was the modernism of Günther, intent upon doing justice to Hegel, and there was the modernism of Hermes, which, by reviving Kant, eschewed Schelling and Hegel. These figures (and their condemnations) were fifty years removed from the variety of modernists (so difficult to define) who fell in one form or another under curial censure between 1890 and 1920. In fact, our history of Roman Catholic theology in the first half of the nineteenth century shows that modernism was a later stage of the never resolved meeting between Catholicism and modernity.

The commitment by Roman Catholic scholars and intellectuals to resolve the tension between faith and knowing, between theology as a science and science defined transcendentally, set loose powerful tremors. They were later weakened by opposition and neglect; but the issue of the self and divine revelation could not be buried, for it was the very spirit of the times. Modernism, far from being a failed attempt at fashioning a modern theology out of the wellsprings of the past century, was, in fact, a middle realm. Its geography lay between two periods of free and full encounter with the modern world: the first began amid Romanticism and idealism at the end of the eighteenth century; the second in the last third of the twentieth century. As our history has shown, the mainstream of Roman Catholic theology strove to be faithful to the tradition of the church and to employ the thought-forms of modern philosophy. Although they came to enjoy a lasting reputation, Hermes and Günther were on the margin of a movement whose center was Baader and Drey.

Envoi

The second half of the nineteenth century witnessed the emergence and expansion of a modern revival of medieval scholasticism as the normative thought-form for philosophy. The spirit of the earlier time lived on in Tübingen and Munich, in figures such as Paul Schanz and Alois Schmid, in Frohschammer and Schell, but the time of dialogue and freedom was gone.[30] By World War I, which marks the far limit of all that belongs to the nineteenth century, modernity was feared and neoscholasticism was in full control in Catholic life. Drey and Möhler were no longer studied; Baader and Görres were unknown; Schelling and Hegel were labeled pantheists responsible for all that was uncontrollable and impious in troubled times.

There was a Schelling renaissance in the years following 1900. Short-lived, it seems to have been an interlude leading to existentialism. Brief academic books on Schelling—on his transcendental philosophy or aesthetics but not on his philosophy of revelation—were published. Paul Tillich was part of that Indian summer of idealism; he wrote two dissertations researching Schelling: one on guilt and one on myth. Not only the young Tillich but thinkers like Eduard von Hartmann and Martin Heidegger took Schelling seriously. Heidegger wrote that "Schelling is the thinker from this entire era of German philosophy who is particularly creative and all-encompassing."[31] And, in a rare autobiographical remark, he recalled:

> One (decisive influence) was Karl Braig, a professor of systematic theology, and the last in the tradition of the speculative school of Tübingen, which gave significance and scope to Catholic theology through its dialogue with Hegel and Schelling.[32]

Surprisingly, from Martin Heidegger we receive a last, faint picture of Schelling as mentor for a past dialogue between modern philosophy and Roman Catholicism.

Tracing any remaining presence of idealism in Catholic theology in the century after Schelling's death, from 1854 to 1954, requires careful work. We would be amiss, however, if we did not at least point out some signs of the continuation of the history we have been narrating. Heidegger mentioned Karl Braig. Braig was professor of philosophy and theology at Freiburg from 1893 to 1919. The author of books on aesthetics, parapsychology and transcendental philosophy, he was a rare Catholic channel into our century of some of the ideas of modern philosophy.

A contemporary of Braig was Herman Schell. To the displeasure of Rome, this Würzburg professor labored on a vital apologetic. The nineteenth century was now only a decade away from its end, but Schell argued that Catholicism's great need was a self-interpretation through the creativity and philosophy of modern culture. Schell had been greatly influenced by the writings of Staudenmaier and Kuhn. Schell's direct contact with Schelling and with the highpoint of Roman Catholic intellectual life in the early part of the century came through Jacob Sengler. Sengler was a student of Schelling in 1827 in Munich, and his first writings, published before 1840, reflect the philosophy of religion of that decade. Schell's work was not acceptable, and his writings were placed on the *Index*.

In the 1920s, when few read or understood idealism, Eric Przy-wara, that extraordinary Jesuit explorer of religious consciousness, pre-served the open spirit of the earlier dialogue. Reflecting his superior knowledge of idealism, he wrote:

> Schelling was the express fulfillment of Romanticism. He brought together the objective primacy of the divine with the subjective primacy of the religious dimension. Schelling's philosophy of mythology and revelation appear as the fulfillment of Baader and Görres. In myth and revelation God is the determining, primal ground and source of all life in nature and spirit. And so, all knowing, action and art flow forth from the dimension of reli-gion.[33]

Hans Urs von Balthasar's first book was an examination of the German soul in apocalyptic times. *Prometheus* surveyed terror and eschatology, secular and Christian morality and aesthetics, in German thought from Fichte and Goethe through Novalis and Schelling to Hegel. This youthful enterprise of the great Swiss synthesizer offers an original reading of Schelling. Schelling, von Balthasar concludes, was writing an eschatology whose poles are the fall and the divine abyss. Freedom and necessity and indifference float above the primal ground of the All. This is a system of mysticism and physics for an age unfolding between Luther and Boehme and Nietzsche. "Schelling labored on a never finished bridge from subject to object, from myth to Christianity; in the last analysis he did not know where to place the foundation stone."[34] Part of the recent Schelling renaissance that began in 1954 has been the contributions of W. Kasper, X. Tilliette, G. Vergauwen, K. Hemmerle. Their works are not theologies or philosophies but studies of Schelling and show anew his attractiveness for the Catholic mind.

The genius of the nineteenth century and the format of the philoso-phy that we call "modern" found their source and climax in Kant, Schelling and Hegel. Recent decades have seen their readmission as legitimate thinkers into the halls of discussion within Roman Catholic theology. Contemporary culture is subject-centered and process-formed; nothing can change that or return culture to an earlier time of eternal objectivity. When transcendental philosophy becomes the content instead of the form, it often ends in atheism or pantheism.

The first generation of Protestant and Catholic theologians to respond to the great idealists, the thinkers from 1795 to 1835, may have been more careful and wiser than Strauss, Günther, Feuerbach and Marx. In their subjectivity, there was a place for the object; in their process, a ground. Two decades beyond Vatican II, we have again within Catholicism systems and methodologies that begin with subjectivity and freedom. They also strive to do justice to objective revelation, past and present. Perhaps this reappearance of nineteenth-century styles of theology explains the rebirth of interest in the history of that century.

We have narrated only part of the history of modern subjectivity and freedom in Roman Catholicism. The affinity, however, of Western Catholicism with Romanticism is not ambiguous. The mystical, the liturgical, the panentheistic, the heroic, the Gothic, the sacramental— these inevitably make Catholic blood rush. Roman Catholicism breathes easy and flourishes when the times are Romantic. Despite its perennial display of the rationalism of the Middle Ages, when an Enlightenment dominates the culture of an epoch, Catholicism appears awkward, indigent and immature. It was Romanticism that introduced idealism and solicitously led an empty intellectual life back to a position more to the center of the European stage. Since 1963, in some striking ways we have entered into a more Romantic atmosphere. Within this cultural shift is the polar vitality of a Roman Catholicism intent upon renewal.

One truth that Schelling and Hegel illumined was the movement and dialectic in cultural history. The history of Roman Catholic theology—between Enlightenment and neoscholasticism—displays that dialectic. As strong as an epoch may be at its birth, it too will mature, age, lose strength and fade away. At its height of power, a movement in art, philosophy or religion already contains the first signs of its disintegration. The ambitions of the idealist system were not fulfilled; the world never received the promised all-encompassing idea to guide sublimely its thought and its life. Romanticism disintegrated into a cluster of disparate movements whose focus upon the heroic, the will, the unconscious and the night became extreme as the century neared its end. Idealism appeared to thinkers, preachers, artists no longer as the advocate of freedom and insight, but as a dusty system with all too obvious limits. Inasmuch as the next generation was more traditional and conservative, it had no desire to dabble with pantheism. As we noted, into this vacuum came historical research and neoscholasticism. These two movements dominated Roman Catholic life for roughly a hundred years.

But by 1950 the pendulum of history was swinging again. Scholastic philosophy and theology seemed oppressive and eminently sterile. Meanwhile, historical study was bringing a new freshness to the fathers of the church, opening up the history of liturgy and catechetics, explaining the fuller meaning and context in medieval culture of the scholastic genuises. Vatican II responded to all these movements and to a drastically new pastoral situation. Rapidly the Roman Catholic world entered an era where freedom, diversity and cultural responsibility were again values in theology and church life. So, our present time resembles the age of Sailer and Möhler and Döllinger more than it does that of Kleutgen or Garrigou-Lagrange.

The historical preparation for our present theology reaches back from Vatican II through five decades to the first half of this century. But the roots of those theologians and their ideas lie further back—in Möhler, Drey and Sailer; in Hegel, Schelling and Kant. We do not know if we are at the second stage of a modern theology begun around 1800, or at the beginning of an entirely new era. Only the spirit of the times will reveal the right balance of sources and innovations for the end of this century.

Only a knowledge of the past century explains why our times, too gifted and too anxious, include existentialism and evolution, mysticism and psychology, political theology and transcendental method. This book has been a theme and variations on the nineteenth century. Not that the theologians and philosophers were only variations on Schelling. They were always more than that. But their systems, articles and encyclopedias were based upon a way of thinking drawn from Romanticism and idealism. They saw no need to give up believing in a unique revelation in history. The leitmotif remained the same: to believe and to understand.

Call it spirit in personality and culture, the harmony of the infinite and the finite, or revelation in psyche and landscape as well as in Scripture and tradition—the theme is always worth pursuing through its variants. For between believing and understanding there is dialectical music: grace within the human personality, and history within the life of God.

Synchronology

	Philosophy	Roman Catholic Theology	Culture
1780	Kant, *Critique of Pure Reason* (1781) ——, *Prolegomena to a Future Metaphysics* (1783) Herder, *Ideas for a Philosophy of Human History* (1784)	Sailer, *Doctrine on Reason* (1785) ——, *Lectures on Pastoral Theology* (1788) Baader, *On Heat* (1786) Stattler, *Anti-Kant* (1788)	Mozart, *The Marriage of Figaro* (1786) Goethe, *Egmont* (1787) David, *Death of Socrates* (1787) Haydn, Middle String Quartets (1789) French Revolution (1789) American Constitution (1789)
1790	Kant, *Critique of Judgment* (1790) Fichte, *Doctrine of Science* (1794) Schelling, *On the Self* (1795) ——, *Ideas for a Philosophy of Nature* (1797) ——, *On the World-Soul* (1798) Schleiermacher, *Addresses on Religion* (1799)	Stattler, *General Ethics* (1790) ——, *True Relationship of Kantian Philosophy . . . to Christianity* (1794) Schlegel, *On the Study of Greek Poetry* (1795) Baader, *On . . . Nature* (1798)	Goethe, *Faust* Fragment (1790) Haydn, London Symphonies (1791) ——, *Creation* (1798) Blake, *The Ancient of Days* (1794) Mozart, *The Magic Flute* (1795) Napoleon as Consul (1799–1804) Hölderlin, *Poems* (1799)
1800	Schelling, *System of Transcendental Philosophy* (1800) ——, *Presentation of My System* (1801) ——, *Bruno* (1802) ——, *Lectures on Academic Studies* (1802) ——, *Philosophy and Religion* (1804)	Salat-Weiller, *The Spirit of the Newest Philosophy* (1803) Görres, *Aphorisms . . .* (1803) ——, *Belief and Knowing* (1805) Weber, *Attempt . . .* (1803) Windischmann, *Ideen zur Physik* (1804) Thanner, *Transcendental Idealism* (1805)	Haydn, *The Seasons* (1801) Arnim-Brentano, *Das Knaben Wunderhorn* (1805) Beethoven, *Eroica* (1804) Goethe, *Faust I* (1808)

—— , *Essay on Freedom* (1809)
Hegel, *Difference between Fichte and Schelling . . .* (1801)
—— , *Phenomenology of the Spirit* (1807)
Eschenmayer, *The Non-Philosophy . . .* (1803)

Hermes, *The Inner Truth of Christianity* (1805)
Sailer, *Basic Teaching on Religion* (1805)
Zimmer, *Philisophical Teaching on Religion* (1805)
Schlegel, *On the Language and Wisdom of the Indians* (1808)
Baader, *Contributions to a Dynamic rather than a Mechanical Philosophy* (1809)

Grimm, *Fairy Tales* (1812)
Napoleon, Defeated in Russia (1812); Waterloo (1815)
Beethoven, *Symphony #7* (1812)
—— , *Fidelio* (1814)
Byron, *Childe Harold* (1812–1818)
Schubert, *Erlkönig* (1815)
—— , *Trout Quintet* (1819)
Gericault, *Raft of the Medusa* (1819)

1810

Jacobi, *On Divine Things . . .* (1811)
Schelling, *Denkmal* (Response to Jacobi) (1811)
—— , *Clara* (1810)
—— , *Ages of the World* (1813–)
Hegel, *Logic* (1811)
—— , *Encyclopedia* (1817)
Fichte, *System of Morals* (1812)
Schopenhauer, *The World as Will . . .* (1819)

Görres, *History of Asian Myths* (1810)
Baader, *On the Concept of Time* (1810)
Drey, *Revision of . . . Theology* (1812)
—— , *Praelectiones Dogmaticae* (1815–1834)
—— , *Short Introduction to Theology* (1819)
Hermes, *Introduction to . . . Theology* (1819–1829)

1820

Hegel, *Philosophy of Right* (1821)
Schelling, *Philosophy of Mythology* (1828)
—— , *Philosophy of Revelation* (1829)

Möhler, *The Unity of the Church* (1825)
—— , *Anselm* (1827)
Baader, *On the Freedom of Intelligence* (1826)
Döllinger, *Handbook of Church History* (1828)
Günther, *School for a Speculative Theology of Positive Christianity* (1828)
Eos (1829)

Constable, *Hempstead Heath* (1821)
Beethoven, *Symphony #9* (1823)
C.D. Friedrich, *Polar Sea* (1824)
Pushkin, *Eugene Onegin* (1825–31)
Thomas Jefferson (d. 1826)
Schubert, *Symphony #9* (1828)

Philosophy	Roman Catholic Theology	Culture
	1830	
Hegel (d. 1831)	Klee, *System of Catholic Dogmatics* (1831)	Mendelssohn, *Reformation Symphony* (1830)
Hegel, *Lectures on the Philosophy of Religion* (1832)	——, *Encyclopedia of Theology* (1832)	Goethe, *Poetry and Truth* (1831)
Schelling, "Preface" (to V. Cousin's Writings [1834])	Hermes, *Dogmatics* (1831)	German, Zollverein (1833)
	Möhler, *Symbolics* (1832)	Chopin, *Ballades* (1836)
	Döllinger, *Church History* (1833)	Coronation of Queen Victoria (1837)
	Baader, *On Evolutionism and Revolutionism* (1834)	Schumann, *Kreisleriana* (1838)
	Kuhn, *Jacobi and the Philosophies of His Time* (1834)	Delacroix, *F. Chopin* (1838)
	Günther, *Janus . . . on Philosophy and Theology* (1834)	
	Windischmann, *Fr. Schlegel's Lectures on Philosophy, 1804–1806* (1837)	
	Görres, *Christian Mysticism* (1836)	
	Drey, *Apologetics* (1838–1847)	
	1840	
Feuerbach, *Essence of Christianity* (1841)	Staudenmaier, *The Philosophy of Christianity* (1840)	A. von Humboldt, *Cosmos* (1845)
Schelling-Paulus, *Philosophy of Revelation* (1842)	——, *Critique of Hegel* (1844)	R. Wagner, *Tannhäuser* (1845)
Engels, *Schelling, The Philosopher in Christ* (1842)	——, *Christian Dogmatics* (1850)	A. Dumas, *Count of Monte-Cristo* (1845)
Kierkegaard, *Either/Or* (1843)	Baader, *Occidental and Oriental Catholicism* (1841)	Viollet le Duc, Restoration of Notre Dame (1845)
——, *The Concept of Anxiety* (1844)	Kuhn, *On the Principle and Method of Speculative Theology* (1841)	Schumann, *Piano Concerto* (1846)
Marx and Engels, *Communist Manifesto* (1848)	——, *Catholic Dogmatics* (1846–1862)	Mendelssohn, *Elijah* (1846)
Schelling (d. 1854)	Deutinger, *Basic Outline of a Positive Philosophy* (1843)	
	Döllinger, *The Reformation* (1846)	

Abbreviations

ADB	*Allgemeine deutsche Biographie* (Leipzig, 1875–1912)
AW	F. Schelling, *The Ages of the World* (New York, 1967)
BB	D. Baumgardt, *Franz von Baader* (Halle, 1927)
BD	H. Fuhrmans, ed., *F.W.J. Schelling, Briefe und Dokumente* (Bonn, 1962–), 3 vols.
CK	J. Geiselmann, *Geist des Christentums und des Katholizismus* (Mainz, 1940)
GF	K. Hoeber, ed., *Görres-Festschrift* (Cologne, 1926)
GGS	J. Görres, *Gesammelte Schriften* (Cologne, 1926)
HD	*Hochland*
HJ	*Historisches Jahrbuch*
HKG-KG	R. Aubert et al., *Handbuch der Kirchengeschichte, Die Kirche in der Gegenwart* (Freiburg, 1971)
HPBl	*Historisch-politische Blätter für das katholische Deutschland*
JMSB	H. Schiel, ed., *J.M. Sailer, Leben und Briefe* (Regensburg, 1952), 2 vols.
KA	F. Schlegel, *Kristische Ausgabe* (Paderborn, 1958–)
KE	J.S. Drey, *Kurze Einleitung* (Tübingen, 1819)
KThD	H. Fries, G. Schwaiger, eds., *Katholische Theologen Deutschlands im 19. Jahrhundert* (Munich, 1977), 3 vols.
KThNJ	G. Schwaiger, ed., *Kirche und Theologie im 19. Jahrhundert* (Göttingen, 1975).
LThK	*Lexikon für Theologie und Kirche* (Freiburg, 1st ed., 1930–1938; 2nd ed., 1957–1967)
OUS	F. Schelling, *On University Studies* (Athens, 1966)
PhJ	*Philosophisches Jahrbuch*
PL	G.L. Plitt, *Aus Schellings Leben. In Briefen* (Leipzig, 1969), 3 vols.
PW	H. Fuhrmans, *Schellings Philosophie der Weltalter* (Düsseldorf, 1954).

RGG	*Die Religion in Geschichte und Gegenwart* (Tübingen, 3rd ed., 1956–1965)
RS	R. Haym, *Die romantische Schule* (Berlin, 1914)
SGPP	H. Fuhrmans, ed., F.W.J. Schelling, *Grundlegung der positiven Philosophie* (Turin, 1972)
SPD	X. Tilliette, *Schelling. Une philosophie en devenir* (Paris, 1970), 2 vols.
SW	F. von Baader, *Sämtliche Werke* (Leipzig, 1851)
SWC	F.W.J. Schelling, *Werke* (Stuttgart, 1856–1861)
TAW	L. Scheffczyk, ed., *Theologie im Aufbruch und Widerstreit* (Bremen, 1965)
TQ	*Theologische Quartalschrift* (Tübingen)
VAR	P. Funk, *Von der Aufklärung zur Romantik* (Munich, 1925)
WGTh	K. Werner, *Geschichte der katholischen Theologie seit dem Trienter Konzil* (Munich, 1866)
ZKT	*Zeitschrift für katholische Theologie*
ZRG	*Zeitschrift für Religions- und Geistesgeschichte*

Notes

Introduction

1. H. Heimsoeth, *Metaphysik der Neuzeit* (Oldenbourg, 1952), p. 105. Translations from the German are my own except where otherwise indicated.

2. Cited in G. Goyau, *L'Allemagne religieuse* (Paris, 1905) 1, p. 161; cf. E.W. Zeeden, "Die katholische Kirche in der Sicht des deutschen Protestantismus," HJ 72 (1952) 433 ff.

3. KThNJ, p. 126. "Study the history of modern Catholic theology and you cannot overlook the deep fissure running through it—the beginning of the nineteenth century. That line separates not only the Enlightenment from its successor, the Romantic, but marks a deep separation of all theological epochs after scholasticism from that period which begins in the nineteenth century" (TAW, p. xl).

4. For a survey of the state of Schelling studies, see T.F. O'Meara, "F.W.J. Schelling: A Bibliographical Essay," *The Review of Metaphysics* 31 (1977) 283 ff.

5. PW, pp. 83 ff.

6. H. Fuhrmans, "Einleitung," to F. Schelling, *Über das Wesen der menschlichen Freiheit* (Stuttgart, 1974), pp. 3 f.

7. See S. Prickett, *Romanticism and Religion* (Cambridge, 1976); G. Marcel, *Coleridge et Schelling* (Paris, 1971); G. Orsini, *Coleridge and German Idealism* (Carbondale, Ill., 1969); T. McFarland, *Coleridge and the Pantheist Tradition* (Oxford, 1969).

8. Hans Urs von Balthasar, *Prometheus* (Heidelberg, 1947), p. 206.

9. PL 3, p. 97.

10. C. Welch, *Protestant Thought in the Nineteenth Century* (New Haven, Conn., 1972), pp. 1 f.

11. In 1834, J.E. Kuhn, a leading theologian of the Catholic Tübingen school, wrote a book sketching the attitude of Roman Catholics toward idealism. Before he began his survey of Kant, Jacobi, Fichte and Schelling, he pointed out that neither theology nor revelation can any longer avoid the post-Kantian philosophical stance that lay claim to subjectivity as the absolute. A state of war between philosophy and revelation is not necessary if theodicy and natural revelation are abandoned as the foundation of religion. Beyond Kantian criticism and dogmatic orthodoxy (alternatives made prominent by a work of Schelling published in 1795) lie the realms of mediate and immediate con-

sciousness: their ground and objects are the task of philosophy as *Wissenschaftslehre*. Kuhn distinguished between this modern science of knowing and the traditional metaphysics of Plato and Aristotle. This science of knowing is general and ultimate; metaphysics is a limited philosophical discipline. To treat the absolute with the approach of the new philosophy but with the content of metaphysics leads to pantheism. Philosophy really means the science of knowing as an investigation of the objects, means, borders and laws of all knowing. "All science comes through a unified bond between empirical and *a priori* knowing. . . . It is nothing other than the doctrine on consciousness in general to the extent that consciousness is the source of all knowing and presents the scope, the content, the context and the limits of human consciousness apart from this or that object" (*Jacobi und die Philosophie seiner Zeit* [Mainz, 1834], pp. iv, vii, 15 ff). In 1834 Kuhn took for granted that educated thinkers and competent theologians had accepted a post-Kantian perspective. That did not mean necessarily the exchange of a historical revelation in Christ for the philosophy of religion by Schelling or Hegel, but it did imply as obvious taking over the approach, if not the ideology, of idealism.

12. E. Wolfinger, *Der Glaube nach J.E. von Kuhn* (Göttingen, 1972), pp. 34 f.

1. The Jena Romantics

1. Hesse, *Under the Wheel* (New York, 1970), pp. 63, 66.

2. BD 2, p. 63.

3. SWC 1, p. 193.

4. H.J. Sandkühler, *F.W.J. Schelling* (Stuttgart, 1970), p. 67.

5. *Einleitung zu den Ideen zu einer Philosophie der Natur*, SWC 2, p. 6.

6. "Just as natural science brings idealism out of realism with its intellectualization of the laws of nature into the laws of intelligence, so transcendental philosophy brings realism from idealism as it materializes the laws of intelligence into the laws of nature" (SWC 3, p. 352).

7. W. Schulz, "Fichtes und Schellings philosophische Entwicklung im Grundriss," *Fichte-Schelling Briefwechsel* (Frankfurt, 1968), pp. 36, 40.

8. SWC 3, p. 603.

9. SWC 3, p. 602.

10. SWC 3, p. 682.

11. SWC 6, p. 57.

12. VAR, p. 197.

13. The opinion of Schelling's friend, C.J. Windischmann, and of others; see G. Bürke, *Vom Mythos zur Mystik* (Einsiedeln, 1958), pp. 100, 188.

14. E. Benz, *Theologie der Elektrizität* (Wiesbaden, 1971), p. 690.

15. H. Korff, *Der Geist der Goethezeit* (Leipzig, 1966) 3, p. 316.

16. BD 1, p. 157.

17. SWC 6, pp. 127 ff.; 1, p. 193; cf. SPD 1, pp. 388 ff.

18. Fragment #105, *Athenaeum* in KA 2, p. 180. We have no monograph on Schelling and Schlegel; see E. Behler's introductory essays "Schelling und die Frage nach der Form der Philosophie" and "Die Entstehung der Schlegelschen Spätphilosophie" in KA 8, pp. xxvii ff. and KA 1, pp. xviii ff. Unfortunately, Schlegel was

not included in KThD; for a bibliography, see E. Behler, *F. Schlegel* (Reinbek, 1966); K. Peter, *F. Schlegel* (Stuttgart, 1978).

19. BD 1, p. 153.

20. Letter of July 1798 (*Aus Schleiermachers Leben* [Berlin, 1862] 3, p. 78). Nevertheless Schlegel composed a poem explicitly referring to the *Weltseele*, albeit dwelling on motifs of Prometheus and uncertainty (KA 5, p. 302).

21. "Einleitung," KA 8, p. xxxvii.

22. KA 11, p. 118.

23. Quoted in Behler, *F. Schlegel*, p. 73; cf. KA 2, p. 204.

24. Transcendental Philosophy (Jena Lectures, 1801–1802), KA 12, p. 105; cf. H. Eichner, "Einleitung," KA 2, p. lxxx; Schelling, *System of Transcendental Philosophy*, SWC 3, p. 628; L. Dieckmann, "The Metaphor of Hieroglyphics in German Romanticism," *Comparative Literature* 7 (1955) 306 ff.

25. KA 18, p. 112.

26. KA 18, pp. 5 ff.

27. KA 19, p. 9; 18, p. 140.

28. KA 19, p. 3.

29. KA 19, p. 43

30. *Aus Schleiermachers Leben* 3, p. 315.

31. "Vorrede," *Jahrbücher der Medizin*, SWC 7, p. 131.

32. BD 1, p. 187. Schelling in November suggested that Fichte spend some time with him in Bamberg. He assured Fichte that his Catholic physicians were influential with the Bavarian ministers so that Fichte had nothing to fear from the government in Munich over his religious views that were causing difficulty in Berlin (BD 2, pp. 202 f.).

33. BD 2, p. 420.

34. "Einige Bemerkungen . . . ," *Magazin zur Vollkommnung* 2 (1800) 255 f.

35. Brown's *Elementa medicinae* (Edinburgh, 1784) was widely known in Germany. Röschlaub, in the introduction to the two volumes of his collected essays *Untersuchungen über die Pathogenie* (Frankfurt, 1798–1800), states that they are an elaboration of Brownian theory. See J. Neubauer, "Dr. John Brown and Early German Romanticism," *Journal of the History of Ideas* 28 (1978) 367 ff.; G.B. Risse, "Kant, Schelling and the Early Search for a Philosophical 'Science' of Medicine in Germany," *Journal for the History of Medicine and Allied Sciences* 27 (1972) 145 ff.

36. Schelling wrote to Goethe: "The new system of medicine is practiced here theoretically as well as practically with a precision which can be viewed nowhere else. I have found various friends of my writings in natural philosophy who have asked me to offer some lectures" (BD 1, p. 188). Schelling's writings on natural philosophy prior to 1800 consider polarity and organic development as ontological laws (see SWC 2, p. 331).

37. SWC 4, p. 352.

38. BD 1, p. 36; SPD 1, p. 182.

39. SWC 5, pp. 117 f.

40. A presentation of how the baroque prepared Bavaria for Romanticism can be found in H. Grassl, *Aufbruch zur Romantik* (Munich, 1968); see D. Mahnke, *Unendliche Sphäre und Allmittelpunkt* (Halle, 1937); G. Bürke, *Vom Mythos . . .* , pp. 194 f.

41. BD 2, p. 3.

42. BD 2, pp. 40 f.

2. First Disciples: Bavaria and the Rhineland

1. VAR, pp. 17 ff. Weiller was lauded for his work in education against "the children of darkness," whereas Schelling was described as the bestower upon medicine of a philosophical foundation. Weiller was soon to prove an untiring enemy of Schelling.

2. See E. Weiss, *Montgelas* (Munich, 1971).

3. BD 1, p. 105.

4. VAR, p. 5. A Landshut professor wrote: "The relationships of the professors here are the relationships of devils—almost literally: rudeness, impoliteness, hellish meanness, envy, calumny dominate" ("P.A. Feuerbach," ADB 6, p. 734). In 1809, Clemens Brentano warned Joseph Görres, who was interested in a position in Landshut, that there he would find "Enlightenmentism, demonism, intrigues, lying, phony piety, fashion-religion, patriotism, rustic simplicity, childishness and satanism" (J. Görres, *Gesammelte Briefe* [Frankfurt, 1955] 2, p. 72).

5. KThD 1, p. 55.

6. KThD 1, p. 56.

7. See T. Frost, *The Secret Societies of the European Revolution, 1777–1876* (London, 1876).

8. See R. Stölzle, *Ein Kantianer an der katholischen Akademie Dillingens und seine Schicksale, 1793/94* (Fulda, 1911), p. 1.

9. Steffens, *Was ich erlebte* (Leipzig, 1838), p. 406.

10. Sailer, *Neue Beiträge zur Bildung der Geistlichen* (Munich, 1811) 2, p. 270.

11. JMSB 1, pp. 312, 357; 2, pp. 26 f.

12. K. Eschweiler, "Joh. Mich. Sailer und sein Verhältnis zum deutschen Idealismus," *Wiederbegegnung von Kirche und Kultur in Deutschland* (Munich, 1927), p. 294.

13. JMSB 2, pp. 279, 292.

14. J. Geiselmann, *Von lebendiger Religiosität zum Leben der Kirche* (Stuttgart, 1932), p. 22. Georg Schwaiger disagrees: "The organic mode of thought of Romanticism helped him to join in an organic, vital unity on both sides of the church, the visible, fallible form on earth and the invisible, supernatural inner side" (KThD 1, p. 91).

15. Sailer, *Grundlehre der Religion* (Munich, 1814), 2nd ed., p. 103. One incomplete edition of Sailer's works counted 41 volumes. If there is one constant theme in his writings from the point of view of the philosophy of religion it is the dialogue with Kant. For Sailer this, and not Schelling, was the intellectual world that went beyond the Enlightenment. From the *Teaching on Reason* of 1785 and the *Lectures on Pastoral Theology* of 1789 to the 3-volume *Handbook of Christian Morality* of 1817, the philosophical problematic is Kantian.

16. *Grundlehre*, p. 127.

17. Ibid.

18. Cited in CK, p. 9.

19. Eschweiler, p. 319. Through Jacobi's influence in Munich, Sailer procured the reinstatement of his colleague Zimmer. Jacobi, however, was no friend to Roman

Catholicism, which he described as an "intolerable religious materialism" (G. Fischer, *J.M. Sailer und Jacobi* [Freiburg, 1955], p. 211).

20. VAR, pp. 170 ff. Sailer's positive attitude toward Schelling was short-lived. Schelling's controversy with Jacobi and his entrance further into religion only made Sailer more fearful. And yet, under the impact of the book on freedom, Sailer is supposed to have said: "Schelling is a man penetrated by God and immortality" (JMSB 1, p. 479). In 1822 Sailer became bishop of Regensburg, having previously been refused that ministry by Rome. In 1825 he witnessed the coronation of his pupil and spiritual son as Ludwig I. When Ludwig was planning a university professorship for Schelling, Sailer advised against it. By then it was clear to the old churchman, who reached his 81st birthday in 1832, that Schelling and the church were each intent upon their own supremacy.

21. Joseph Weber was born in 1753 in Donauwörth and was educated by both the Benedictines and the Jesuits. His interests lay with the sciences and he developed an instrument for measuring electricity. Ordained a priest, he began his teaching career in the subjects of canon law and catechetics at Dillingen in 1781. His first major work defended Kant against Stattler, but he soon began to question the Enlightenment. His studies in Landshut of Schelling's writings led to lectures on them after 1803. In 1804 he returned to Dillingen and devoted himself to more pastoral theological work. He died in 1831. Schelling and the appearance of Romantic idealism, full of possibilities for the renewal of Catholic intellectual life, remained the great event of his life. See H. Trefzger, *Der philosophische Entwicklungsgang von Joseph Weber* (Freiburg, 1932).

22. J. Salat, *Denkwürdigkeiten* (Landshut, 1823), p. 264.

23. BD 1, p. 322. Alois Gügler, a Swiss student of Zimmer and Sailer in Landshut from 1802 to 1804, founded in Lucerne a school of Catholic students of Schelling who also had connections with Drey and with Tübingen. Gügler recalled Zimmer's lecturing on Schelling: "This professor, so educated in philosophy, lectured on Schelling's thought with enthusiasm, careful clarity, thoroughness and depth" (J.L. Schiffmann, *Lebengeschichte . . . Gügler* [Augsburg, 1833] 2, p. 35).

24. P. Schäfer, *Philosophie und Theologie im Übergang von der Aufklärung zur Romantik* (Göttingen, 1971), p. 64.

25. Zimmer, *Philosophische Religionslehre* (Landshut, 1805) 1, pp. 1 f.

26. Ibid.

27. Ibid., pp. 212, 230.

28. Ibid., p. 215; SWC 4, p. 126.

29. Ibid., pp. 252 f.

30. Ibid., p. 266.

31. BD 1, p. 407.

32. In Ignaz Thanner (1770–1825) we have yet another Catholic Enlightenment theologian who incarnated the passage from Kant to Schelling. He had been influenced by Lessing as well as by Kant but study in Landshut led him to prefer Schelling. As the title of one of his books puts it, Kant, Fichte and Schelling are the escalation of idealism. Schelling's philosophy of identity shows us the ground of all, and it is eternal, vital, developing knowledge. In his *Encyclopedic Introduction* Thanner writes: "Living spirit, the essential, manifests its scientific form through productive unity and organic fullness mutually intertwined. Academics name this identity-in-totality. . . . In this

spirit rest the correct method as well as the entire richness of true knowledge, and of the form and material of knowing" (p. 75). Thanner tended to overlook the philosophy of nature; he wrote on academic studies and composed a dialogue on immortality resembling Schelling's *Clara*. He employed the aphorism genre, so popular with the Romantics, to interpret the speculative theology of church dogmas through the new philosophy: *Aphorismen der speculativen Dogmatik* (Salzburg, 1816).

33. OUS, p. 102.

34. KThD 1, p. 111.

35. See A. Sonnenschein, *Görres, Windischmann und Deutinger* (Bochum, 1928); A. Dryoff, *C.J. Windischmann und sein Kreis* (Cologne, 1916).

36. PW, p. 86.

37. See M. Braubach, "Zur Beurteilung des jungen Görres," and R. Reisse, "Die Weltanschauung des jungen Görres (1776–1806)," in GF; F. Nothardt, *Görres und sein "Rothes Blatt"* (Pforzheim, 1932).

38. Cited in J. Sepp, *Görres und seine Zeitgenossen* (Nördlingen, 1877), p. 75.

39. M. Koppel, "Schellings Einfluss auf die Naturphilosophie Görres," PhJ 47 (1934) 346.

40. SWC 2, p. 489.

41. GGS 2:1, p. 65. Schelling had written: "Art is paramount to the philosopher because it opens to him the holy of holies, where burns, in eternal and original unity—as if in a single flame—that which is divided into nature and history" (SWC 3, p. 628).

42. GGS 2:1, p. 169.

43. GGS 2:2, p. 12.

44. SWC 5, p. 120.

45. Letter of Nov. 15, 1804, in J. Görres, *Eine Auswahl* (Cologne, 1927), p. 220.

46. GGS 3, p. 11.

47. GGS 3, pp. 21 ff.

48. A. Stall, *Fr. Karl v. Savigny* (Berlin, 1929) 2, p. 191.

49. PL 2, p. 137.

50. *Mythengeschichte der asiatischen Welt, Auswahl*, pp. 198 f.

51. GGS 3, p. 414.

3. Würzburg and the Catholic Enlightenment

1. BD 1, pp. 184 f.

2. *Entschliessung* . . . , cited in F.X. von Wegele, *Geschichte der Universität Würzburg* (Würzburg, 1882), 2, p. 465.

3. Paulus came to Jena as a young professor in 1789. In fact Schelling was born in the house where earlier Paulus had come into this world. By 1803 Paulus was Schelling's enemy and at the end of his life the philosopher was involved in a bitter lawsuit with the exegete in Berlin, in 1845.

As Funk observed, the ideological relationships in Bavarian intellectual life at this time were remarkably confused; this new mixture of Protestant scholars only added to it (VAR, p. 148). The northern scholars were seen, whether they were or not, to be representatives of a secular Enlightenment and were presumed to be Prussians and Protestants. The Bavarians and other southerners were Catholics, pre-Enlightenment in supernatural faith and baroque in piety. Yet the northerners were opposed to Napoleon and advocated a limited monarchy; the Bavarians perceived ideas such as German unity, political freedom, republicanism as little more than slogans.

4. BD 3, pp. 18, 27; see A. Blackwell, "Three New Schleiermacher Letters Relating to His Würzburg Appointment of 1804," *Harvard Theological Review* 68 (1975) 333 f. F. Schlegel also applied for a position in Würzburg, which he failed to receive despite Schelling's support (PL 2, pp. 42, 142).

5. L. Günther, "Schelling in Würzburg," *Würzburger Universitäts-Almanach* 18 (1936–1937) 32 ff. See S. Merkle, "Würzburg im Zeitalter der Aufklärung," *Archiv für Kulturgeschichte* 11 (1914) 166–95; K. Schilling, *Die Kirchenlehre der Theologia Wirceburgensis* (Munich, 1969).

6. J. Salat, *Schelling in München* (Heidelberg, 1845) 2, p. 2.

7. Kant began this trend in writing books on the structure of a university with his *Streit der Fakultäten* (1798), and Fichte continued the genre. Schleiermacher wrote on the makeup of a theological faculty for the new university in Berlin. Among the Catholics, I. Thanner, the senior Döllinger, J.S. Drey and F. Staudenmaier published writings all drawing upon Schelling's influential book of 1802.

8. OUS, p. 82.

9. OUS, p. 96.

10. OUS, p. 102.

11. OUS, p. 97.

12. W. Dilthey, *Aus Schleiermachers Leben* (Berlin, 1863) 4, p. 579.

13. SWC 4, p. 129.

14. SWC 6, pp. 169 ff.

15. SWC 6, p. 178.

16. SWC 6, pp. 572, 558.

17. *Philosophie in ihrem Übergang zur Nicht-Philosophie* (Erlangen, 1803), p. 1.

18. Ibid., pp. 25, 30, 104. In 1804 Eschenmayer wrote to Schelling's reactionary colleague at Würzburg, J.J. Wagner: "Here is the point where I differ from Schelling: for him God is the absolute, for me the image of reason is the absolute, and God is beyond both" (BD 1, p. 320). In a letter in response, Schelling explains that he does not hold that the absolute is the ultimate self and that the subsistent subject is God. Rather there is "the eternal," which is the absoluteness of absoluteness or the indifference of subject and object. This would be the same as "God." Schelling was revising his natural philosophy to go beyond the absolute, to combine transcendent consciousness with transcendent godhead. This would appear to Hegel to be "the night in which all the cows are black."

19. SWC 6, pp. 38, 40.

20. J.F. Marquet, *Liberté et existence* (Paris, 1973), p. 233. "Is *Philosophy and Religion* the anticipation of the new freedom, a meteor signifying something new, a new horizon? Or does the change come in Munich with the writings of the mystics and with Franz von Baader after 1806? Certainly the idea of a fall and the removal of God not only from the self but from the earlier absolute are important. But in 1804 at Würzburg, these views are dangling from an idealist system waiting for a new approach demanded by the waves of religion and theology swirling around Schelling's career in Würzburg" (SPD 1, p. 478).

21. "It is well known how the general tone of dogmatic indifference spread through Catholic intellectual life. It is all too understandable how rationalist tendencies appeared

in Catholic theology that sought to disrobe dogmas of their supernatural character. . . . Nevertheless, the profound reforms of academic life, which go back to the 'Catholic Enlightenment' brought new life for biblical and historical theology and thereby helped dogmatic theology too" (A. Reatz, *Reformversuche in der katholischen Dogmatik zu Beginn des 19. Jhr.* [Mainz, 1917], p. 7).

22. N.W. Wendehorst, "Würzburg," LThK 10, p. 1276.

23. For an overview of the Catholic Enlightenment see W. Heizmann, *Kants Kritik spekulativer Theologie und Begriff moralischen Vernunftglaubens im katholischen Denken der späten Aufklärung* (Göttingen, 1976). Also, L. Swidler, *Aufklärung Catholicism, 1780–1850* (Missoula, 1978), which focuses on liturgy and the church and is marred by neglecting the groupings of Roman Catholic thinkers before and after Schelling; the latter—Romantic idealists—did not view themselves as of the Enlightenment.

24. Paulus, now unfriendly to Schelling, was included in the bishop's censure. Horst Fuhrmans believes it was the professor of New Testament who attracted the bishop's attention (BD 1, p. 293). The studies of Fechenbach by Wegel and Roesch do not mention this conflict with Schelling.

25. *Sextus* (Würzburg, 1804). Schelling did not take Berg seriously. The students mocked Berg, and a Catholic disciple of Schelling, J.C. Goetz, responded with a mediocre defense *Anti-Sextus* (Heidelberg, 1807). On Berg, see J.B. Schwab, *Franz Berg* (Würzburg, 1869). Berg's successor was Franz Oberthür, who brought an interesting mix of Roman Catholicism and the Enlightenment to patristics and pedagogy. See the studies on him by O. Volk, R. Stölzle, A. Lindig, L. Faulhaber. On Köppen and Berg as Romantic philosophers of nature, see J. Esposito, *Schelling's Idealism and Philosophy of Nature* (Lewisburg, Pa., 1977), pp. 164 ff. Two other Catholic critics of Schelling were J.J. Wagner and K.J. Kilian. Wagner was at Jena in 1798 as a student of Fichte, and Schelling assisted in his call to Würzburg. Wagner then turned against Schelling and attacked *Philosophy and Religion* in his university lectures. Schelling never took him seriously. See L. Rabus, *J.J. Wagner, Leben, Lehre, Bedeutung* (Nuremberg, 1862); BD 3, passim. Kilian was a priest and had been Caroline Schlegel's physician at Jena. Once close to Schelling and Hegel, the Romantics' intrigues alienated him from the movement. At Würzburg, he worked to turn the medical and science faculties against Schelling.

26. BD 3, p. 59. Hegel wrote to Schelling in November 1803, inquiring as to how he liked Würzburg and mentioning that at Weimar, Schiller was at work on Wilhelm Tell (BD 3, p. 29). Schelling wrote back: "Our situation is good, a pretty house and the enjoyments of the climate and the area. . . . There are certain reactions from the point of view of the clergy and others: without success, laughable" (BD 3, p. 56).

27. The review was in the *Jenaer Allgemeine Literaturzeitung*, #39, #41 (February 1805).

28. BD 3, p. 47.

29. Köppen, *Schellings Lehre oder das Ganze der Philosophie des absoluten Nichts* (Hamburg, 1803).

30. Salat, *Über den Geister der Verbesserung im Gegensatz mit dem Geist der Zerstörung* (Munich, 1805), p. 175.

31. Weiller, *Versuch eines Lehrgebäudes der Beziehungskunde* (Munich, 1802).

Weiller continued to write books on religious education and in 1813 he was still attacking Schelling in his *Grundriss der Geschichte der Philosophie* (Munich, 1813).

32. BD 3, pp. 198 f. "The situation of Schelling in the years 1803 to 1806 is determined greatly by a furious press campaign against him. [Journals] . . . carried mocking, ridiculing articles written by Salat and Weiller in almost every issue" (BD 3, p. 27).

33. BD 3, p. 263. Some state, incorrectly, that the refusal of an oath of loyalty to the new regime was Schelling's reason for leaving Würzburg. In this new reorganization the university became again officially Roman Catholic, and the new movements in German culture faded into the background. Kantians, however, such as Franz Berg, also lost their positions. Schelling knew that the older Catholic element would reorganize the university along traditional lines (PL 2, p. 78).

34. BD 3, p. 294. "We see now that the intermediate philosophy [at Munich] was the result of a beautiful agony of the system of identity during the years at Würzburg" (M. Vetö, *F. Schelling, Stuttgarter Privatvorlesungen* [Turin, 1973], p. 52).

4. A Dark Romanticism and a Subterranean Man

1. SPD 1, p. 501.

2. See L. Hammermaier, *Gründungs- und Frühgeschichte der bayerischen Akademie der Wissenschaften* (Munich, 1954). This academy is not to be confused with the one for fine arts, which at its foundation in 1808 had Schelling as its general secretary. Schelling's address before the king was his only complete work to be translated into English and published during his lifetime.

3. PW, p. 80.

4. PW, pp. 80 ff., 121 ff.

5. PW, p. 79.

6. H.U. von Balthasar, *Prometheus* (Heidelberg, 1947), p. 240.

7. BB, p. 231. Baader's brother Clemenz, a priest, worked for the abolition of celibacy, for church reform and various Josephist causes. Long before Nietzsche, Baader in 1818 spoke of cultural figures and movements who were "the murderers of God" (SW 2, pp. 58, 81).

8. Cited in K. Poppe, ed., *Baader, Schriften* (Stuttgart, 1969), p. 112. See F. Lieb, *F. Baaders Jugendgeschichte. Die Frühentwicklung eines Romantikers* (Munich, 1926).

9. SW 3, p. 249. See H. Grassl, *Fr. von Baaders Lehre von der Quarternar und die Dreiheitsspekulationen seiner Zeitgenossen* (Munich, 1949); J. Sauter, *Baader und Kant* (Jena, 1928), pp. 540 ff. Schelling's *Ideas for a Philosophy of Nature*, published in 1797, show some similarities to the *Contributions to a Fundamental Physiology* of 1796; see BB, p. 184.

10. SWC 2, p. 546; 4, p. 147.

11. PL 2, p. 101.

12. *Caroline. Briefe aus der Frühromantik* (Bern, 1970) 2, p. 420.

13. SWC 7, p. 120. As early as 1802 Schelling designated his philosophical

Anschauung as mysticism and spoke positively of the great Protestant and the "crystal-bright" Catholic mystics; see SWC 3, pp. 537 f.

14. *Kritische Fragmente*, SWC 7, p. 247.

15. SW 15, p. 381.

16. PL 2, p. 101.

17. BD 1, p. 416.

18. SWC 7, p. 352.

19. SWC 7, p. 366. These analogies are based upon medicine and show that the triad of medicine, natural philosophy and idealism has been joined by mysticism. The reference is to an article by Baader on an analogy between knowing and sexuality published in Schelling's *Jahrbücher* in 1808.

20. SWC 7, p. 375.

21. R. Brown, *The Later Philosophy of Schelling* (Lewisburg, Pa., 1977), p. 127. "Apart from the explicit mention of Baader by name, the entire essay resounds with Baader's philosophical themes" (Sauter, *Baader und Kant*, p. 543).

22. SWC 7, pp. 360 f.

23. Ibid.

24. Ibid.

25. SWC 8, pp. 55 ff. In a letter, Schelling remarked of Jacobi: "[He] knows how to trick the world . . . an unbelievable pretension joined to an emptiness of heart and spirit" (PL 2, p. 270).

26. Letter of 1815, SW 15, p. 280.

27. SW 3, p. 285. Cf. K. Fischer, *Franz von Baader. Versuch einer Characteristik seiner Theosophie und ihres Verhältnisses zu den Systemen Schellings* (Erlangen, 1865), pp. 22 ff.

28. For letters breaking off the relationship in December 1824, see SW 15, pp. 420 f.

29. SW 15, p. 159. On Hegel and Baader, see H. Grassl, "Ein Brief Hegels an Baader," *Hegel-Studien* 2 (1963) 105 ff.

30. SW 15, p. 464. Minister E. Schenck must have been surprised to receive from Baader a description of Schelling's philosophy of nature (which had so inspired Baader and Görres twenty years earlier) as "anti-religious" (SW 15, p. 438).

31. AW, pp. 205 ff. See T.F. O'Meara, "Process and God in Schelling's Early Thought," *Listening* 14 (1979) 223 ff.

32. Letter printed in C. Kahn-Wallerstein, *Schellings Frauen* (Erlangen, 1959), pp. 236 f.; for further documentation see SPD 2, pp. 103 f. In a letter to his devout Lutheran mother in 1815, Schelling wrote: "The lie that I have become a Catholic is, most likely, meant maliciously. . . . I am sorry it causes you pain. To deny it is beneath me. Otherwise, worrying about the present regime would not hold me back [from such a denial], a worry which, moreover, is not necessary. From different sides there are denials in the journals. . . . Don't worry: my happiness lies not in the hands of men but with God" (PL 2, p. 352).

33. C. von Höffler in T. Borodajkewicz, *Deutscher Geist und Katholizismus* (Leipzig, 1935), pp. 64, 126.

34. Hegel, *Vorlesungen über die Philosophie der Weltgeschichte* (Lasson, 1920) 4, pp. 886 ff.

35. SWC 14, p. 324.

5. Founder at Tübingen: Johann Sebastian Drey

1. Because of his Würzburg experience Schelling deplored the mix in Tübingen of Protestant and Catholic theologians (PL 2, p. 381).

2. "Revision des gegenwärtigen Zustandes der Theologie," in J. Geiselmann, CK, pp. 83 ff. Elsewhere Drey mentioned that half a century had passed since scholasticism had faded into the background (KE, p. 5).

3. KThD 1, p. 111. Drey reviewed Thanner's essay on theology and Schelling, the *Aphorismen . . .* , in TQ 1 (1819).

4. On Schleiermacher and Drey, see R. Stalder, *Grundlinien der Theologie Schleiermachers* (Wiesbaden, 1969).

5. KE, p. 1. W. Fehr observed in Drey's own copy of the KE the name "Schelling" written in Drey's hand next to a passage on theological science (*Method and System in the Dogmatics of J.S. Drey, Founder of the Catholic Tübingen School* [Yale, Diss., 1970], p. 19).

6. KE, p. 3.

7. KE, p. 10; cf. pp. 7 ff.

8. KE, p. 65.

9. Schelling rejected the position that revelation was a special "action God performed" (OUS, p. 92). He observed that incarnation and mysticism meet in nature (OUS, pp. 88 f.). For the early Schelling, incarnation and symbol find their material in nature intuited as the place of idealism's disclosure of the absolute.

10. Drey, *Apologetik* (Mainz, 1838) 1, p. 199. Drey states that an apologetic mean would lie between rationalists and supranaturalists, a polarity set by in Schelling's early letters on dogmatism, and adopted by many thinkers up to Paul Tillich. For a study of the influence upon Drey in works other than KE, see Fehr, *Method and System . . . .*

11. Journals in CK, pp. 187 ff.

12. KE, pp. 4, 22.

13. KE, p. 33.

14. "Aphorismen . . . ," TQ 8 (1826) 268 ff.

15. SWC 4, p. 145.

16. SWC 4, pp. 360 f., 382.

17. SWC 4, p. 405.

18. SWC 5, p. 505.

19. OUS, p. 89.

20. KE, p. 150.

21. *Giessener Jahrbuch* 1 (1834) 100.

22. KE, p. 57.

23. OUS, pp. 82, 84 f.

24. OUS, p. 95.

25. SWC 5, p. 293 (author's translation; cf. OUS, p. 90).

26. OUS, p. 85.

27. "Ideen zur Geschichte des katholischen Dogmensystems," CK, p. 245.

28. *The Great Chain of Being* (Cambridge, Mass., 1936), p. 323.

29. SWC 2, p. 39; cf. p. 534.

30. SWC 3, p. 279.

31. SWC 7, pp. 346; SWC 4, p. 422.

32. From Drey's journals cited in CK, pp. 138 ff.
33. KE, p. 41.
34. "Vom Geist und Wesen des Katholizismus," cited in CK, p. 205.
25. "Vom Geist und Wesen . . . ," cited in TQ 1 (1819) 197 f.
36. "[In Drey] we have the first Catholic theologian who, with dialectical development, shows the way to determine the idea of revelation in the context of science. Kuhn and Staudenmaier follow him" (J. Geiselmann, *Die Katholische Tübinger Schule* Freiburg, 1964, p. 31). Drey's journals are filled with notes on the theology of tradition; CK, pp. 148 ff.
37. O. Braun, "Briefe Schellings an seine Söhne," HD 9 (1911) 322 f.

6. The System-Builders

1. SWC 9, p. 221.
2. E. von Schenk, "Die Bischöfe J.M. Sailer und G.M. Wittmann," *Charitas* (Regensburg, 1838), pp. 251 ff. Schenk, a convert from Protestantism, had heard in person Schelling at Jena, "in the first fire and truly titanic power of his youth" (M. Spindler, *Eduard von Schenk* [Munich, 1931], p. xxvii).
3. J. Salat, *Schelling in München* (Heidelberg, 1845) 2, p. 115; H. Fuhrmans, "Schellings Briefe aus Anlass seiner Berufung nach München im Jahre 1827," PhJ 64 (1956) 277. Schenk urged Schelling upon the king: " . . . That doubt against religion might not have the upper hand through a philosophy of pure reason but rather, that philosophy would present the necessity and need for revealed religion" (M. Huber, *Ludwig I von Bayern und die Ludwig-Maximilians Universität in München, 1826–1832* [Würzburg, 1939], p. 34).
4. Ringseis, *Erinnerungen* (Regensburg, 1886–1891) 2, pp. 240 ff.
5. M. Doeberl, "Bausteine zu einer Biographie des Bischofs Sailer," HPBl 155 (1913) 805.
6. Salat, *Schelling* . . . , 2, pp. 56 f.
7. VAR, p. 61.
8. "Dokumente zu Schelling Forschung, II," *Kant-Studien* 47 (1955) 277.
9. Ringseis, *Erinnerungen* 2, p. 259. The theological faculty, unlike the philosophical and historical, had no universal geniuses or famous figures. Some of the theology professors had been influenced by Sailer. A pastoral and moral tone pervaded the lectures in many of the theological disciplines. In exegesis there was an emphasis upon textual research; Christianity was presented within the framework of the idea of the kingdom of God. Döllinger's chair in church history did not keep him from lecturing in canon law, exegesis, scriptural canon and the history of dogma. He and his friend Möhler (who was active in Munich for only a short time before his death), brought some distinction to the theologians. Heinrich Klee, whom his students equated with the gifted Möhler, arrived in 1839 as Möhler's successor. Schelling as well as Sailer, Windischmann and Görres had been his mentors. While at Bonn, Klee wrote a *System* and an *Enzyklopädie*; both were responses to Hermes and the Rhenish Kantians, and both were formulated with the help of ideas from Schelling and Hegel (KThD 1, pp. 380 ff.). On the Munich theological faculty, see H. Witetschek, "Die Bedeutung der theologischen Fakultät der Universität München," HJ 86 (1966) 107 ff.

10. M. Frank, ed., *Schelling. Philosophie der Offenbarung 1841/42* (Frankfurt, 1977) (Paulus's text).

11. SWC 12, p. 231.

12. SWC 13, pp. 268, 348.

13. SWC 11, p. 65.

14. SWC 11, pp. 193, 198.

15. SWC 13, pp. 327, 318; 14, p. 277.

16. SPD 2, p. 467.

17. SWC 14, p. 77.

18. SWC 14, p. 124.

19. SWC 14, p. 142.

20. SWC 14, pp. 239, 296.

21. Staudenmaier, "Andenken an Fr. von Schlegel," TQ 14 (1832) 644, 650.

22. J.W. Goethe, *Briefe, Gedenkausgabe* (Zurich, 1949) 18, p. 543.

23. Cited in E. Behler, "Zur Theologie der Romantik," *Hochland* 52 (1959) 342.

24. "Die Entwicklung der Philosophie . . . ," KA 12, pp. 130 f.

25. SWC 7, p. 339.

26. KA 11, p. 26.

27. PL 2, p. 302. On the rediscovery and use of Indian thought by the Romantics and idealists, see S. Sommerfeld, *Indienschau und Indiendeutung romantischer Philosophen* (Zurich, 1943).

28. Letter of Nov. 13, 1817, cited in KA 8, p. cxlii.

29. KA 8, p. 588.

30. Letter of July 1828 in J. Korner, *Krisenjahre der Frühromantik* (Bern, 1969) 2, p. 448.

31. Doeberl, "Bausteine . . . ," p. 805.

32. Cited in A. Dempf, "Der frühe und späte Schlegel," *Weltordnung und Heilsgeschichte* (Einsiedeln, 1958), p. 93.

33. Korner, *Krisenjahre* . . . , 2, p. 448.

34. KA 14, pp. 233 f.

35. Behler, "Zur Theologie . . . ," p. 352.

36. E. Behler, "Einleitung," KA 10, p. lxviii.

37. GGS 4, p. 453; see J. Grisar, "Görres religiöse Entwicklung: Die Rückkehr zum katholischen Glauben," *Stimmen der Zeit* 112 (1927) 332 ff.

38. K.A. von Müller, "Görres Berufung nach München," GF, p. 222.

39. H. Raab, "Görres und die Geschichte," HJ 93 (1973) 74.

40. See H. Kapfinger, *Der Eoskreis, 1828–1832* (Munich, 1928). A more successful periodical was begun in 1838 by Görres and his son, the *Historisch-politische Blätter*. Reports and analysis from all areas of culture characterized the issues. The first volume discussed French politics, poverty and the legal system, bishops in Poland, Catholics in Scotland. For lengthy surveys, see the "Introductions" to GGS 16.

41. *Briefe* 1 (Munich, 1825), pp. 291.

42. "Die wahre und falsche Geschichte," *Eos* 12 (1828), in GGS 15, p. 49. Hegel reviewed some of Görres's early lectures on the nature of history in the *Jahrbücher für wiss. Kritik*, Nos. 55 seq. (1831).

43. W. Schellberg, "Neue Görresfund," GF, p. 2.

44. Görres cited in E. Conrads, *Der Wandel in der Görres'schen Geschichtsauffassung* (Münster, 1937), p. 15.

45. Görres in ibid., p. 21.

46. "Preface" to Görres's edition of writings of Henry Suso (Regensburg, 1884), p. lxxii.

47. PW, p. 89. "The genius of Görres was certainly for Schelling a kind of challenge. And we could cite, following Fuhrmans, many pages which seem to have colored the first drafts of *Weltalter* and the *Philosophy of Mythology*. The difficulty which remains . . . is the manifest allergy of Schelling to Görres's writings" (SPD 2, pp. 589 f.).

48. PL 3, p. 97.

49. SPD 2, pp. 398, 403, 426.

50. A. Dempf, *Görres spricht zu unser Zeit* (Freiburg, 1933), p. 55.

51. GF, p. 96.

52. I. Sepp, *Görres* (Berlin, 1896), p. 179.

53. M. Koppel, "Schellings Einfluss auf die Naturphilosophie Görres," PhJ 47 (1934) 67.

54. "In *The Christian Mystic* Görres created a monument of the religious spirit which is a crowning achievement. It is a gathering together of all the streams of late Romanticism which search into all that is puzzling and mysterious. . . . In it we have the rediscovery of the piety of the Middle Ages through Wackenroder, Tieck and Novalis, the research into the history of myth through Creuzer and Grimm, the organic worldview of the early Schelling and the theosophy of the late Schelling, the philosophical and theological undertakings of Baader and Günther, the popular interest in parapsychological phenomena, the medical system of Ringseis and his Romantic predecessors, and the full enterprise of renewal in Catholic life. In this sense, Görres's *Mystik* is a *summa*, a presentation of Catholic Spätromantik" (G. Bürke, *Vom Mythos zur Mystik* [Einsiedeln, 1958] p. 243).

55. Görres, "Die Berufung deutscher Gelehrten nach Berlin," HPBl 9 (1842) 48 ff.

56. Review of Baader's writings in TQ 14 (1832) 135.

57. "Mein Cursus philosophicus in München . . . ," SW 15, pp. 114 ff.

58. E. Benz, *Die abendländische Sendung der* Östlich-orthodoxen Kirche (Wiesbaden, 1950), p. 831.

59. SW 15, p. 593.

60. SW 10, p. 256.

61. SW 8, p. 187.

62. SW 8, pp. 229 ff.

63. SW 8, p. 3.

64. SW 5, pp. 371 f.

65. F. Hartl, *Franz von Baader* (Graz, 1971), pp. 40 ff.

66. See the writings of E. Benz on Baader and nihilism, socialism, eschatology and Marxism.

7. Between Schelling and Hegel

1. K. Eschweiler, *J.A. Möhlers Kirchenbegriff* (Braunsberg, 1930), pp. 167 f.

2. Staudenmaier, "Über den unpersönlichen Gott des Pantheismus . . . ," *Jahrbücher für Theologie und christliche Philosophie* 1 (1834) 302.

3. Staudenmaier, *Darstellung und Kritik des Hegelschen Systems* (Mainz, 1844), p. 5.

4. KThD 2, p. 99.

5. Review of Schleiermacher's *Der christliche Glaube* in TQ 15 (1833) 699. "And so now we have clearly the principle upon which Schleiermacher built his dogmatics. It is not the spirit of Christ who explains himself out of his divine origins; it is the human personality which somehow piously raises itself in faith toward . . . revelation" (ibid., p. 523).

6. B. Caspar, "Einleitung," F.A. Staudenmaier, *Frühe Aufsätze und Rezensionen* (Freiburg, 1974), pp. 12 f.

7. Staudenmaier, "Über den unpersönlichen Gott . . . ," p. 313.

8. "Das göttliche Prinzip in der Geschichte . . . ," *Jahrbücher für Theologie . . . ,* 4 (1835) 5 ff. Staudenmaier had joined the large group of intellectuals who with Schelling and Schleiermacher and Drey addressed the topic of the nature of a university and a theological school; *Über das Wesen* (Freiburg, 1939).

9. *Jahrbücher für Theologie . . . ,* 4 (1835) 30, 35. The *Enzyklopädie der theologischen Wissenschaften als System der gesamten Theologie* (Mainz, 1834) begins by setting aside amalgamations of biblical and patristic texts; the encyclopedia, Staudenmaier wrote, is a system, an arrangement of multiplicity in totality, to let the central Christian ideal unfold organically in all of religious science. Schelling's philosophy up to 1809 is present in the structure and general philosophy of religion.

10. Staudenmaier, *Die Philosophie des Christentums* (Giessen, 1840), p. 226.

11. Staudenmaier, *Der Geist der göttlichen Offenbarung* (Giessen, 1837), p. 37.

12. Ibid., p. 39.

13. Ibid., p. 113. Staudenmaier speculated that the first awakening of our consciousness of God coincides with the first divine revelation to us. Originally for the human race these were the same; in Eden primal man and woman were caught up in the awareness of metaphysical identity which was also grace and revelation (*J.S. Erigena* [Frankfurt, 1834], pp. 23 ff). Did Staudenmaier agree with Schelling that history is not only a moral but an ontological fall?

14. The quote is from a review of books by Günther, TQ 14 (1832) 107 ff.

15. "Schelling appears as someone from the past . . . " (*Die Philosophie . . . ,* pp. 287 ff.).

16. Staudenmaier, "Über die Philosophie der Offenbarung von Schelling," *Zeitschrift für katholische Theologie* 8 (1842) 247 ff.

17. Staudenmaier, *Die christliche Dogmatik* (Freiburg, 1850) 3, p. 61.

18. K. Eschweiler, *J.A. Möhlers Kirchenbegriff*, pp. 18 ff.

19. I. Döllinger, ed., *J.A. Möhler, Gesammelte Schriften* (Regensburg, 1840) 2, p. 229.

20. J. Fitzer, *Möhler and Baur in Controversy, 1832–1838* (Missoula, Mont., 1974), p. 15.

21. Möhler, *Die Einheit in der Kirche* (Mainz, 1825), pp. 9, 50.

22. Ibid., p. 15. Möhler did not hesitate to employ as a description of Christianity phrases such as "the religion of the spirit" or "the true philosophy." "Whoever conceives of the gospel as the revelation of the highest reason whose acceptance in faith ought to express the spiritual life of the human person according to the facet of psychic life we call faith, must, to be consistent, view the church as the living objectification of

the gospel. The Christian religion is one with true philosophy and the teaching of the church is one with the gospel" ("Anselm," *Gesammelte Schriften* 1, p. 143).

23. J. Geiselmann, *Die Katholische Tübingen Schule* (Freiburg, 1964), pp. 572 ff.

24. *Einheit* . . . , p. 112.

25. Möhler's dynamic ecclesiology led him to work actively on practical issues of church reform such as liturgical renewal, clerical celibacy, etc. See KThD 2, p. 89; W. Leinweber, *Der Streit um den Zölibat im 19. Jh.* (Münster, 1938).

26. *Einheit* . . . , p. 93.

27. Ibid., p. 117.

28. J. Geiselmann, "Der Wandel des Kirchenbewusstseins und die Kirchlichkeit in der Theologie J. Möhlers," *Sentire Ecclesiam*, ed. J. Danielou (Freiburg, 1961), pp. 615 ff. On the shift to Hegel, see Geiselmann, "Zur Einführung . . . ," in J.A. Möhler, *Symbolik* (Cologne, 1960), pp. 96 ff.

29. For Möhler's evaluation of Schellingian philosophy, see his discussion of revelation, philosophy and religion with Bautain; "Sendschreiben an Herrn Bautain," *Gesammelte Schriften* 2, pp. 196 ff.

30. *Symbolik* drew forms not only from Plank but from Marheineke. The latter's *Grundlehren der christlichen Dogmatik* (1819) showed influences from Schelling: from the *Lectures on University Studies*, from *Philosophy and Religion*, from the *Essay on Freedom*. The second edition of this work shows its author's turn to Hegel; see F. Zoeller, *Marheinekes Grundlehre der christlichen Dogmatik in ihrer Abhängigkeit von Schelling* (Erlangen, 1909).

31. F. Wolfinger, *Der Glaube nach J.E. von Kuhn* (Göttingen, 1972), pp. 20 ff.

32. Kuhn, "Über den Begriff und das Wesen der speculativen Theologie oder christlichen Philosophie," TQ 14 (1832) 411 f.

33. SPD 2, p. 243.

34. Kuhn, *Jacobi und die Philosophie seiner Zeit* (Mainz, 1834), p. 524.

35. Ibid., p. 59.

36. Kuhn, "Die Schellingsche Philosophie und ihr Verhältnis zum Christentum," TQ 26 (1844); 27 (1845).

37. Ibid., TQ 26 (1844) p. 219.

38. Ibid., TQ 27 (1845), p. 39.

39. Wolfinger, *Der Glaube* . . . , p. 155.

40. KThD 2, p. 140.

8. The Decline of the Munich Circle

1. L. Kastner, *Martin Deutingers Leben und Schriften* (Munich, 1875) 1, p. 6. Kastner completed only one volume, covering the years up to 1852, in the life of his "teacher and friend" (p. 2). It is interesting to see how the writers from the period 1870 to 1919 lost a certain feeling for the era of Romantic idealism.

2. H. Beckers (1806–1889) liked to call himself "the last Schellingian" (A. Dryoff, "Martin Deutinger als Vorläufer der Wertphilosophie," PhJ 28 (1915) 458.

3. KThD 2, pp. 272 ff.

4. SW 15, pp. 635 ff. Baader, in these pages, presents a remarkable critique of

idealist trinitarian thought through the Latin and Greek fathers. Schelling would have agreed that the Trinity was the absolute. He, however, affirmed a dual life-scenario in God. The divine, esoteric life is complete and inaccessible to us. (Here Schelling recalls the distinction made by the German mystics between the godhead and God.) The exoteric life is the concrete realization and unfolding of God's life in cosmic history— much more than revealed information about God.

5. Kastner, p. 8.

6. M. Deutinger, *Grundlinien einer positiven Philosophie* (Regensburg, 1843– 1853) 1, pp. 15 ff.

7. Ibid., 3, pp. 384–86.

8. Ibid., pp. 138, 144.

9. Ibid., p. 394.

10. Ibid., pp. 401 ff.

11. Deutinger, "Philosophische Meditationen über den letzten Grund des menschlichen Wissens," *Siloah* 2 (1850) 711. "The time has come to unite the true supernatural content of scholastic theology with the natural method of subjective philosophy and to replace the empty form of the Middle Ages and the emptied content of modern philosophy with a positive system in which object and subject, knowing and faith, are brought in full harmony with consciousness" (p. 731).

12. Kastner, p. 595. Scholars agree that Deutinger's aesthetics is closer to Hegel's than to the works of Schelling from 1800 to 1804. See W. Neckmann, *Das Wesen der Kunst in der Aesthetik M. Deutingers* (Salzburg, 1966).

13. Deutinger, *Über das Verhältnis der Poesie zur Religion* (Augsburg, 1861), p. 11.

14. From a lecture cited in Kastner, p. 378.

15. *Grundlinien* 1, pp. 10 f.

16. Deutinger, "Der katholische Standpunkt aller wahren Kritik," *Beilage zur Augsburger Postzeitung* (1845), 101 f.

17. Dryoff is the advocate of a close connection between Schelling and Deutinger, whose work "is essentially rooted in certain positions of Schelling" (p. 459). On the perhaps greater influence of Baader, see KThD 2, pp. 272, 284.

18. Deutinger, *Das Prinzip der neueren Philosophie . . .* (Regensburg, 1857), pp. 383 ff., 434 ff.

19. Ibid., pp. 356, 252.

20. Ibid., p. 261.

21. Ibid., p. 293.

22. Deutinger, "Philosophische Briefe," *Abendblatt zur neuen Münchener Zeitung* 32 (1856) 125. Deutinger is reviewing the published form of H. Beckers's address on Schelling for an anniversary of the Bavarian Academy. On Deutinger and Döllinger, see L. Dotzler, "Über das Verhältnis M. Deutingers zu I. Döllinger," *Jahrbuch für altbayerische Kirchengeschichte* (Munich, 1963), 130 ff.

23. I. Döllinger, *Chronik der Ludwig-Maximilians-Universität für das Jahr, 1870– 1871* (Munich, 1872), p. 109.

24. "The agreement of Professor Döllinger with Schelling's natural philosophy was so great that Döllinger would have given the lectures on that topic at the university if Schelling had not come in 1803" (J. Speigl, *Traditionslehre und Traditionsbeweis in*

der historischen Theologie I. Döllingers [Essen, 1964], p. 1). Döllinger senior wrote a book on the popular topic of university studies; it owed much to Schelling's lectures on that topic held after 1802. See J. Friedrich, *I. v. Döllinger* (Munich, 1899) 1, pp. 35 ff.

25. KThD 3, p. 14.

26. A. Rio, *Epilogue à l'art chrétien* (Fribourg, 1870) 2, p. 195.

27. G. Goyau, *Lettres de Montalambert à Lamennais* (Paris, 1933), p. 175.

28. S. Lösch, *Döllinger und Frankreich* (Munich, 1955), p. 102.

29. See Döllinger, *Geschichte der christlichen Kirche* (Landshut, 1833–1835), cited in "Memoir," to Möhler's *Symbolism* (New York, 1844), p. 33.

30. Döllinger, *Akademische Vorträge* (Nördlingen, 1889) 2, pp. 47 ff.

31. Speigl, p. 70.

32. For a comparison of Döllinger and Möhler on historical process in the church, see Speigl, pp. 42 ff.

33. "Die Schellingsche Philosophie und die christliche Theologie," HPBl 11 (1843) 585 ff; 753 ff.

34. TAW, p. 262.

35. Döllinger, *Chronik*, p. 109.

Conclusion

1. A. Jung, *Fr. W.J. von Schelling und eine Unterredung mit demselben im Jahre 1838 zu München* (Leipzig, 1864), p. 52.

2. E. Corti, *Ludwig I von Bayern* (Munich, 1960), p. 158.

3. Ibid., p. 210.

4. VAR, p. 62. See also SGPP, p. 35.

5. PL 3, p. 600.

6. "Die Berufung deutscher Gelehrten nach Berlin," HPBl 9 (1842) 48 ff.

7. R. Haym, *Hegel und seine Zeit* (Berlin, 1857), p. 6.

8. Cited in M. Frank, ed., *F. W.J. Schelling, Philosophie der Offenbarung (1841/42)* (Stuttgart, 1977), p. 9.

9. The liturgical theologian R. Liliencron, cited in H. Pölcher, "Schellings Auftreten in Berlin (1841) nach Höhrerberichten," ZRG 6 (1954) 196.

10. A.B. Marx in ibid.

11. F. von Tschudi in ibid., p. 199. See A. Koktanek, *Schellings erste Münchener Vorlesung, 1827/28* (Munich, 1959).

12. Frank, ed., *Philosophie* . . . , p. 43.

13. Pölcher, "Schellings Auftreten . . . ," pp. 202 ff.; see A. Dempf, "Kierkegaard hört Schelling," *Weltordnung und Heilsgeschichte* (Einsiedeln, 1958), pp. 56 ff.

14. Pölcher, "Schellings Auftreten . . . ," p. 207.

15. Letter of Oct. 30, 1843, in W. Bolin, ed., *Ausgewählte Briefe* (Leipzig, 1904) 2, p. 127; cf. Frank, *Philosophie* . . . , p. 18.

16. L. Trost, F. Leist, *König Maximilian II von Bayern und Schelling, Briefwechsel* (Stuttgart, 1890), p. 280.

17. Ibid., pp. 115 f., 261.

18. C. Hinrichs, "Schelling und 'der Konflikt der modernen Welt' in Rankes 'Epoche der neuren Geschichte,' " in W. Berges, ed., *Zur Geschichte und Problematik der Demokratie* (Berlin, 1958), p. 88.

19. L. von Ranke, *Das Briefwerk*, W. Fuchs, ed. (Hamburg, 1949), p. 377; cf. P. C. Hayner, *Reason and Existence* (Leiden, 1967).

20. PL 3, p. 180.

21. O. Braun, "Briefe Schellings an seine Söhne," HD 9 (1911) 322 f.

22. Ibid.

23. Baader, Letter of 1838, SW 15, p. 569.

24. Cited in R. Reinhardt, "Die katholisch-theologische Fakultät Tübingen," KThNJ, p. 74.

25. J. Kleutgen, *Philosophie der Vorzeit* 1 (Innsbruck, 1878), p. 10. Cf. G. McCool, *Nineteenth Century Catholic Theology* (New York, 1977).

26. Cf. B. Casper, "Hegel in der Sicht Kleutgens," KThNJ, pp. 167 ff.

27. Kleutgen, *Philosophie der Vorzeit* 1, pp. 8 ff. "What was opposed to the truth of the Middle Ages was not idealism, which the churchmen of the new era did not take time to master or have the intellectual power to grasp, but simply a general fear of what was other: the *venenum Protestantismi*" (KThD 2, p. 145).

28. Cf. T. Hartley, *Thomistic Revival and the Modernist Era* (Toronto, 1971).

29. G. Schwaiger, "Die Münchener Gelehrtenversammlung von 1963 in den Strömungen der katholischen Theologie des 19. Jahrhunderts," KThNJ, p. 127. We find the attitude of the Vatican toward the assembly (do not exchange obedience and conformity with the magisterium for freedom, philosophy of a profane nature and modern science) in the letter to the archbishop of Munich, *Tuas libenter* (Dec. 21, 1863); *Acta Sanctae Sedis* 8 (1974) 436 ff.

30. On P. Schanz, see H. Fries in KThD 3, pp. 190 ff.; Schmid wrote essays on Schelling, Baader and Görres as well as Möhler; his *Wissenschaftliche Richtungen . . .* (Munich, 1962) is a good summary of Catholic thought at that time. Schell's *Die neue Zeit und der alte Glaube* (Würzburg, 1897) and Frohschammer's *Einleitung in die Philosophie und Grundriss der Metaphysik* (Munich, 1858) also look back at Schelling and at the present changing times.

31. M. Heidegger, *Schellings Abhandlung über das Wesen der menschlichen Freiheit (1809)* (Tübingen, 1971), pp. 4, 2.

32. M. Heidegger, "A Recollection," *Man and His World* 3 (1970) 4.

33. E. Przywara, *Humanitas* (Nuremberg, 1949), p. 303.

34. H. U. von Balthasar, *Herrlichkeit* (Einsiedeln, 1965), 3:1, p. 904. Schelling lived on in a vital way in Slavic thought. He was very much at the center of Russian circles devoted to German idealism and Romanticism where Khomiakov, Soloviev, Berdiaev and Kirjeuski studied him. See W. Setschkaroff, *Schellings Einfluss in der russischen Literatur* (Leipzig, 1939).

Bibliography

LITERATURE ON THE HISTORY of Roman Catholic theology after Trent, apart from neoscholasticism, is sparse. Until recently there has been only the occasional doctoral dissertation, inevitably in German. In English, hardly an article, much less a book, has been written on Roman Catholic intellectual life in Germany in the eighteenth and nineteenth centuries.

A rediscovery of the vitality of the early nineteenth century began in Germany after 1900, and a few books on figures such as Sailer or Staudenmaier appeared before the Second World War halted this process of rediscovery. J. Geiselmann studied the manuscripts of the theologians of the Catholic Tübingen school to introduce to the world Drey, Möhler and Kuhn. S. Lösch, P. Funk and K. Eschweiler produced scholarly monographs on this period; they were pieces for a larger mosaic. E. Przywara and H.U. von Balthasar were aware of the riches of the Catholic nineteenth century and of Schelling's position there. In the 1930s, Yves Congar reintroduced Möhler's theology of church and tradition in such a way that it had a major impact upon the ecclesiology of this century and upon Vatican II.

Recently a second generation of interest in the nineteenth century has set to work, its most significant contribution being the three volumes edited by H. Fries and G. Schwaiger: *Katholische Theologen Deutschlands im 19. Jahrhundert*. Bibliographies in these volumes list monographs and articles, often in inaccessible tomes, dealing with more than thirty German philosophers and theologians from the period from 1775 to 1900. This collection is a symbol of the increasing number of books and articles written in the last decade in Germany on the nineteenth century, especially the first half.

From the point of view of Schelling studies, Horst Fuhrmans's *Schellings Philosophie der Weltalter* presents in detail Schelling's intellectual move into religion, mysticism and Christianity. X. Tilliette's massive study *Schelling. Une philosophie en devenir* offers in his lengthy notes a great deal of material relating Schelling to the Catholic theological world of his time.

German authors give some access to Catholic Romantic and idealist theology, but the English reader has very few aids. M. Schoof's *A Survey of Catholic Theology, 1800–1970* is a hundred pages of ideas on some modernists (mostly French) and some theologians (mostly from Tübingen). The book is representative of most non-German literature: it fails to present a historical picture, singles out condemned modernists from different periods and countries, and overlooks the deeper cultural dynamics of the period. Loisy and Renan are lumped together with Hermes and Günther; Sailer and Drey are omitted.

Alexander Dru's *The Contribution of German Catholicism* does understand the diversity of periods in German Catholicism over the past century; the volume is, however, no more than an outline. G. McCool's *Catholic Theology in the Nineteenth Century* is about the second half of the nineteenth century. With the exception of sections on Drey and on France, it is a study of J. Kleutgen, the German Jesuit largely responsible for the successful reintroduction of neoscholasticism. The book is, then, a history of the *reaction* to the Catholic Romantic idealists, to the circles around Schelling, to the earlier age of theological exploration and confidence. P. Gottfried's *Conservative Millenarians* looks at the Catholic intellectuals in Munich from the point of view of social theory.

The following bibliography is of general works on Roman Catholic intellectual life in the late eighteenth and the nineteenth century. For bibliographical information on individual figures, articles in Fries-Schwaiger should be consulted.

J. Altholz, *The Churches in the Nineteenth Century* (Indianapolis, 1967).

R. Aubert, *Die Kirche in der Gegenwart, Handbuch der Kirchengeschichte* (Freiburg, 1971).

R. Bauer, *Der Idealismus und seine Gegner in Osterreich* (Heidelberg, 1966).

J. Bellamy, *La théologie catholique au XIXème siècle* (Paris, 1904).

H. Bruck, *Geschichte der katholischen Kirche in Deutschland im 19. Jh.* (Münster, 1887–1908).

J.A.M. Brühl, *Geschichte der katholischen Literatur Deutschlands vom 17. Jh. bis zur Gegenwart* (Leipzig, 1854).

F. Buuk, "Zur Geschichte der Theologie des 19. Jahrhunderts," *Scholastik* 18 (1945) 54 ff.

B. Casper, "Begegnung. Geschichtspunkte für eine Geschichte der katholischen Theologie im 19. Jahrhundert," *Begegnung* (Graz, 1971), pp. 569 ff.

V. Cramer, *Bücherkunde zur Geschichte der katholischen Bewegung im 19. Jahrhundert* (Mönchen-Gladbach,1914).

J. Diebolt, *La théologie morale catholique en Allemagne au temps du philosophisme et de la restauration, 1750–1850* (Strassburg, 1926).

D. Dietrich, *The Goethezeit and the Metamorphosis of Catholic Theology in the Age of Idealism* (Las Vegas, 1979).

A. Dru, *The Contribution of German Catholicism* (New York, 1963).

K. Eschweiler, *Die zwei Wege der neueren Theologie* (Augsburg, 1926).

──, *J.A. Möhlers Kirchenbegriff. Das Hauptstück der katholischen Auseinandersetzung mit dem deutschen Idealismus* (Braunsberg, 1930).

M. Ettlinger, *Geschichte der Philosophie der Romantik bis zur Gegenwart* (Dempter, 1924).

L. Foucher, *La philosophie catholique en France au XIXème siècle avant la renaissance thomiste et dans son rapport avec elle (1800–1880)* (Paris, 1950).

H. Fries, G. Schwaiger, *Katholische Theologen Deutschlands im 19. Jh.* (Munich, 1975).

H. Fuhrmans, *Schellings Philosophie der Weltalter* (Düsseldorf, 1954).

P. Funk, *Von der Aufklärung zur Romantik* (Munich, 1925).

B. Gams, *Geschichte der Kirche Christi im 19. Jh. . . .* (Innsbruck, 1854–1856).

J. Geiselmann, *Geist des Christentums und des Katholizismus* (Mainz, 1940).

P. Gottfried, *Conservative Millenarians: The Romantic Experience in Bavaria* (New York, 1979).

G. Goyau, *L'Allemagne religieuse. Le Catholicisme* (Paris, 1905–1909).

M. Grabmann, *Die Geschichte der katholischen Theologie seit dem Ausgang der Väterzeit* (Freiburg, 1933).

P. Hadrossek, *Die Bedeutung des Systemgedankens für die Moraltheologie in Deutschland seit der Thomasrenaissance* (Munich, 1949).

H. Herberg, *Eine Ideengeschichte der neueren katholischen soziallehre* (Bern, 1933).

E. Hocedez, *Histoire de la théologie au XIXème siècle* (Paris, 1951).

H. Honecker, "Die Wesenszüge der deutschen Romantik in philosophischer Sicht," *Philosophisches Jahrbuch* 49 (1936) 199 ff.

H. Kapfinger, *Der Eoskreis, 1828 bis 1832* (Munich, 1928).

K. Leese, *Philosophie und Theologie im Spätidealismus* (Berlin, 1929).

J. Lefon, *La crise revolutionnaire*, in A. Fliche, V. Martin, *Histoire de l'Eglise*, 20 (Paris, 1949).

G. McCool, *Catholic Theology in the Nineteenth Century* (New York, 1977).

M. Nedoncelle, *L'Ecclésiologie au XIXème siècle* (Paris, 1960).

J.C. Powell, "Perspectives on Protestant and Catholic Thought in the Nineteenth Century," *European Studies* 10 (1980) 247 ff.

A. Reatz, *Reformversuche in der katholischen Dogmatik Deutschlands zu Beginn des 19. Jahrhunderts* (Mainz, 1917).

O. von Redwitz-Schmoeltz, *Geschichte der katholischen Literatur Deutschlands* (Vienna, 1861).

L. Scheffczyk, *Theologie im Aufbruch und Widerstreit* (Bremen, 1965).

A. Schmid, *Wissenschaftliche Richtungen auf dem Gebiete des Katholizismus in neuester und gegewärtiger Zeit* (Munich, 1962).

F. Schnabel, *Die Katholische Kirche in Deutschland. Deutsche Geschichte in XIX Jahrhunderte* (Freiburg, 1947).

M. Schoof, *A Survey of Catholic Theology, 1800–1970* (New York, 1970).

G. Schwaiger, ed., *Kirche und Theologie im 19. Jh.* (Göttingen, 1975).

──, *Zwischen Polemik und Irenik* (Göttingen, 1978).

M. Schweitzer, "Kirchliche Romantik," *Historisches Jahrbuch* 48 (1928) 389–460.

J. Silbernagl, *Die kirchenpolitischen und religiösen Zustände im 19. Jh.* (Landshut, 1901).

G. Sloyan, "Developments in Religious Education since 1800," *Living Light* 2 (1965) 82 ff.

A. Sonnenschein, *Görres, Windischmann und Deutinger als christliche Philosophen* (Bochum, 1938).

L. Swidler, *"Aufklärung" Catholicism, 1780–1850: Liturgical and Other Reforms in the Catholic "Aufklärung"* (Missoula, Mont., 1978).

X. Tilliette, *Schelling. Une philosophie en devenir* (Paris, 1970).

H. Tuebeen, *Die Freiheitsproblematik Baaders und Deutingers und der deutsche Idealismus* (Würzburg, 1929).

L. Veit, *Die Kirche im Zeitalter des Individualismus. 1648 bis zur Gegenwart* (Freiburg, 1933).

H. Weber, *Sakrament und Sittlichkeit. Eine moral-theologische Untersuchung zur Bedeutung der Sakramente in der deutschen Moraltheologie der ersten Hälfte des 19. Jh.* (Regensburg, 1966).

P. Weins, *Die Reichgottesidee in der katholischen Dogmatik des 19. Jh.* (Freiburg, 1921).

B. Welte, "Zum Strukturwandel der katholischen Theologie im 19. Jh.," *Auf der Spur des Ewigen* (Freiburg, 1965).

K. Werner, *Geschichte der katholischen Theologie seit dem Trienter Konzil bis zur Gegenwart* (Munich, 1866).

Index of Names